MR NASTY

This is a note from

CAMERON WHITE

MR NASTY

MISADVENTURES IN THE DRUG WORLD

MAINSTREAM
PUBLISHING
EDINBURGH AND LONDON

This edition, 2004

First published in Great Britain in 2004 by
MAINSTREAM PUBLISHING COMPANY (EDINBURGH)
LTD
7 Albany Street
Edinburgh EH1 3UG

ISBN 1 84018 906 1

A catalogue record for this book is available
from the British Library

Typeset in Anklepants and Galliard

Printed in Great Britain by
Cox & Wyman Ltd

For Octopuschick

CONTENTS

INTRODUCTION

IT'S NOTHING PERSONAL, IT'S STRICTLY BUSINESS

I clocked Gillespie in the canteen on Friday morning. He was sitting with a group of boggle-eyed student pals bragging, no doubt, about his brush with the police.

I bided my time.

Eventually, he rose and moved away from his impressionable acolytes. I'd banged out a couple of lines of the devil's dandruff and was primed to explode. I'd show him how to make an impression.

I followed Gillespie into the main corridor, down the steps to the university's front entrance.

I hung back while he stopped to chat with some friends. It would be better if our little discussion was held in private.

He was on the move again, walking towards the toilets facing the front hall. I followed him in.

We were alone.

He was positioned in front of one of the urinals. With his back to me he couldn't see me coming. My first punch was low, right into the small of his back, on the money, crunching his kidney. He doubled up: the bastard fell to his knees. I followed up, quickly slamming my fist into his mouth. His lips split against his teeth.

It felt righteous.

Now he was down but still conscious, flat on his back. I straddled him and locked my left forearm into his throat, forcing his Adam's apple back to block his airway: 'You've been a silly boy Gillespie, haven't you?' He was fighting for breath as I pushed down harder on his neck, squeezing the air out. 'What did you tell the police?'

'Nothing. I didn't tell them nothing,' he gasped, his face turning purple, blood frothing between his pulped lips.

'You'd better be sure that it was nothing,' I said, "cos if you land me in the shit, I'm gonna take a 10lb masonry hammer, start with your stupid feet, and work my way up until you either stop breathing or stop moving. You understand me?' To emphasise my point, I hit him flush on the nose with my right fist.

I let go of his neck and he gagged, desperately trying to force air back into his lungs. 'I won't tell them a thing. I promise,' he wheezed through his bruised windpipe.

'Be sure that you don't.'

I patted one of his cheeks and stood up to leave. 'If the cops ring my doorbell, I'll break every bone in your body, you little prick.'

I left him spread-eagled on the floor, floundering on the urine-streaked tiles. I had made my point. Word would get round that I didn't suffer fools, gladly or otherwise. It would enhance my reputation as the Irish boy from the wrong side of the tracks, who played by the rules of the East End streets. I was the dealer. Nobody messed with me. Unless they wanted to end up being fed through a tube.

As far as I was concerned, the summary justice I had just meted out to Gillespie was entirely warranted. I had plenty to protect beyond my liberty. My afternoons in the university canteen, moving pills to the as-yet-unenlightened masses, were just for openers. I was ready to fight my way to the top, and didn't care who blocked my path. Anyone who posed a threat to me was a potential victim.

It was July 1986: I was a testosterone-fuelled 18 year old bursting with resentment and ambition. These were the first steps of a journey that would take me from London's chemically fuelled clubland to the smack-ridden streets of Sydney, making the move from recreational chemical consumer to dealer to being ultimately consumed and almost destroyed by drugs.

This book isn't meant to be a confession. I'm not looking for absolution for the things I've done. The price I've paid for my misadventures in the drug world has already been a high one. I bear few physical scars, but managed to eviscerate my psyche as I immersed myself in a world in which the rules and social mores of normal, decent society quite simply don't apply. I wear the psychological wounds I sustained during my journey like tattoos on my soul.

This book contains specific experiences from a decade spent at the outer limits of drug culture. The geography might change but the basic principles of my thirst for money, power and narcotics themselves remain the same. If you've never experienced the rush, the buzz of gambling with your own life, then my motivation may puzzle you at times, but the end result of my actions should be viewed with absolute clarity – when you're lying on a bare mattress with the agony of heroin withdrawal lacerating your brain, all the romance of living on the edge and playing by your own rules disappears pretty damned quickly. I'm not expecting you to learn from my mistakes, but when you're staring down at that mirror with its carefully chopped-out lines of coke, take a good hard look and think carefully about where you might end up. I know, because I've been there.

What follows is a series of snapshots in time of my journey through the junk culture of our narco-planet. It is a cautionary tale for consumers and dealers alike. I have changed the names of everyone who participates in this story to protect both the innocent and the guilty. The events though, much as I now wish I could change some of them, are pretty much described as they happened.

MR NASTY

Drugs have had a dramatic impact on my life, taking me from the dizzy heights of being a strutting, Armani-clad narco-deity to pain you wouldn't wish on a fly. It's your life. Make your own choices.

MR NASTY

LONDON

OLD SKOOL DAZE

So, who died and made me Mr Nasty?

I am the youngest of three sons born to a bog-standard working-class mother and father. We lived in the same council flat my parents moved into as newlyweds, furnished on the never-never.

My ma worked as a nurse on the nightshift at St Thomas' Hospital in London. She was the breadwinner, struggling to hold the family together. She's Irish Catholic, the matriarch who dragged us three boys to mass every Sunday. More significantly, she instilled in us the importance of a decent education, so we could make something of ourselves.

My ma was hardened to the seamy side of life, dealing, as she did, with the violent aftermath of East End street brawls; stitching up knife wounds and gunshot victims. My da worked as a second-hand office furniture salesman for Lenny Ablett, a local wheeler-dealer and small-time hood. Working for Lenny was hard graft: my old man was paid on commission. No sale? No money.

He was a strict disciplinarian. A fearful character who would take a strap to us when we stepped out of line. A bit of a bully, if the truth be told.

Da was prone to gambling his earnings away on the horses, and nights down the pub, in Neasden or Kilburn mostly, pissing his commission up against a wall. He was out of sight and usually out of his mind, far removed from the wife and kids who waited, sometimes fearfully, for his return to the East End. I was scared of him.

It was hard and when there was trouble, no stranger to our doorstep, we pulled together, as families do.

The tallyman would come to our door every Friday evening to settle up. A fiver here, a tenner there, borrowed when Dad hadn't sold the battered desks and filing cabinets needed to put food on the table.

We were no different from other families on the estate who used the tallyman to pay the bills during hard times. He was a local institution, noting debts and settlements in the thick ledger he always carried.

I was seven years old when the tallyman came to our flat one December evening in 1975. As I opened the door to the familiar face of Mr Goldblatt, all smiles and hair-ruffling bonhomie, I sensed things were different: Goldblatt was not alone. Two heavies stood behind him, their unsympathetic stares fixing me like a statue.

'Is your father in, sonny?'

'Dad, Dad, it's the tallyman.'

My father came through to the hallway. The debt was not going to be repaid this time. My da was in too deep. Goldblatt and his henchmen were here to collect as they saw fit.

They took the telly and the radio; the silver cutlery canteen my mother inherited from her nan, the only possession she truly treasured; even the second-hand bike my brother bought from the proceeds of his paper round. Neighbours gathered outside to watch as the procession of our worldly goods continued. For them it was entertainment, the twentieth-century equivalent of a public flogging. My ma sat in the front room: alone, sobbing quietly, blotting out her pain and humiliation.

Da didn't go to the pub that night. I remember watching him as he sat in silence at the kitchen table, brooding, cursing the forces compelling him to trudge from one dead-end sales pitch to another. Momentarily he turned his head to look at me. I remember that look. It was a look of defeat and pain. At that moment, I can remember resolving that I wouldn't end up like my father, dragging his family along as he ran round in circles trying to make ends meet. I would have a better life, away from the deprivation and the drudgery that surrounded me. I was going to break out and make a fist of it. The Goldblatts of the world would live in fear of my power and reputation.

As I moved into my teenage years I became a child of my times; an emotional stakeholder in Thaatchi PLC. What I took from these formative years of the 1970s and early 1980s was that getting by like my parents wasn't enough: I wanted to get on.

It was, like the sea change in pop music during the 1960s, a generational thing. Then the kids wanted rock 'n' roll rather than the limp-wristed ballads that had been churned out by Brylcreemed troubadours. The '80s saw a heightened level of aspirational yearning, surpassing the desires for greater social freedom and better sounds on your stereo that had been on everyone's wish list during the previous two decades. The Thatcher years of the '80s shaped my creed of greed. It was acceptable to be ambitious. It was OK to seek to climb the ladder, be it to a new social level or to a financial one. I just couldn't be bothered with all the hard work that was required to be successful. If there was another route to fast cars and wine bars then I was sure as hell going to find it, exploit it and make it work for me.

My mother's obsession with providing her children with a good education paid dividends. Both my elder brothers qualified as barristers but the intricacies of the British legal system held little interest for me at that time. I was a self-proclaimed businessman. I wasn't quite sure what that business would be, but avarice and envy were already poison in my veins. Although my brothers and I were all ambitious, pride and reserve rendered them more staid than me. As the youngest, I was Mr Vivacity. Like many teenage boys, I had brushes with the law, and my parents thought I ran with the wrong crowd. But I slogged through school and, surprising one and all, continued on to university.

I passed my A levels and gained a place on a business studies course at the University of Westminster. It did teach me fundamental economic principles: the joke about economists is that when you show them how something works in practice, they'll explain why it couldn't work in theory. And university provided me with a laboratory where I could put academic business principles to the test in the real world. Uni became my first kosher dealing arena.

I began taking Ecstasy as soon as I took up my place at university. Pills were everywhere in the clubs and everybody was doing them. I'd smoked dope since my early teens and was more than eager to trade up to a new high. The pivotal moment for me came in March 1986 when I did my first deal. It wasn't pre-planned but from that moment, my future for the next decade became preordained. It happened by chance. I was in a club in the West End of London with a few friends. We were seated in the chill-out room coming up on our first pills of the evening when a figure appeared out of the gloom.

'Anyone got a spare E?'

We collectively shook our heads, but I felt the first stirrings of the thrill of making a fast buck with minimal effort. Our group had bought our pills from a bulk dealer who operated out of a pub in the Holloway Road in north London. He retailed them to us at £15 each as we bought in bulk in batches of 20 pills at a time. This was way below the going rate at end-of-line distribution in the clubs. I knew that the two spare pills I had nestling in the pocket of my jeans were worth far more than I'd paid for them so I made my move.

'I've only got one spare. You can have it for twenty-five.'

'OK, sorted.' And that was that. A few discreet fumblings later the exchange was made and I was a tenner up on the deal. Not exactly big money, I know, but in my book it was money for nothing and that was the best kind of deal there was. The next time we went clubbing I had ten pills in my pocket, which were gone within an hour. I didn't have to trawl through the club making a sales pitch to the punters. I simply stood by the bar and waited for someone to ask me if I had any gear on me. There was always someone who hadn't come prepared for the evening and who was desperate to join the party. I had a supplier and I had customers: I had become a dealer. Within a few weeks I had expanded my activities, becoming the main supplier of pills on my degree course. Most of my fellow students were chinless wonders from the Home Counties who were experiencing the bright lights of the big city for the first time. They had more money than sense, but didn't have the connections to procure the illicit substances which would fuel their term-time parental rebellion. It was like shooting fish in a barrel.

Through the dosh I earned, I quickly became a scenester on the London club circuit. And that nearly got me killed. What did I know? I was a teenager. I thought I was immortal. Narco-entrepreneurs are well advised to avoid such delusions and cultivate a more practical trait: invisibility.

I'm an individual who doesn't stand out in a crowd. My appearance is utterly unmemorable; a useful attribute in any illicit enterprise. I've never owned a flashy car, worn outlandish clothes, or dyed my hair. I try to spend money quietly, and go to bed early on school nights. A regular poster boy for playing it straight in Squaresville.

But I wasn't. I was identifiable to the people who mattered. I was already cultivating my look. I wore the right clothes, but didn't blow the bank balance. I started to develop the 'aura' of a dealer. It's almost impossible to define, but dealers seem to radiate an invisible force which dictates that you can stop me and buy one but don't, under any circumstances, try and fuck with me. It's always better to keep it understated. I learnt early on that screaming blue murder into someone's face isn't nearly as effective as whispering in someone's ear that you're going to have to break their fingers unless they don't get their shit together and come around to your point of view.

I was to all intents and purposes invisible to Joe Public, but my suppliers, their associates and my customers sure as hell knew who I was, and I was to move a mountain of pills and speed across London. I was to be a Face, a Name, a dealer to be reckoned with. This chameleon-like quality, the ability to blend in with my surroundings, be it the sobriety of a lecture theatre or the mayhem of an East End pub festooned with cartoon villains, was to instigate most of the drug connections I was to make over the next ten years. Whatever situation I was in, I had the savvy and the attitude to carry it off.

I didn't care whom I stepped on as I climbed up the ladder. Beneath my carefully manufactured, unremarkable façade, something deep inside – a mean streak, a coldly relentless determination, the killer instinct – would drive me to the top.

Violence doesn't come naturally to me. Sure, I can display staggering callousness and cruelty, but always use my fists only as a final sanction. Gillespie's beating? Necessity. He had been busted with three of my pills in a club, and I needed to send a message that runners took the rap themselves. I had to make them understand that giving up their supplier to the cops was quite simply not an option.

It's unattractive, I know, but truthfully, I felt little remorse for the Gillespies of the world. Sometimes you have to get down and dirty, do the job yourself, but the rough stuff wasn't really a part of me, a factor in my core philosophy. Actually hurting someone doesn't float my boat. I preferred to leave that side of things to other people. It was the fact that I could engineer a situation to meet my own needs which gave me the thrill. If someone required a going-over, then I could make it happen. I didn't have to actually do it myself. I could say the word and one of my crew, who over time I carefully assembled from amongst my school buddies, could do it.

My actions were calculated carefully, weighing risks and evaluating outcomes. Mindless thuggery is generally best left to professionals, and I learned to let hired hands turn the awkward squad into hospital cases.

Drug dealing is an insane business, but I never doubted my

chosen vocation. The pursuit of hard cash became my mantra, but my memory of the tallyman meant that money was more than keeping score. My rise through the drug hierarchy generated respect from the criminal fraternity who orbited my world. The power to inspire fear in others is as addictive as any narcotic. I craved it. I didn't have to be the one who dished out the punishment. It was enough for me that the victim knew that I was responsible for making it happen. After all, violence usually causes some kind of comeback and I didn't feel the need to get tagged by the law for giving someone a slap or breaking out the heavy artillery. Best to leave it to the foot soldiers.

Taking down someone like Gillespie meant little. He wasn't a player. I knew that I would be dealing with people who wouldn't think twice about cutting me to pieces if I crossed them. I wanted to be a part of that. I wanted the danger, the adrenalin, the rush, but I also didn't feel the need to get banged up in a police cell for my sins. I was to cut others into the business who would take those risks for me. My part in the violence that regularly poked its nose from under the duvet as the business expanded was mainly on a cerebral level. It's all about reputation and that's something that can be carefully constructed with a little creative energy and some business partners who are carefully selected for their psychopathic tendencies.

Did this need for respect motivate me more than the need for a better life for myself? I think that both motivations played a part and drove me onwards and upwards.

You may think that I am cold-blooded, heartless, a cash-bot-sans-scruples but . . . failure was unacceptable. I had to win, to prove myself, to better myself, to drag myself away from being just another kid from a council flat with a chip on his shoulder, and to hell with the pain I inflicted on others. Drugs can kill and I make no excuses for the business I conducted, or the manner in which I facilitated it. It takes a lot of bottle to stick a gun in someone's face and mean it. I meant it all. It may not have been my finger on the trigger all the time, but I was pulling the strings within the team of drug mercenaries I put together. I was nasty by nature, pure and simple. I think I really got to understand the power of fear as an emotion from both sides. I knew how to manipulate a situation whereby people were scared of me, or at least of my perceived reputation. I also understood the concept of being scared shitless when I was on the receiving end of serious intimidation. I think that it was this understanding that made me sometimes blasé about the risks I took and which would inevitably lead me into deeper and deeper trouble. I began to run from one disastrous situation to the next, incrementally screwing up even more each time I was to re-involve myself in the drugs business. I felt that the normal rules didn't apply to me and that I was somehow greater than any threat posed to me. I was wrong.

The socio-economic backdrop of the time was perfect for me. London in the second half of the 1980s was driven by the pursuit of a fast buck and an easy life. Yuppie ethics ruled. Dosh poured forth like a fountain, and I was happy to go with the flow. Halcyon days.

Working people aspired to and achieved their dreams: home ownership, a nice car, two weeks abroad in the sunshine every year. The streets of east London presented an opportunity to someone with enough balls to take a chance on life.

The pubs and clubs created a social scene that ran in parallel to my family's straight life, but was underpinned by criminal activity. You want a new car stereo? A knock-off MTV shirt? Two grams of coke and a quarter of grass? Welcome to the market economy, my son.

My parents' generation had found their potential social distractions to be fairly limited. Nightclubs were only for the rich and glamorous. It was more a case of spending Saturday night down the local boozer than cruising through to the early hours of Sunday morning in some swanky Soho nighterie. The 1960s had introduced prohibited drugs into the mainstream, even popular beat combos of the day smoked a bit of dope and experimented with acid. Heroin was always around but junkies were still the exception to the rule until punk exploded in the late '70s. Kids took speed and tabs as harder drugs began to appear on recreational shopping lists along with the usual quarter ounce of Lebanese Red.

It was the money explosion of the '80s that really fuelled the drug wave on both sides of the Atlantic. Young people found themselves with more disposable income than ever before. A work-hard-play-hard ethic developed which covered all the social tribes from City bond traders and their bottles of Bollinger to blissed-out clubbers dropping their third pill of the night. There was plenty of money to pay for the non-stop party as the economy went into overdrive while the decade progressed and the recession-ridden '70s became a distant memory.

The clubs began to change from cheesy discos which were little more than lager-fuelled meat markets to carefully constructed environments which would enhance the experience for those who wanted to party on drugs. The rave scene hit in 1986–7. Thousands of clubbers would decamp from the towns and cities and drive in convoy to dance up a storm in some rain-soaked mud bath of a field with some piss-poor sound system thumping out a relentless bass line. Dropping an E became as normal as smoking a fag. It became essential to enjoy the music and your surroundings to the full, and let's face it, early on, some of the floor fillers were pretty dire. Screw the melody, just keep kicking in with rampaging beats and faux air-raid sirens. The baby boomers of the '50s and '60s had spawned a new breed of teenager: independent, ambitious, cashed up and searching for the next new thing to try. Ecstasy was the new drug of choice. Total entertainment in tablet form.

It's simplistic to believe evil pushers loiter by ice-cream vans with free samples, luring their unwary young victims with a hypnotic whisper: 'Go on, kid, try it, it's fun.' Attitudes to hard drugs changed considerably in the '80s. The fear factor dissipated; it became acceptable to do a couple of lines of an evening or drop a pill to keep your feet moving. Even heroin became hip for a while, although the stigma of being a smackhead still meant that you were pretty much ostracised from society unless your allowance from daddy meant you could support your habit without having to nick the lead off a church roof.

Kids on the thrill ride began to prefer gobbling Ecstasy to a quiet pint in their local. Their parents quaffed bitter and rum-and-blacks, perhaps smoked spliffs to Bob Marley records. My generation wanted to leave its own footprint in the sand.

As a business studies student, I could see the opportunities for supplying the demand around me as plainly as the nose on Michael Jackson's face. If the boys and girls wanted disco biscuits and amphetamines to switch on their Saturday night, someone would find a way to flip their switch. And that someone was me.

I immersed myself in the subculture; perfected my chameleon abilities, met the right people, did the right things, and powered onwards and upwards.

If I knew then what I know now, would I have done it differently? Possibly. But my journey was travelled at 1,000mph. The boundaries between civil society and the narco-zone of pushers, dealers, pimps and killers became so blurred it was impossible to tell where and when the lines crossed and it wasn't without its potential pitfalls.

Selling drugs is a high-risk business. It's illegal, secretive and dangerous. Professional longevity is rare, personal catastrophe common. During the next few years, politicians and police, media and medics would pump up the volume of their concern about 'the drugs problem'. Ecstasy became the bugbear of the tabloid media and those who dealt in this insidious new threat to society were in league with the devil.

Did they mean me?

Fucking A. My take on 'the drugs problem' was to be a player and get to the top of the scene powering up around me. And the first of Mr Nasty's rules for a successful business operation: make sure you know your product.

Ecstasy, or MDMA (methylenedioxymethamphetamine), was first synthesised in Germany in 1912 as a slimming aid but fell out of favour before the Second World War when amphetamines became fashionable for wannabe stick insects. The drug that changed a generation didn't reappear until the 1970s, when progressive US-based therapists discovered it helped relationship counselling. The euphoric element of the E-experience helped married couples loosen up and contributed to bringing a sense of harmony into discussions over the merits of married life.

Today, most production centres on labs in the Netherlands and Belgium: very handy if you're running a distribution network in the United Kingdom, with Amsterdam only an hour's flight away.

The coalescence of drug culture, its fusion with music, fashion and nightclubbing started almost imperceptibly with LSD in the early 1980s. Embryonic house tunes were thumping out of Chicago, and the amphetamine-fuelled, 120-drilling-beats-per-minute of Hi-Energy exploded from the global gay club scene.

Acid can freak out the unprepared or inexperienced. Imagine your brain as a personal computer: LSD rebuilds its desktop.

There was one old hippy in Islington who hadn't spoken for 20 years after dropping acid. He was said to have been tripping when he looked in the mirror and saw a dinosaur's head staring back at him.

LSD is powerful, and not for lightweights. You should have someone straight around to talk you down and dose you up with vitamin C if the trip goes tits up. Never drop acid if you're feeling overly anxious, or are prone to playing with sharp objects.

The best trips often happen in a stable 'set and setting': the set is your mind, the setting your physical environment. I remember dropping a tab of white lightning in a stroboscopic club landscape. Acid can give you a sense of synaesthesia, that cross-perceptual juice that lets you taste colours, hear smells and puts engines beneath your sensory wings. Several hundred other people raved around us as we danced to a baseline that could collapse tall buildings and boogied to the rhythms in our heads.

The mid-'80s acid-house scene, with its retro-psychedelic lightshows and smiley-face motifs, demonstrated clubbers wanted release from their lives' pressured drudgery, a temporary escape,

MR NASTY

23

fun. But even the most seasoned grand wizards of the cosmic club scene found LSD too intense.

The solution? MDMA. Haven't you ever wondered who first realised that the kids would buy into the MDMA lifestyle, big time? And it is big. In the mid-'80s around half a million Ecstasy tablets were munched down in the United Kingdom every weekend. And sales were by no means restricted to weekends. Now, tell me who the hell wouldn't want a piece of the action? I did.

Take MDMA and you feel loved-up, happy and energetic. No vile next-morning crash after your night at Party Central. You can get up on Monday morning and go into work feeling fresh. And it keeps your weight down: how many chubby pill monsters do you see out and about? Ecstasy is the perfect play pill.

The social commentators waxing lyrical about the 'rEgeneration' of youth culture insisted that 'it's all about the music'. Maybe it was for them – but for the rest of us, the 1980s were pretty tame until Ecstasy appeared. Punk, new wave, new romantics, retro soul boys, each new fad came and went in the early '80s, but it wasn't until the pills started to be popped that a youth movement with mass appeal began to develop.

I've got two words for the so-called guardians of our social history who insist that it's the soundtrack of our lives which shapes each era of youth culture and they're not Happy Birthday. Because from 1985 onwards it became *all* about the drugs: going out on the weekend became an event, not a necessary chore in the composite make-up of being a teenager. The music, the parties, the clubs and the culture provided the social pretext – the amphitheatres and the context for total hedonism – the drugs enhanced the moment.

By 1986, London's club scene was exploding. Peter Gatien, an eyepatch-wearing Canadian, had opened a venue called Limelight in a deconsecrated church on Shaftesbury Avenue. It brought a novel sophistication to UK clubbing, lifting the experience above and beyond punters' low expectations of a Saturday night in the smoke.

Limelight had earpiece-wearing doormen, changing interior installations and sexy staff who looked smart and smiled when you tipped. The music was edgy, the cocktails potent and you could eat sushi after midnight.

You had to queue to get in but, if the door-goons didn't like your look, or your name wasn't on some arcane list, you'd end up looking elsewhere for entertainment. Developed from Gatien's eponymous boîte in lower midtown Manhattan, Limelight pioneered today's club culture: not only did its velvet ropes and VIP room create a hierarchy within the city's nightworld, but its management reached out to selected clientele and offered them an extended surrogate family with whom to indulge their narco-fuelled hedonism.

Limelight immediately attracted star DJs and high-voltage bohemian American scenesters, flying in on cheap airline tickets from now-defunct carriers like People Express. Drugs were just one aspect of a fashion, music and art scene that was amping up London's presence as the nexus between the US and Europe. These new clubs were different from the discothèques of the '70s. They were slick and expensive, and people went to them to dance rather than spend a night on the prowl for the opposite sex. On E you were everybody's best friend. You could spend an hour in deep conversation with a girl you'd just met and the thought of hitting on her wouldn't enter your head. Everybody was just there for the shared experience and euphoria that the drugs provided. Clubbing had reached a new level. The socio-economic changes and greater societal freedom of the '80s meant that London was overflowing with a young population who wanted to spend their hard-earned cash in the pursuit of pleasure, be it buying a Porsche or a pill. The city felt vibrant and happening. Saturday nights down the pub were a thing of the past to anyone under the age of 25.

A younger generation had noticed Limelight's success and now wanted to reinterpret club culture for themselves and their peers. A scruffy student like me would never feature on Limelight's guest list. But why would I want to when DJs like Pete Tong, Paul Oakenfold and Danny Rampling, early adaptors to the mid-1980s rise of happy-house culture, were catering to a new generation with banging Balearic beats?

Oliver Peyton's clubs, Shoom and Raw, had a different vibe from Limelight, built more around Euroland scenesters who would import Ecstasy, initially for friends. The clubs had a stark, minimalist feel as opposed to Limelight's lounge-lizard opulence. Shoom and Raw tapped further into what the kids wanted and gave it to them. They had large dance floor areas and dispensed with overworked designer trappings, boasting practical bars and comfortable seating instead. When you're off your head you can just sit on the floor, it really doesn't matter. Out went the glitter balls and in came the lasers and strobe lighting. Throw in a few strategically placed podiums for the poseurs and shape throwers and you've got yourself the ideal of what a decent nightclub in the mid-'80s should be. The kids reacted. Limelight had paved the way, but why queue up for two hours, pay £20 to get in and another fiver for each drink when a tenner could see you through the night at Raw, provided you had paid for your drugs already. Pretty soon every clued-up club owner was stripping out the chrome and mirrors, painting the walls black and installing a kick-ass sound system to attract the punters in. The DJs exploited this social network, getting paid to play their beats by pilled-up punters chugging Evian like it was water, and building the room's loved-up vibe.

The punk generation had grown up and moved on; the new kids on the block wanted peace and love in a 12-hour pill that would energise them at 140 beats per minute.

Shoom and Raw became my weekend stomping ground. The crowd was younger, and there were no lame dress codes. My customer base was already on the floor, and I had the connections to walk into the room and deal successfully. I was still pretty low rent in the grand scheme of things. I didn't buy pills in batches of more than 50 and was running around the clubs selling the gear myself. This was turning out to be hard work after all. I had more spare cash than any of my fellow students or peers in the clubbing community, but I was basically operating as a street dealer as 1986 came and went.

MR NASTY

All this ambitious teenage business studies student needed to kick-start life as a narco-entrepreneur was a move up the ladder.

What had started as an easy-money, instant-margin opportunity with plenty of potential really needed to become a proper business for me.

My clueless peers thought I was the man. I ran with a crowd alien to these Home Counties kids who treated university as a four-year round of dinner parties and parentally sponsored time-wasting, rather than a leg-up in life.

My drinking partners infested the underbelly of society, the East End's drug subculture. These were the mates I had grown up with and who hailed from the council estates of Hackney. I had a core group of friends I had been to school with. I knew them and trusted them and they never cast judgement over what I was doing. Illegal activity was always on the menu for kids on the skids. It was to these schoolfriends that I would turn in order to facilitate my move up in the drugs hierarchy. My East End friends wouldn't answer to Sebastian or Jocasta, be found at the pony club gymkhana, or enjoy Sunday lunch with Mater, Pater and that nice Annabelle 'who's just your age, darling'. My action revolved around meeting the right faces, making the right waves and cutting the right deals.

It meant I could move a few pills amongst the gutless college crowd who were primed to inform on my arse if collared by John Q. Law.

My punters may have been witless provincial twunts, but they ordered regularly. I enjoyed chipping away at their student grants via pills for thrills, with a little hash for cash thrown in as a sideline. Life was sweet as long as I kept my supplier the same way.

I first hooked up with Dom 'the Bomb' in mid-1987. He was running pills and whizz for a crew of north London heavies called the Doherty brothers. Dom was a big blast on a short fuse – he thought a belt was something you hit below and kicking what you did once somebody was down. He could provide me with pills at a cost of £10 each, providing I bought in batches of 50 pills or more. This wasn't exactly a bargain-basement price, but I wasn't at the level yet where I could buy 1,000 pills a time for a few quid each: in the early days of Ecstasy, pills were bloody expensive. Dom the Bomb had me over a barrel just as much as I squeezed the university crowd for maximum margin.

For an impoverished student, £500 was a hefty investment. I hustled a loan from one of my brothers for the first batch. I told him it was to buy a Vespa and he didn't ask too many questions when I repaid him out of my profits a couple of weeks later, saying I had changed my mind about the scooter. At this time none of my family knew what I was up to. They figured I was the diligent student who went out a bit more often than was good for my education. If they'd been wise to the situation they would have freaked, but I managed to keep things low key as far as my family was concerned. The rewards were cut glass.

I made the pick-up from Dom every Wednesday night, so I had enough time to cater for the weekend rush. We would meet in his local pub in Finsbury Park and conduct the ritual of him counting the money as I checked the goods, in the gents' toilet. Mission accomplished.

I could move the Es amongst my fellow students at £25 each. Show me another business that returns a 150 per cent profit on investment, and I'll show you my wedge.

Maximum impact protects your margin because it negates your personal risk. So I embarked on a strategy of intimidation to keep customers in line: pills were only for personal use. If I caught anyone dealing them on without express permission, then they'd be on the business end of a slap on the snout.

Curiously, despite my heavy-handed methods, my popularity never wavered. I had what punters wanted, and I was the only person they knew who could get it for them. Many drug dealers go tonto at this point, they start confusing business and pleasure: their clientele end up telling them that they only like them because they supply their drugs – if I'd wanted a new friend, I would've bought a puppy.

Perhaps amoral is the wrong way to describe my outlook at the time: I rationalised it as strictly business. I provided a service. If someone came to me complaining of a bad trip then I just stopped dealing with them. Once a deal was done I couldn't care less what the kids did with the pills. They could feed them to their little sister for all I cared. I was in it for myself. To hell with the consequences.

Minor irritants, like Gillespie, aside, business was solid. But the risk of getting busted or encountering ultra-violence always lurked like a dorsal fin. And my resentment of being a street-tier dealer grew.

Why should I be shouldering maximum risk, running my arse off around campus, supplying a client base too diverse to provide me with any security?

This chippiness triggered a shift in my motivation that set me on the path to bigger, but not necessarily better, things. Narco-self-sufficiency soon paved the way to avarice, and a lust for cash and kudos amongst the drug business's elite.

I was actually studying quite hard in conjunction with my more nefarious nocturnal activities. This probably held me back a bit in expanding my business. I spent a couple of years living off a small-scale dealing enterprise before finally deciding that I would be better suited to a management role. My first big move was in early 1988, when I stepped up and decided to bulk wholesale the tablets of dance wisdom. It was my third year at university and I was starting to plan ahead. Unlike most of my contemporaries at college, I didn't aspire to being a marketing executive for a white-goods manufacturer. It was time to delegate some of the responsibility in my clandestine business. I started by dealing 10 pills at a time, for £20 a pop, to a few trusted associates. They disposed of the product for me at a small mark-up, which paid for their own pills. I was still buying pills from Dom the Bomb. His price had dropped to £8 each, which was still, quite frankly, extortionate. However, we had a relationship. Volatile as he might have been, I knew that Dom wouldn't rat me out if the law came knocking on his door. He always delivered and I could mess him about from time to time, for instance by paying him a few days late. He knew I was good for it and would always come up trumps with the gear, on the nail. Trade flourished. I had taken the first step up the hierarchy away from the dangerous, hands-on approach you meet on the street.

When making the dealership decision, your drug(s) of choice should be whatever's in greatest demand: and you'll find that demand directly reflected in the values and mores of the youth culture around you.

Youth culture is the barometer of any new wave of drug dealing. Forget the smackheads who constantly can't come up with the cash. Don't even think about distribution down at street level: go after the money train with passengers onboard, who can pay for your products and punch your ticket. E was to be my motherlode, my ticket that exploded. The market was tailor-made for people like me.

The late 1980s provided a springboard for young drug entrepreneurs to win their narco-MBAs and enter a business which had been covered predominantly by old-school criminals in the past. I was a completely different breed to these veteran armed robbers. These lags had had their fill of 'over the pavement' work, taking down security vans and suburban banks. The 1980s found many of these villains on Spain's Costa del Sol, beyond the reach of UK extradition treaties and conveniently out of the UK Ecstasy scene, allowing young entrepreneurs like myself to thrive in their place. These crims had cash, but had missed out on the no-questions-asked late 1980s London property boom.

Instead, they financed large quantities of cocaine into the UK in a temporarily successful attempt to turn those shores into a mini-Miami, where coke is endemic.

Boy, did they get that wrong.

When recession hit as the '90s dawned, Charlie proved too pricey even for yuppified City types, and grunge-fertilised 'heroin chic' blossomed and died like a hothouse plant among the beautiful and damned within a couple of years.

As the fattening old-timers sat in Spain, bleating about how much they missed decent fish and chips and a pint of proper beer, the UK's drug explosion blew by them. They tried to play catch-up as the millennium loomed during the fag end of the decade, but never got to ride the drug wave crashing from the dance floors of the clubs, and the kids there who wanted the total experience – full throttle, no holds barred.

Not all of the old-school criminals were that dumb though and some of them made the move into drugs where they quickly established heavy-duty distribution operations. I was low level in what I was doing. I wanted to be where the people who supplied the people who supplied the people who supplied Dom the Bomb were, if you catch my drift. This would take me into a new business arena where your business partners and competitors wrote a whole new rulebook, but I knew full well what I was getting into. This was bandit country. It's a curious elite who make it to the pinnacle in the drugs game. The rest are on a long-term vacation within Her Majesty's Prison Service, or some State or Federal Penitentiary going nowhere. And they are the lucky convicts.

It takes a nano-second to die. A bullet from a .45 will hit you at a velocity of between 1,200 and 1,500 feet per second. Hideous. Even if it's a professional hit and the 'termination consultant' is an experienced assassin using one hollow-point .9 millimetre round to the back of the head.

Taking someone out of the game is a worst-case scenario. Murder attracts heat for the protagonist and heat is bad for business. And this is strictly business, right?

Defensively, it's best to understand what might get you killed, by whom and when. This is essential knowledge as you rise, level by level, toward the higher end of the drugs food chain. Even trading up from being a street dealer to a distributor could potentially put you in the line of fire. It's astounding how quickly your knowledge of firearms increases. How often you look over your shoulder when you hear the sound of a motorbike closing in behind you. I pity the pizza delivery guys: how many have had a Colt automatic or Beretta pointed at them by a player who's pissed someone off and dealt his last hand in the world of proscribed pharmaceuticals?

It's that easy to die. It happens all the time, you just don't know it. We're too solipsistic to worry ourselves with the details of another shooting in a messy paragraph at the bottom of page 21. We filter out the casualty reports on the local evening news bulletin. Civilians neither need nor want to know the law of the jungle.

Nobody respects an amateur at any level in the drug world. You are competing with professionals who maintain, within their organisations, some of the best expertise money can buy. Joe Schmo could have a degree in international finance from Yale for all you know. Combine it with a back room full of Uzis and MP5 machine guns, and twitchy-trigger-fingered troops ready to use them . . . are you getting the picture? These were the people I wanted to emulate, but I would need to think about whether the risks were acceptable for the potential rewards on offer.

It was a no-brainer really. A gap in the market. Demand outstripping supply. Profit margins escalating though the roof at every level of the distribution networks – 200, 500, 1,000 per cent. Too good an opportunity to waste.

The DJ plays discs, my runners knock out wraps and pills, and everyone gets paid. The punters snog, trip and go home together under the ether. We count our cash. Everyone's happy.

Aren't they?

As time passed we clocked into 1989 and my studies finally started drawing to a close. I had begun to take on more than I could handle in preparation for a post-university life living off the fat of my criminal activities and spent most of my time running around after customers. At weekends my phone rang red-hot. This was too much to deal with on my own.

My recruitment drive began in earnest when I decided to trade up from shifting a few pills to becoming a fully fledged wholesale distributor. The decision to trade up at this point was mainly a financial one. Sure, you make a reduced margin as a distributor as opposed to a street dealer, but then again the risk of getting busted is significantly less and you are moving a lot more product, so you actually make a lot more money. My instincts had served

MR NASTY

me well up to now and they were telling me that now was the time to make a move for a bigger score. My student market would soon become impractical to service directly and I needed a greater supply to pump down to my runners who were always whining that I never had enough gear. I needed help though if I was going to trade up and I looked to my roots for a resource pool.

Naturally, my self-image as businessman of the year entrenched in concrete my belief that I was to be the brains of this outfit. But brains needed hands, arms and legs to move on up. My future strategy was to handle the actual Ecstasy as little as possible. And since I was starting to carry heavy money, I sussed I was putting myself on offer for a rip-off. Protection and some added influence in keeping the customers in line was required.

I'm no wallflower when it comes to a tear-up. But, physically, I'm not built to inspire fear in big-deal suppliers or predatory competitors at this level. My prime requirement was for some backup for the rough stuff that can occur when cash and drugs collide.

Aiden Mooney Murphy: 6ft 5in. of pure malevolence. OK, he wasn't exactly mastermind, but that was my job; Murph was qualified for his. I knew because I was at school with the guy. The hardest bastard in the yard, Murph was to be my enforcer. His role was simple: bodyguard, pure muscle, violence for hire. He had an inherent genetic capacity for thuggery. Murph was my key weapon in maintaining order with suppliers and distributors alike.

He joined me for two reasons: aged 21, he was lumbered with a prize cow of a wife and a couple of mini-Murphs, so he needed the cash; and the Murphster enjoyed the sheer exhilaration of physically threatening anyone who crossed our path. Murph used to actively seek out opportunities for violence. My role was simply to channel his energies into something more structured.

His favourite game was Bash the Student. He only tolerated me because we had grown up together. Murph had the uncanny ability to sniff out college kids anywhere. I'd lost count of the times spent in The Bricklayer's Arms in Bethnal Green, when

Murph would devastate the evening of some hapless bastard only looking for a good night out. His inherent resentment and bitterness, born of his own ignorance and poverty, would manifest itself in the use of his fists.

His favourite route to beating someone up was jumping the queue for the pool table. A few cross words would inevitably ensue, and result in Murph delivering a severe hammering with a pool cue to some poor fool. He repeated this in pubs throughout east London and established a reputation as someone you didn't fuck with under any circumstances. No landlord had the bottle to bar Murph, and his Missus allowed him out to play every weekend, probably glad that it wasn't her on the end of his fists.

Our involvement began when I ran into him in the pub one Friday night. I had just picked up 200 pills from my new source, the Doherty brothers, and was about to start 3 hours of cabbing around inner London to distribute them.

Dom the Bomb had got himself busted with 2,000 tabs of acid, and was looking at a long stretch in Pentonville Prison. This, and the sheer quantities of E that I was moving, meant that I was now positioned to deal directly with the Doherty brothers, who had been Dom's suppliers. I was now taking his place in the food chain. The Dohertys represented an interesting proposition as suppliers: they reliably obtained the gear I wanted, but they supplied me under constant fear of impending doom. There was no way I could be late in paying the brothers and they set the prices. No argument.

Tonight was different because half the consignment was earmarked for one specific third-party distributor, an individual called The Weasel. It meant travelling to The Elgin pub in Ladbroke Grove, west London. My manor was east and north-east London, and I wasn't thrilled about leaving it.

It was time to show that I wasn't a total mug. Two pints of lager and twenty quid later, Murph was onboard as my partner in what I envisaged as a full-tilt assault on the higher end of the narcotics world. I needed him to prove to everyone that I was a genuine player. Murph wasn't a total plank though and he knew exactly what I was up to; that I was earning some serious bunce from the pill business. This was a trial run and Murph was happy with a couple of tenners in his back pocket. However, if we were to work as a team he wanted a cut of the profits. I told him that he'd get a percentage of what we earned on a weekly basis. I didn't tell him what percentage and as it turned out Murph was happy to put himself about for me for a couple of hundred quid a week. We carried on that way until the business went international and Murph, myself, and the other two schoolfriends who were to join our happy band were to form an equal partnership. But, on this first occasion together he did it simply for kicks and a little beer money.

Entering The Elgin that Friday night with a pocket full of grade A tablets was a turning point for me. I went in first to scope the place out. Murph joined me at the bar about two minutes later.

He inspired fear in others by his physical presence alone, and I felt that instant connection between fear of him and my power. Usually The Weasel was a real pain to deal with. He never had the cash upfront, and often tried to pull stunts like sale-or-return. But tonight, he produced cash on the nail. He didn't seem in the mood to haggle, either. He couldn't wait to escape from The Elgin, as far away as possible from Murph, who delighted in giving him the thousand-yard stare that only true psychopaths can carry off with conviction.

Although I was trying to get other people to actually distribute the product on the ground, I was fed up with the continual moaning and backbiting that came with trading up to be a wholesaler. I wanted more money and less risk and had chosen to move a couple of rungs up the ladder, but now I had to get more merchandise to market. I had to get the gear into as many clubs as possible if I was to really become a distributor. Murph was the answer to my prayers. I had found my muscle for hire and, more importantly, I had found a route to the holy grail of Ecstasy distribution: 'owning the door'.

This is how it worked. Our clientele were in the clubs. For me to scoot around selling a few pills here and there to punters who

MR NASTY

wanted to get frizzed before they went clubbing was too time-consuming. I needed distribution at dance floor level itself.

This carried two key requirements for it to be a good risk: exclusive, hassle-free distribution in each club, and our own dealer 'on the floor' in every venue.

To get exclusive distribution you firstly have to ensure that you can get the merchandise into the specific venue, then, vitally, lock down the dealing environment so that nobody else can poach on your turf. That inevitably leads to unpleasantness. So, to get our pills into the room we had to own the door for each club we targeted.

The owners and managers of the clubs were easy to bypass if you could control the people providing security. They decided which customers entered the premises and which didn't. We did this relatively easily. Our stick: Murph's unique premeditated carnage skills. Our carrot: a wedge of banknotes.

Murph was funding his expanding family on social security. He didn't have the savvy to hold down even the most menial of jobs – apart from working the doors of clubs and bars, cash-in-hand. He knew the people we had to reach and how to get them to play ball, so we just bought our way in with hard cash and kickbacks.

The first club we took over in terms of drug distribution was a place I'll call Utopia, a cavernous barn in Hackney, which could hold 2,000 kids every night from Thursday to Saturday. It played a heady mix of uplifting house music, techno and trance, the perfect musical backdrop for the pill-poppers.

We reached our pumped-up clubbers through a sole distribution arrangement that proved pretty cost-effective: the guys who controlled the door got £100 each night. In exchange, our runner had carte blanche to enter and deal in the main room with no hassle from internal security; he only had undercover cops to worry about. Anybody else who was a known dealer was either barred from entry at the door, or sorted out by Murph inside the venue if they were insane enough to try it on. We owned the action.

Connecting with these door-controlling animals was slightly

bizarre. Each of them was checked by the house every night when they arrived and again at the end of their shift in the early hours of the morning. The cash that they had in their pockets was accounted for, before and after each evening's work. The owners and managers of the venues either trusted nobody or were trying to establish their own pet dealers in each club.

This posed a problem: how do we actually get the money to our tame doormen? The answer was Murph's hobby: the gyms.

London's gyms are a weird mix of under-the-counter steroids and pumped-up narcissism. I invariably found myself meeting Murph mid-afternoon at some fairly sordid workout room, usually above a shop or warehouse. This was the witching hour for bouncers who wanted to work their pecs, thighs and tris. The lunchtime office crowd had long returned to their desks, PCs and out-trays.

It was like hanging out in a prison's physical education facility. Between 3 p.m. and 5 p.m., the establishments I began to frequent were inhabited by meat-pounding monsters. These guys would lift the equivalent weight of a small car for kicks.

Business was always conducted by Murph, as he tended to be in sync with the steroid-induced mood swings of our target security staff. It amazed me how many of these tough hombres were actually gay. The attitude and scripted verbal diarrhoea they spouted was a total act for most of these muscle marys.

It further confounded me how the totally heterosexual, and utterly bigoted, Murph conducted business so easily with the iron-pounding pansies we dealt with. Live and let live, says I. Murph's doctrine was pure violence to all and sundry that didn't obey 'Murphy's Law'.

Maybe he wasn't as dumb as I thought he was. Credit where it's due, he sorted out those vital door connections.

A hundred quid a pop was dosh well spent, considering that we could cream two to three grand from each venue during a weekend, pure profit, ready for re-investment.

Most of the money was coming from pills rather than speed, which was fine by us. Pills are easier to hide, palm and sell than the paper wraps of amphetamines, which measured about an inch across by half an inch wide.

More importantly, Es represented a product where the profit margin was a minimum of 50 per cent.

We built on our first successful door coup, Utopia, very quickly to establish presence in half a dozen east London clubs. This was my next quantum leap up the food chain, but it created two problems. Firstly, I needed a much greater supply at a better wholesale price than I was currently paying the Doherty brothers, yet I couldn't afford to break our relationship. It wasn't the type of business arrangement that you simply backed away from. Secondly, I needed a master vendor to take the gear into each venue we controlled. This master vendor would take the product through the door at each location to our specified, pre-selected, in-house dealer. They would usually skim a percentage of the asking price as his or her slice of the drop. My main concern though was keeping things sweet with the Brothers D.

I was first introduced to John, Mick and Pat Doherty at one of the bars that they managed in Manor House, north London, in March 1989. An evening of bragging and threats on their part cemented an enduring business relationship between us. I never felt at ease with them, but they were to be my suppliers, so I had to set my personal concerns, like if I would walk out of the pub with fully functioning kidneys, aside. They had ploughed their profits into outright ownership of several bars and clubs in north London, as well as a couple of car repair shops through which they pumped their drugs and cleaned their cash.

The eldest of the brothers, John, called the shots. Usually John kept his nose clean, but when I first met mano-a-mano with him at one of the clubs he owned, he didn't. After several hours of scoping each other out, and snorting large amounts of Colombian marching powder together, John finally accepted that I wasn't an undercover cop. He realised that I could be useful to the Dohertys' organisation by getting their gear into certain East End venues.

He marked my card from the giddy-up. 'A word to the fucking

wise, Mo . . .' (Mo was my pseudonym amongst the dealing fraternity.) 'You only move our fucking gear, OK?'

'Yeah, yeah. No problem, John.'

'Don't you ever yeah, yeah me, you little fuck. If we even get a fucking sniff that you're fucking holding out on us, we'll nail your fucking legs to the floor with fucking railway spikes. Understand?'

'No problem, John. It's your gear and nothing else.'

If you played ball with the Dohertys then everything stayed safe: regular supply, efficient distribution, no heat from the gendarmes, and, most importantly, no aggro from the brothers themselves.

They needed to be kept happy: Pat Doherty had a disturbing attachment to high-calibre, fully automatic weaponry. Totally out of our league at that time.

These boys were at the top of the drugs ladder. You couldn't have wished for a better connection at the supplier tier. The Dohertys seemed to operate across north London with apparent immunity from the police. They allegedly had some influence with the Local Area Drug Squad, and could lean on certain key individuals if I had any serious issues regarding potential raids. They themselves didn't stray far from their north London manor in terms of dealing, but you could never really tell with the Dohertys: they had gained an indirect foothold in the East End via supplying my operation and I knew of several other 'drug franchises' that they ran in other parts of London.

Narco-commerce was changing the topography of London's gangland. By the late 1980s, Islington was the hub of criminal action north of the River Thames. The neighbourhood was home to two big families, the Adamses and the Whites (no relation).

The Adams clan was the more notorious: the family had a pedigree in armed robbery, protection rackets and drugs, and had made inroads into north and south London during the '80s and '90s. South London was open turf: its black community was still dealing weed; the dominant force there was the Arif brothers, who specialised in old-style security-van heists to finance their heroin dealing. Smack was mainly the province of the Turkish

MR NASTY

community in London – it still is – and the north London crime families sensibly steered clear and focused on pills and Charlie.

In east London it was just my expanding operation competing with a few chancers and a bunch of Essex wideboys on the make.

The influence of the IRA in north and east London was also a factor. Every Friday in the pubs, some fellas would pass round a bucket for donations for the roaring boys over the water. These impromptu fundraisers provided a conduit of funds for Provo terrorists: they, in turn, provided useful US connections for the supply of drugs, particularly cocaine, to certain London crime families.

The Dohertys only focused on the drug business, and had been savvy in picking up on the new wave of chemicals being pumped into London. In those days, there were no clandestine pill labs, although speed was manufactured in the provinces – bulk production but low profit margins. So the Dohertys stayed in distribution and steered clear of production.

Narco-commerce created a new breed of crim, with a different modus operandi to the old school East End gangsters wasting their days away in The Fox pub in Dalston. Out went the criminal 'code of ethics'. In came firearms and ultra-violence.

The Adams mob was pretty insular and too difficult for an outsider like me to penetrate. The Dohertys were more sophisticated: they had firm international supply connections and a highly organised distribution network. Although they had heavy contacts in Belfast, they avoided the internecine warfare that sporadically flared up between the Adams and other crime families in Islington.

The Dohertys had made their reputation earlier in the '80s and now lived in million-quid mansions on tree-lined streets within inner London. Their capacity for new-style ultra-violence had got John, Pat and Mick to the top and kept them there. They were gangsters in the classic mould: fast cars, big shooters and an incredible devotion to their elderly Irish mum.

The big advantage of dealing with premiership narco-entrepreneurs like the Dohertys was that they always had what I required available at short notice. My job was to make sure that I could pay for the gear 'on the fucking nail', and keep my mouth shut if I was put under pressure.

In hindsight, the Dohertys must have had a lot of faith in me. At the time it was like riding a roller-coaster.

My connection with the Dohertys gave me a certain kudos. It was sexy to be seen out and about with respected villains like the three brothers. The coke flowed freely and the bar was always open. Speed and pills of every description were at the top of my shopping list and the Dohertys always delivered.

The Brothers D were based in Muswell Hill and had no direct street-level operation on eastside turf, so they had no way of knowing how fast our operation was expanding. We never had enough pills on the floors of the clubs to meet demand, and I couldn't be everywhere at the same time. The cab fares alone were eroding my profit margin.

I increased the orders from the Dohertys to 500 pills and 300 grams of speed a week.

But the margins on the whizz were lousy, and we needed nearly 20 times the amount of Es each weekend to ensure our customer base didn't want for anything and start looking for other suppliers.

There was only one solution to this problem: start planning to bring the stuff into the country ourselves. But it would be too much for Murph and myself to handle on our own: time for another recruitment drive. Again, I looked to cohorts from my younger days.

Grahame 'Gray' Gillet had been the best soccer player at our school. He'd had a trial at Tottenham Hotspur when he was 16, and they were ready to take him on as an apprentice with a big career laid out for him, but one Friday night on a blind bend, Gray took a tumble off his Vespa and smashed his left leg in four places. He never kicked a ball in anger again. He may not have been a dab hand on a moped, but he was a good driver and that's what I had in mind for him. If I could set up a direct distribution channel from a European supplier then I would need people to drive the gear over to the UK.

At 6ft 3in. tall, Gray was initially recruited as the workhorse. His day trips to Amsterdam would begin later that year, 1989. Between him and Murph, I could control the in-house dealers and ensure that they weren't skimming too much off the top or, worse, selling their own supply in preference to our product. It was our gear only, or you'd receive a sharp smack on the snout from Gray or Murph.

Any drug distribution network requires workhorses who do the legwork to move the product, be it to wholesale buyers, distributors, or at street level. You need someone to actually carry your drugs to the end destination, which your operation is geared up to supply.

A common error that many nascent drug barons make is to combine the roles of the mule or workhorse with that of the enforcer.

The individual physically moving the product is just there to get the gear onto the dance floors. It's first-year man management to make them understand theirs is a vital role within the overall operation. The enforcer can tag along if there is any risk on a particular run, but his skills are better employed in extracting payment or implementing a preordained dialogue with competitors who may disrupt your business.

At this stage the Doherty brothers were pleased that I was buying more speed and pills from them with minimal fuss. And with Murph and Gray onboard, I was more confident about getting the merchandise to the point of sale.

Once a week though, I would have to endure a night out with the Brothers D to collect our order. It was always slightly surreal. I think these three Anglo-Irish psychopaths had a genuinely soft spot for me. Perhaps I gave them a sense of legitimacy, something all dealers crave as they move on up. They always introduced me as having 'been to fucking university and all that fucking shit'. In whichever of their venues they held court that night, I was encouraged to engage their associates and bumpy-knuckled foot soldiers in banal banter as the Dochertys hoovered huge mounds of Bolivian accelerants.

To be honest, they scared me shitless. I had started to bring Murph or Gray along with me, just in case. Sure, the Dohertys had given me my start in the business, but it didn't hurt to show you had real physical power within your organisation. Gotta have muscle if you want to hustle.

I was young and ambitious. I'd come this far on ego, wit and attitude. I reckoned I could take on almost anybody. As our business expanded I started to look for alternative routes of supply behind the Dohertys' backs. I was soon to find myself taking the shuttle plane from City Airport in London to meet with our new connections in Amsterdam every fortnight. Probably better the Dohertys didn't know about it.

Throughout all this, I was holding down a day job. I worked in local government if only to have at least some legitimate income to put the boys in blue off the scent. I had left university in July 1989 and was in a bit of a quandary about what I was going to do next. I realised that I had to legitimise myself to a certain extent to avoid any heat from Plod or the Inland Revenue. I was living way beyond my means, in fact I had no legally recognised source of income. Working my way up through the marketing department of some faceless corporation didn't really appeal and I needed a job which would give me time to keep expanding my real job: dealing pills and speed. I actually applied to Camden Council for a job as a parking officer, but at the interview it was deemed that I was overqualified and I was sent over to see the manager of the Superannuation Division who had a vacancy for a pensions officer. After an amiable chat I was offered the job and it proved to be perfectly suited to my needs. The position entailed me being out of the office a lot visiting pensioners in the borough, which made room for my other, less than socially benign activities – management were pretty lax in checking where I actually was at any given time. The division also worked on a flexitime system. If I so desired, I could clock in at 10 a.m., clock off for lunch at noon, return at 2.30 in the afternoon and leave at 4.00 p.m.: a three-and-a-half-hour day. Sure, I would invariably have to make up the time at some point or other and occasionally found myself working a 14-hour day, but it gave me the leeway to keep my narco-empire on track. I wasn't exactly using the skills I'd learnt on my degree course, but I wasn't planning a career in local government. Like most members of the dealing fraternity I fully expected to get out of the game and retire after a few years, so a stint as a council pensions advisor was no skin off my nose.

The work itself was pretty easygoing and I wasn't exactly chained to my desk on a nine-to-five basis, but I was still spending time with the Dohertys, controlling the overall supply and gearing up to organise a continental pipeline to reduce our reliance on the Brothers D. Gray was doing most of the legwork and Murph was keeping our runners in the clubs cool: I rarely touched a pill or a wrap. The cash profits were beginning to overflow from several shoeboxes under my bed. But mixing my day job and nocturnal narco-commerce became problematic. By night, I was Mr Nasty in east London's burgeoning drug and club scene – by day, I was a mild-mannered clerk in the Superannuation Division at Camden Council.

I worked from offices in King's Cross, itself London's epicentre for low-rent street-level smack 'n' crack dealing. My arrogance convinced me that my own narco-action was elevated from the sleazy crap going down on the side streets around my office.

Reality was that the difference was largely imaginary – the end results were similar and the motivation was exactly the same: hard cash, not to feed a habit, but to feed my ego.

Communication was a serious problem. I couldn't really have people phoning into my open-plan office at work to discuss the finer points of knocking out whizz and pills.

We only had one cellular phone between us at that time. Technology in the late 1980s did not stretch to the micro-sized mobile fun gizmos currently spewing from Finland and Japan. This baby was the size of a house brick. Battery life was measured not in hours but in minutes. The brick took three days to charge up.

I was responsible for the phone, but I couldn't carry it around as an accessory. Mobile telephones were expensive status symbols for wealthy yuppie city boys. Even the Council's Director of Finance didn't have one. So your humble civil servant carried the brick around in a rucksack, which I toted everywhere.

One slight problem was that its ringtone had the quiet subtlety of an inter-continental ballistic-missile launch. Luckily for me, my colleagues were stupid, incurious, or both.

It became apparent that I needed to further beef up the ranks of my operation when, one afternoon, my parallel careers collided spectacularly.

Part of my job at Camden Council entailed visiting pensioners to ensure they were being catered to and supported at acceptable levels by the local authority. As I mentioned, it got me out of the office.

Usually, this involved swinging by sky-rise council tower blocks to see elderly widows or widowers. Apart from the counter staff at the local social security office or supermarket checkout, I was often their only human contact.

These visits usually consisted of several hours of listening to how it was so much better in ye goode olde days as I drank several gallons of weak tea. To this day I can't bring myself to touch the stuff.

I was at Mrs McQuigley's when the bloody phone demonstrated its mild and mellow ringtone. Mrs McQuigley wasn't seeing 90 again: her faculties, like her weight and her dreams, were mostly behind her. The old biddy thought that we had returned to the days of the wartime Blitz. She panicked and started searching for her gas mask, as Nazi bombers were doubtless overhead.

The phone kept ringing. She kept flapping.

'It's them Jerry whatchermacallits, doodlebugs . . .' she warned me. As she rolled under the kitchen table, I abandoned futile attempts to reassure her, and answered the phone. It was Murph. He had seriously fucked up.

Pushed for time, I'd given Murph the simple task of running 50 pills over to a distributor I was cultivating, a routine tube journey from Angel Islington to Westbourne Grove: 30 minutes tops.

Murph still lived off social security. He hoovered his narco-income straight up his nose in gargantuan amounts. His paranoia was off the scale and in my ear.

Murph had caught the train at the Angel, sat down and stuffed the gear between the seat cushions directly behind him. But he had neglected to retrieve the goodie-bag when he got off at the Grove.

Picture the scene.

The Widow McQuigley was turning her gaff upside down, screaming about an impending firestorm and mustard-gas bombs, as I was trying to calm an extremely agitato Murph.

The pill bag had his prints on it: given his hobby as a psychopathic lunatic, PC Plod had taken Murph's fingertips for a stroll across the old ink-and-blotter many times before.

Clear thinking and a quick decision were required. If Murph was pulled up on a charge which might involve a custodial sentence, would he grass me up as the boss of our little firm? I didn't trust him enough.

Simple.

'Mrs McQuigley, your pension payment will be with you in the first post tomorrow. Now, *sit down there and shut the fuck up, please.*'

She complied immediately. I explained to her, as calmly as I could, that the war had been kaput for more than 40 years, and that the only evil emanating from Germany these days was some dire pop music perpetrated by women who didn't shave their armpits. I legged it to Westbourne Grove. Taaaaxi!

Murph was frantic. Even by his standards, he hadn't got all the dots on his dominoes.

We spent the next three hours riding trains on the Metropolitan line, moving from carriage to carriage, groping between the seats, to no avail.

'I got it, I got it,' Murph said, suddenly inspired. 'It's so fucking easy. All we have to do is ring up the lost property office.'

'And what the fuck are we going to tell them?' I asked. 'Excuse me, but I seem to have lost 50 tabs of pure MDMA on one of your trains. Has anybody handed them in?' Even Murph realised it was dumber than a bar of soap.

We sweated it out for a while.

'Whoever found them either didn't realise what they were, and chucked them . . .' Murph said.

'Or more likely, clocked the pills and did a runner with five hundred quid's worth of my merchandise,' I said. 'The bloody bastard.'

Either way, Murph was in the clear, but the limitations of our set-up had hit home. We needed more help, fresh blood. Murph and Gray had two brain cells between them, and one had run off leaving the other to die of loneliness.

So by autumn 1989, I decided that I needed some support at my level of the operation. I brought in a Vice President. He was to be my right-hand man and help me clean up our cash flow. I was also about to embark on my first trip to Holland for a major score, and would need someone to oversee that side of the operation and help Gray with driving the drugs back to the UK.

Gary Baptiste was right for the job. He was my best friend from my schooldays and someone I knew wouldn't knife me in the back at the first sign of trouble.

This is where the worlds of legitimate and illicit business contrast: a VP in the legitimate commercial world is often someone with long service within a specific sphere, but insufficient talent to move up and take extra responsibility. So the corporation keeps them safe with a grandiose title and a few more spondoolicks in the breadbasket. But no more power.

As my VP, Gary was to back me up in the decision-making process: all organisations suffer from politics and ours was no different. He would help supervise Murph and Gray. He was my voice of sweet reason when key strategies, like which clubs we would take on and which runners would work for us, were set in stone. Gary B was there to cover my back. We both understood our set-up, and its potential pitfalls. He was the one I had to rely on when the wheels fell off, as they invariably did. He was my drug buddy and confidant.

Baptiste was a preternaturally handsome black dude. He was smart, charming and funny. More importantly, I trusted him.

We were making truckloads of cash. I kept mine in shoeboxes. We did our best to spend it out on the town on non-business nights. Our wardrobes were crammed with Armani and Versace and our noses stuffed with pure Colombian blue-flake coke, courtesy of the Dohertys. By this time I had stopped taking pills myself: the headfuck was too much to deal with. My cocaine consumption, however, was becoming pretty serious and, worse still, I had dabbled occasionally with heroin. I didn't know it then, but I was developing a habit which would come back and haunt me during the next few years.

Among the East End's underworld cognoscenti, who we were and what we did was an open secret. Through our connections on the doors, we had instant access to most of the eastside bars and clubs. I didn't socialise with Murph much and it was a rare occasion that his wife let him out to play – and anyway, the sight of blood can really put a crimp in my evening. Murph's nightlife was purely restricted to the weekends when he was patrolling the clubs for me. So, Gray Gillet and I had the attention of many fine fillies as we hung out in these boîtes – until they spotted Gary B and abandoned us to circle him, kittens to his catnip. The greedy bastard. Out of hours, Gary had a talent that I have never seen before or since. Every time he went out, he went home with a different girl. Maybe his knicker-dropping grin helped: his consistent strike rate was flabbergasting.

So Gray and I began to exclude Gary from our social itinerary. When he found out, he'd go into a tremendous sulk, which required some full-on psychological trick-cycling to dispel.

Hits means writs. And in the second half of 1989, we had two new problems directly stemming from our combo's success: hot issues and cold cash.

We were making more than we could spend. What should we do with the surplus cash? And then there was the heat.

The boys and girls in shiny buttons were au fait with the nature of our business. They'd pull each of us in for routine questioning with monotonous regularity. Remember, heat is bad for business. And it was starting to get quite annoying. We were continually being collared by the same detectives from Hackney CID for interview. My answers, even to me, were becoming increasingly unconvincing with repetition.

These two problems were related: to integrate the cash and clean it via the UK banking system would attract attention from the taxation authorities, and thus the police. Things came to a head with Gary's car.

Baptiste had always been flashy. It was in his genes: he groomed to thrill, dressed to kill and loved his rides. He was the only other member of our syndicate who had a day job. He worked as a mechanic at a distinctly dodgy garage which specialised in cutting, chopping and ringing upmarket motors.

None of us had the legitimate income to support our standard of living, so I had imposed a rule that we were to curtail our cash expenditure unless hanging out with similarly minded members of the criminal fraternity. Consequently, the best car we could buy was a second-hand BMW 3-Series – or something scuzzier – because, by this stage, even traffic cops were continually pulling us over just for the sake of delaying us and causing us unnecessary hassle.

The road rozzers supposedly played 'car snooker'. Its rules were simple: they would systematically pull over cars, awarding themselves points on the same scoring system as snooker, so every red car tugged would be followed by another colour, with black being worth maximum; with more red balls on a snooker table than any other colour, red and black were obviously shades to avoid when we bought a new set of wheels, which we each did every three or four months.

The cars were always bought with cash at auctions: the sale of our previous vehicles converted our money into legitimate cash as cheques or banker's drafts. We'd request car buyers to pay one way or the other.

I used to drive silver or grey VW Golf GTIs to avoid the snooker scenario, but still usually got stopped every couple of days.

It was a Wednesday night in November 1989, and Gray had organised to spend an evening with me at a pub on the Hackney Road. We didn't invite Gary B because we were on the pull. It had been a while for both of us. Murph's wife had him locked down during the week. You expected to see her hoofprint branded on the poor sod's forehead as a mark of ownership. I had been screening my calls all day, as Baptiste was ringing every hour saying he wanted to hook up. I was slightly desperate for female company, and reckoned a Gary-free evening was just what the sex therapist ordered.

I was checking spectacles, testicles, wallet and watch before heading for the hoedown of the evening's entertainment, when Baptiste pulled up in his latest ride and parked up outside my flat. The word car covers this vehicle loosely: it was a mack mobile, a motorised pimp palace, a four-wheeled jukebox.

That morning he'd paid thirty grand in cold cash for this two-year-old, bright red Mercedes Benz SL500. The automotive nightmare had been customised by detailers enthralled not by crankshafts, but by Shaft, John Shaft. It flaunted more chrome than a Jewish bathroom; overextended wheel arches; a TV aerial on the boot; 18-inch alloy wheels; jet-black tinted windows; and low-rider suspension, so the whole shooting match sat mere millimetres above the road.

Baptiste was rambling about compression ratios, torque 'and the legendary feel of fine Corinthian leather. Smell it man, just smell that . . .'

My coolant zeroed out and I boiled over.

'You mother-fucking cock-sucking dumb-ass shithead . . .' I began. Then laid down some megawatt verbal.

No one would notice its bright scarlet paint job, I explained to Baptiste, and the vehicle's neon-lit underbody – eerily reminiscent of a spaceship from my elder brother's 1970s Teutonic prog-rock album covers – was unlikely to attract either attention or surveillance.

'And you park it right outside my door you freaking nutter. Why not save time and drive us down to the nick right now . . .'

Gary stammered his apologies.

After 20 minutes or so, now merely furious, I established that although he had bought the car for cash that morning, he had not yet changed the registration over to his name. Technically, the vehicle was in limbo: it didn't belong to anybody.

Baptiste tried not to cry as we drove back from Hackney Marshes in my Golf later that evening.

We had ceremonially doused the Bordello Benz with petrol on a barren spot of wasteland beyond the dog track. Gary couldn't bring himself to administer the *coup de grâce*, so it was up to me to flick a match onto the pyre and put it out of its misery.

This was a clear signal that we needed to devise and adopt a more structured way of cleaning our cash. The answer to our problem was simple, but took up most of my free time during the next two years.

Any legitimate business cash transaction north of £10,000 attracts attention from the Inland Revenue and, often, the police. Internationally, similar rules apply: $10,000 tags a flag on the screens of the IRS in the US, or Australia's ATO. You will have to be very well established before you start thinking about numbered accounts in Zurich or the Cayman Islands.

There are only so many cars you can sell in a year, or horses that come in at 100:1, to justify integrating narco-sized stacks of cash into the banking system legitimately.

Taxation irregularities will get you busted faster than the actual manufacture or distribution of narcotics. Remember Al Capone?

Ideally, you need someone on the inside of the finance world. If that isn't viable, then pick an individual who can learn quickly and play the role. The point of integration of dirty money into the legitimate system is the point of maximum risk: so no ponytails, tie-dyes nor 'attitude' should be a part of your player's make-up.

This may be one part of the operation you should conduct in person. A sharp suit, a pair of glasses and a plausible manner go a long way in allaying bank tellers' suspicions of large cash transactions. Remember, it's the teller behind the till who can raise the flag that could ultimately bring you down.

With the help of an acquaintance on the inside of one of the major UK banking chains, we formulated what turned out to be a highly successful laundering operation.

Banking methods were far less sophisticated in the late '80s and early '90s than they are today. So, although you can apply the principles we used, your chances of getting caught out have greatly increased.

By now, we were generating an annual cash surplus of around £1 million. After our extravagant expenditure on clothes, cars, coke and casinos we had about half a million clear profit to be laundered every year.

We fronted up every bank and building society, opening multiple accounts with each, but at different branches using different IDs.

Baptiste and I were the cash integrators. We looked more convincing than Gray. Murph's coke habit had induced a paranoid psychosis; he believed he was being followed everywhere by the law. For once, his delusions were on nodding terms with the truth as the cops chose this period to notch up the pressure.

Every working day of every week Baptiste and I, in suits and ties, visited these retail banks in a carefully ordered pattern. A separate branch on the same day, at the same time, every week.

I wore a pair of clear glass spectacles to emphasise my ordinariness. Only my £1,000 Donna Karan suit distinguished me from a million wage slaves. Its sartorial subtlety would be lost on a bunch of bank clerks in the burbs.

It was quite easy then to open an account using fake ID and a rented postal address, where you would receive passbooks, ATM cards and bank statements.

In each branch at the designated time and date, we would aim for the same teller, usually female, and turn on the charm. We carried an envelope with a copy of a payslip and cash; depositing identical amounts each week into every account, it looked like we were paying our weekly wages into the bank.

Personal computers helped us run the admin, but the paperwork was incessant.

I'd nominate an arbitrary amount, say £265.40, to deposit while we studiously examined our payslips and complained to the teller what a bloody pittance it was.

Every few months we would drop a four-figure cash-bomb, under the ten grand mark to avoid Inland Revenue attention, into every account. Along with some chat about the car we'd just sold to some nice young chap.

Our methodology was tried and tested, but the running around was frustrating. The secret to success was consistency. The Revenue had the banks install software programmes that flagged any accounts that received cash deposits without incurring withdrawals. We would make a small withdrawal each week, maybe £20, from every account via an ATM card to avoid attention.

So we sorted our laundry, and all ran smoothly.

First, Camden Social Services . . . now, provincial building societies. Was there no beginning to the glamorous life of an up-and-coming drug dealer? Well yes, there was. Only not quite as I'd envisioned it. I was becoming totally hacked off with the Doherty brothers and their way of doing business, which involved me paying way over the odds for the pills and whizz, despite the fact that I was buying in bulk. By the end of 1989 I decided that the time was right to open up a European arm to our operation. I had been thinking it through for several months and was sure that we could successfully bring the drugs we needed into the UK ourselves. I couldn't just drop my deal with the Dohertys, but if we had an alternative supply chain we could triple the amount of gear we were selling without being chained to the Brothers D. I was sure we could buy stuff from the continent more cheaply than we were getting it from John Doherty and his siblings, and we definitely needed more on the floors. Our mission to control the doors of the clubs in the East End had been very successful and we had dealing rights in several of the largest venues. Demand was outstripping supply and although I knew that we could get as much gear as we wanted from the Dohertys, they had us between a rock and a hard place and were basically ripping us off. We would keep our regular order with the Brothers Grimm and look elsewhere to fuel our expansion. I had Baptiste in place to run things once the supply line was set in place, and he and Gray could handle the actual transportation. All I needed was a connection in Europe and I knew just the right man for the job.

MR NASTY

AMSTERDAM

CANDY LAND

I spotted Maud about 100 yards ahead of me as I sauntered down central Amsterdam's Van Baerlestraat. One-time bank teller, part-time drag queen, and now my introductory agent to some big-time bulk dealers, Maud perched on the steps of the coffee shop. He was puffing on a reefer the size of low-gauge drainpipe. He looked round, his peroxide crew cut bobbing in the sunlight, and gave me a laconical stoned wave as I approached. Game on.

Maud was really my brother's friend, but he'd been in the Dam for a while and had some useful connections. Visiting the city as a drug tourist during the past year, I had reached out to build a rapport with him, and we had fostered a mutual trust.

This time was different. The £10,000 nestling snugly in my jacket pocket required me to ask Maud to really stick his neck out for me. I wanted to be hooked up with the connections to sort me out for Ecstasy and amphetamines.

Maud gave me a hug as I drew level with the plume of smoke he was exhaling delicately through his nostrils. 'Hello, stranger. Welcome to Candy Land.' We exchanged greetings and went inside.

It was just before Christmas, 1989, and I was ready to trade up to being a real player in London's drug business and ramp up supply for the festive season. My nerve endings were raw with adrenalin, but I had a sense of incredible excitement. And no fear.

This Dam deal was crucial to my operation in terms of pushing us up a tier. At the time, I had moved up to buying a couple of thousand pills and a kilo of speed a week from the Doherty brothers. But they were asking a high price: I needed a reliable bulk supplier to improve our profit margin. We were making lots of money as things were, but the potential for even greater riches was huge. Quite simply, we needed more gear at a cheaper price.

This meant shopping in the Dam, and if I got the quantities that I was after, we'd generate enough revenue to reinvest in the business and increase our supply exponentially. I was about to move from being a casual visitor buying ten-guilder bags of grass in Amsterdam's coffee shops to my first major score on European soil.

My confidence was high: I reckoned we could move as much merchandise through clubland as we could smuggle in. If I pulled off this purchase, and established a pipeline into the UK, then the sky was the limit.

Maud sat opposite me in the half-full café and passed me a spliff. I took a deep toke and felt my head start to spin as the zero-zero hash congested my lungs. A couple of hits of this very fine Bob Hope wouldn't hurt, but I knew I'd require the fullest use of my faculties for the job ahead.

Maud gave me a knowing wink as he sat draped in his chair, resplendent in an orange T-shirt and brilliant white dungarees. The guy was camper than an Ungaro spring dress.

Most Europeans who dabble with soft drugs make it to Amsterdam sometime, many under the misapprehension that drugs are legal in Holland: they are not. Possession of Class A hard narcotics can land you in serious trouble. There is a tolerance policy, the *gedogen* approach, to soft drugs, like cannabis. In the 1980s you could be found with up to 30g of hash or weed in your possession and that was deemed acceptable for personal use. But the tolerated amount was slashed to only 5g after pressure from Holland's neighbours, who have been in a tizz over their nationals trading contraband drugs across their borders: France has endured periodic trafficking epidemics. The Belgians too have been vociferous in demanding a Dutch crackdown on soft-drug exports.

The political thinking is that the market in Class B and C drugs fosters a socially more corrosive trade in Class A narcotics. They have a point: there's a constant flow of smack across the Dutch–French border, and moves towards the controlled legalisation of heroin in the Netherlands have only fuelled disagreement among the European authorities.

Hard drugs are prevalent on the streets of the Dam's red-light district, although the chances of getting ripped off or, worse still, beaten up for your money, are quite high.

If it's pills that you are after, you're better trying your luck in one of the city's nightclubs.

In Amsterdam, most of the trade in soft drugs takes place in the numerous coffee shops – *koffieshops*, as they are called locally – as opposed to the city's other cafés – *koffiehuis* – where you won't find anything stronger than an espresso. Typically, the coffee shops have a menu behind the bar with a dozen or so varieties of weed and hash listed, ranging from mellow Moroccan hash to locally grown and harvested super skunk. Those of limited spliff-making abilities can buy joints ready-rolled.

But the uninitiated should be warned that some of this stuff can radically impair your functions. It's known as 'card-table baccy', because your legs fold up and under if you overindulge.

The days of peace, love and hippyshit went with the 1960s. Soft drugs are now grown in huge hydroponic weed farms nestling amidst the tulip groves of rural Holland. The smaller, privately owned coffee shops are also a rare breed these days, as organised crime, local syndicates or the Russian gangsteri now control most production and sale. All of the hard-drug trade is the remit of organised cartels and syndicates. Much of Europe's cocaine and heroin passes through the Dutch port of Rotterdam en route to its final destination.

Amsterdam is often described as a drugs supermarket. But in

most supermarkets I've visited lately you don't need to 'know the right people'. And drugs supermarkets don't take credit cards, quelle surprise. So I played Maud in. He regularly met the dope suppliers for the coffee shop he managed. Although he wasn't in the pill biz, he knew people I could talk to and had been busy since my phone call to him the week before.

He helped me in two ways: one involved the introduction; the other was to act as a temporary hired hand to hold the buy-money for the first deal. I never asked him: Maud volunteered for this second role. Perhaps he was a bigger thrill junkie than I had suspected. Drama queen plays gangster.

'So what's the plan, brown eyes?'

Maud was a total tease, an incorrigible flirt who hit on everybody, straight or gay, just to provoke a reaction.

'The plan is simple. We meet these guys, pay for the gear and then ride off into the sunset.'

I wasn't giving him too much information and Maud looked visibly hurt for a second, temperamental soul that he was. But he wasn't going to let me butch him out.

'OK, OK, I get the point,' he said. 'You have to meet me here tonight at 8 p.m. There will be someone here that will be able to sort you out with what you need. You don't need to get all pushy about it.'

If I stuck around, I would infect Maud with the paranoia enervating my system. So I told him that I would be there at 7.55 and departed to plot, scheme and scam from my hotel room.

Mr Nasty's rules for conducting a major deal should be implemented to the letter by both professional buyers and sellers – when the deal actually goes down, the drugs and the money are held separately from the location of the primary parties until the last possible moment. It's not that we don't trust each other. Actually, it's entirely because we don't trust each other. Always keep the buy-money with a friendly third party until you have seen and sampled the merchandise and are totally happy. Taste and try before you buy.

Maud had a battered old Peugeot and was to be my bag man. He may have been a tantrum-prone diva, but I trusted him.

MR NASTY

The best deals are conducted on neutral ground. The principal parties involved in the transaction meet when holding neither drugs nor cash. The transaction's tangible elements are only introduced when both parties bring them in.

If you are conducting the deal on your own territory then there's the risk of a set-up and the cavalry, in the shape of Officer Dibble, riding in. If the deal is done on the supplier's turf then the chances of being liberated from your cash and departing sans goods increase dramatically.

Yay, come to narco-country where the living is easy.

All that afternoon I lay on the bed in my hotel room, tired from the morning's 6 a.m. flight, but unable to sleep. I kept replaying every possible scenario: blue-sky outcomes to worst-case scenarios. Then I'd devise fresh ones.

I had no way of chemically analysing the goods, but I knew what high-quality pills and speed tasted like by now. I hoped I could keep my tongue in my mouth and get the job done.

I was unarmed. What if they had shooters? What if they took my wedge and then gave me the flick off? Worse still, if they were armed, they could take my money and give me one behind the ear for my trouble.

I didn't even want to think about the final part of the process yet. But rogue agents in my brain rehearsed it. For, on this first run back into the UK, I was going to have to carry the drugs back into London on my person.

I had unobtrusively scoped out security and Customs arrangements at London's City Airport for weeks. They seemed lax. But you can't always plan for an overzealous official to piss on your fireworks.

City Airport was my point-of-entry because it was located smack bang in the middle of the East End. It was much quieter than Heathrow, Gatwick or either of the two smaller airports out further east. City Airport's flights were restricted to compact, prop-driven planes; you could clear Customs in about ten minutes.

There was still a high risk. But I would just have to pluck up my courage and take my chances.

My thoughts turned to what I was actually intending to buy: 1,000 pills at the equivalent of £6 per tablet and, with the remaining four large of my cash, 1kg of base amphetamine sulphate. This was a major leap from moving a few pills around town. If this deal went smoothly I would have transformed myself from a two-bit runner to an international trafficker.

Base sulphate is the purest form of speed; snort it and you'll buzz away for 48 hours. Buying base meant that I could step on the shipment: by cutting the powder with ground-up caffeine tablets we could boost a 1kg purchase into 2kg worth of revenue.

Most amphetamines are cut, adulterated with other substances. Some speed has been confiscated by police with a purity as low as 2 per cent. Most will prove to be around 20 per cent pure. Every stage at the lower end of drug distribution involves somehow diluting the product. Which is why, as a buyer, you want to get as close as you can to the source of supply while avoiding concomitant grief.

Even after I'd stepped on the whizz, I would still have a high-quality product for the East End party monsters. At an eventual retail price of £10 per gram, the deal promised market growth and potentially vast wealth generation.

Speed, sometimes called 'poor man's coke', is one of the simplest drugs to manufacture and one of the most lucrative, apart from cocaine and heroin, to distribute. Speed, sulph, whizz, Billy – to use a few of its street names – is a bit of a drug oddity. Officially it is classified in the UK as a Class B drug, but the holder can be prosecuted for possession of a Class A narcotic if it is seized in a cooked-up form, ready for injection. Trafficking, which is what I hoped to be doing, carries a maximum of 14 years' imprisonment in the UK.

After the Second World War, during which both Allies and Axis had supplied uppers to troops under pressure, amphetamines went mainstream and were used to treat depression and obesity during the 1950s and 1960s.

Illicit use in the UK mainland caught on during the mid-1960s Mod period. The short-haired, parka-clad, Vespa-scooting youth would fuel up on pep pills before their rumbles in south coast holiday resorts with equally wired leather-clad motorbike gangs called Rockers. Same belligerence, different uniforms.

Manufacturing methods vary from territory to territory. In Europe, the major catalyst for production is hydrochloric acid. The end product can dissolve your teeth and, with prolonged use, mash your internal organs. In Euroland, you can always tell a speed freak by counting their cavities. Further afield, in Australia, the manufacturing process is completely different and speed is more of a methamphetamine with the core ingredient being ephedrine. Drug gangs buy up huge amounts of over-the-counter cold and flu remedies and distil them down to produce Aussie whizz. Speed comes in powder or crystalline forms, with colours often featuring shades of white, off-white or pink. Pink speed is much coveted because it's purer.

Typically, speed is either snorted or dabbed. Dabbing is plunging your finger into a pile of speed, licking it off and swallowing asap: it tastes vile and you can almost feel your teeth dissolving. It's sometimes flicked into drinks for smooth absorption, or packed into 'Rizla bombs': after the powder is wrapped within the cigarette paper, you swallow it. This doesn't accelerate your bloodstream's absorption rate much, but does minimise the drug's disgusting taste.

Speed's effect is a coarser, less subtle version of the cocaine ride. It lasts longer: a coke bump stays in your bloodstream for around 45 minutes, whereas a snort of speed will stick around for 5 hours. The effects mirror those of cocaine: higher energy levels, loquaciousness, appetite suppression, increased stamina and insomnia.

Speed's downside is brutal – to paraphrase Julie Burchill, taking speed is like overdrawing at the energy bank. What you borrow from the physical energy the chemical creates, you must repay when its traces dissipate. It can seriously harm your sex drive and heart rhythm. Its psychological effects are wicked, and not in a good way. The comedown is nasty. Some call it sulphate crash-and-burn. Most hardcore speedfreaks try to avoid it by continuing to use more gear. And that's how they get a habit. Long-term abuse triggers psychosis.

I remember one of my first speed punters, a student called Danny Towers. Eventually, he bought his crank in 50g bags and ingested the lot within a week. Danny had that Billy Whizz twitch that made him act like an over-caffeinated gerbil, and he believed that the giant spiders that lived under his bed were out to get him.

I crashed at Danny's flat one night, kipping in his bed as Danny, on a bender with the gear, preferred to spend the wee hours staring wide-eyed at rubbish TV.

In the morning, I sauntered through to the kitchen where Danny was preparing breakfast. I watched as he dipped a teaspoon into the open bag of sulphate on the kitchen table and proceeded to sprinkle it liberally over his cornflakes.

'What fucking planet are you on, Danny?'

'Planet Billy, my man, Planet Billy,' he said.

He spooned up a mound of speed-frosted flakes into his mouth. Such is the madness of the hardened speed user, but you had to admire his dedication to the cause of getting totally fucked up.

You can't become physically addicted to whizz that easily, unless you are injecting it, but psychological dependence comes quickly, particularly if you ill-advisedly mainline the stuff. This is serious substance abuse's twilight lounge. Shooting speed creates a neurone-affected buzz, akin to that of crack cocaine.

Mr Nasty's rule on whizz is to remember that the higher you fly, the further you fall: coming down from speed is one of the worst feelings in the world. Imagine your emotional responses having been carved out of your body. Physically, you feel completely drained. Every movement is a chore and mental agility is all but impossible during your recovery from nights with Billy

Whizz. Hitting the real world from amphetamine's dizzy heights is like hitting concrete at 1,000mph.

I brooded on what I was about to unleash on London's drug-buying public. The clock gradually ticked round to 7.30 and I tried to clear my mind of any elements of doubt about the enterprise at hand. Then at 7.45 it was time to make a move.

It was a short walk from my hotel to Maud's coffee shop along Amsterdam's beautiful, canal-lined streets. When I arrived, just before 8 p.m., the café was thronged with people, but I was disappointed not to spy my man behind the counter when I peered through the front window.

Suddenly, I heard a lever window opening. Maud's head popped out directly above me as I stood on the steps.

'Catch.'

He tossed down a bunch of keys and indicated, with a nod, the side door a few yards to the right of the main entrance. Although we'd barely begun, my heart was already thump-thump-thumping.

I walked up the steep stairs. A landing opened out into a chic little kitchenette and front room. Chez Maud was overwhelmed by pot plants, surprisingly all strictly legitimate, which was far from my take on the gruesome twosome slouched on Maud's purple-and-gold flocked sofa. Both looked on only nodding terms with the bathtub. They had mixed and mismatched their Asian and African hippyshit clothes and accessories, and looked like they'd dressed in the dark during an acid flashback.

Hippy Number One rose to his feet and extended a hand.

'Hello, we are happy to be meeting with you.'

You know how when you're listening to playback from a black box retrieved from a crash site, just before the plane goes down you can often hear an alarm sounding in the background? Figuratively, I could hear it now: 99 per cent of all Dutch people speak fluent English, many using better syntax than English speakers themselves. This clown could barely string a sentence together. His handshake was insipid.

'I am Niils and this is Stephan,' Hippy One said.

He indicated with a vague wave his equally tie-dyed cohort, sprawled across the sofa with a joint wedged in his hand. Great! So much for my abstinence earlier in the day. This felt skeletal.

'You are bringing the monies with you?' So Hippy Two had a voice.

'Are you bringing the drugs with you?' Sorry, but I couldn't resist joining in the local patois.

This was a bad scene: I was breaking the rules of running a deal. I had brought the buy-money with me, planning to pass it to Maud to carry it separately. On my signal that the pills were bona, he was supposed to pitch in with the cash. But it wasn't going down like that.

'We have what you want right here.' Niils nodded to Stephan, who produced a bag of pale blue tablets from the inside pocket of his cheap topcoat. The bag looked improbably small.

'Is that the whole thousand?'

It had to be a sample of the full six grand's worth.

'No, we are bringing 150 with us.'

I glanced over at Maud, who had taken a seat in a wicker chair opposite the Chuckle Brothers. He had the grace to look sheepish.

'The order was for 1,000 pills at £6 each. What the hell am I going to waste my time with 150 for? I can pick that amount up in London and save the airfare.' I was annoyed.

Niils and Stephan exchanged blank looks. I could almost hear the oxygen whistling through their ears.

'Please tell me that you have got the speed.'

'Yeah, yeah, sure. One large one of sulphate. Take it easy, my friend,' Stephan said.

His pinprick pupils reinforced my suspicion that he was completely caned. Mr Nasty's rules dictate: don't trust a hippy. And never, ever, trust a junkie.

'Show me the speed,' I snapped.

'You will be showing us the monies first, yeah?'

It was time to take control.

'Look. I've come a long way, too far to be dicked around by a couple of divs like you. The dough's here with me, and you can check it when I'm satisfied that at least you can deliver on the sulphate.'

Stephan produced a snap-lock bag with a miniscule amount of yellowish powder in it.

'What the fuck is that? That's not a kilo.'

'This is what you want. A large one of speed.'

'For Christ's sake, I meant a kilo, not an ounce.'

I moved forwards slightly and they both flinched. They didn't have a clue what they were doing, and were scared shitless too.

'Right. Both of you can just get the fuck out of here right now.'

'But you are not paying us the monies.'

'No kilo and only 150 pills equals no deal and no money. Now the pair of you can just fuck yourselves off right now. Go on, fucking do one.'

They did as I ordered. They rose and shuffled off down the stairs in silence. I sagged down onto the sofa, my adrenalin levels on the wane.

'Bloody hell, Maud, is that the best that Amsterdam has to offer? Where did you find that pair of muppets? Drugs R Us?'

'Oh, don't be so cross with me,' he said. 'That's the best that I could do at short notice. Those two are my suppliers for the shop.'

'No, you moron, those two are the delivery boys. I need to talk to the people who supply them. I'm not getting busted for the sake of a few pills and an ounce of whizz. How the hell do I get to talk to the bigger fish rather than the bottom feeders?'

'I'll have to make some calls,' he said. 'Don't get pissed off with me. I'm doing the best that I can.'

He looked disappointed by the evening's pathetic events.

'Sorry, Maud. It's not your fault. I think I'd better get back to my hotel.'

'I'm sorry, Cam. Meet me back here at noon tomorrow and we'll have another go.'

I trudged back through the red-light district to my canalside hotel. Half of the minibar's contents to the good, I accepted that this was not going to be the cakewalk I'd expected. Those two had been as much use as an ashtray on a motorbike.

The next day dawned with crisp winter sunshine. I decided to take a more positive approach after last night's farce. Breakfasting by the canal on pancakes and syrup, I window-shopped to kill time until the next meet with Maud.

I arrived at the coffee shop at 12 p.m. prompt. Behind the counter, Maud jerked his head towards a table in the corner and held up his hand to signal five minutes. I sat down and waited.

Lou Reed has some well-chosen words about waiting for the man that cranked up on my internal jukebox. They do illustrate a larger truth about narco-time. Occasionally, your life can seem to flash before you in a second. But when you're engaged in buying or selling drugs, it seems to move much slower than real time.

Forty actual minutes later Maud was finally able to bound from behind his counter and join me. He was fizzing with excitement. To him this was some jolly adventure. To me, it was an enterprise that, if we weren't more careful, could see us both banged up in choky. But I didn't want to burst his bubble.

'We're on for tonight,' he said. 'I made some calls and there are some people who can sort you out. We are meeting them at The Roxy later. You owe me several birthday and Christmas presents for this.' I ignored his camp charm.

'Do you know them?'

'No, but these boys are the ones who supply half the coffee shops in Amsterdam with their puff. We are talking about some seriously connected people.'

'Hallelujah for that. I'll meet you there and you can introduce me, then disappear and wait until I need you to bring the buy-money into things.'

'Gosh, I feel just like a gangster.'

'Just as long as you don't start acting like one,' I said, 'we should be OK.'

After recounting my buy-money back at the hotel, I had an afternoon at leisure in Amsterdam. I bought some chocolate from a hausfrau in a shop where I picked up some other essential supplies: a jar of instant coffee, gaffer tape and clingfilm.

I admired the *gevelstenen*, the gablestones high on the old buildings that pre-date the city's French occupation in 1795. Sculpted and coloured, they were an idiosyncratic symbol that revealed much about the person who had owned the house: here was a hide dealer, there a grain carrier and, oh yes, a yawning man, the sign of a druggist.

The *gevelstenen* had guided the Dutch around their city, but baffled the French, who numbered every building. I would need to have my wits about me in this strange terrain.

Walking down to The Roxy that evening I was less enthusiastic about the deal than I had been earlier. If Maud was right, these were not people to mess with. I was pretty sure that they would be tooled up with some kind of weaponry. The best I could manage was my cutting wit.

I'd told Maud to bring the motor with him. After bitching about how hard it would be to find a parking space, he'd agreed. We had arranged to meet outside at 8 p.m.

The Roxy was probably the best nightclub in Amsterdam: small, tasteful, and usually packed solely with the Dutch. This was a small slice of town that remained for locals only. The club's strict door policy kept tourists out. Particularly English tourists. There would be no footie louts crossing this threshold. Maud had assured me he was a regular and could get me in. He was waiting outside in a bright purple jumpsuit.

'Hiya, gorgeous. Don't bother with the queue, I've already smoothed our passage.' He couldn't help smirking when he said this. I was too edgy to bother with the innuendo.

'Here, take this and don't let it out of your sight.'

As surreptitiously as possible, I handed him the wad of £50 notes, folded in half. He palmed same, pocketing it in that tasteful jumpsuit. I was to be 'clean' while I conducted the deal, standard practice in London. Maud was to hold the folding stuff until the last possible moment. I just hoped the Dutch knew the score when it came to getting down and dirty in narco-transactions. I

MR NASTY

took a deep breath and followed him as he strutted past the door staff.

The place was rammed. A long bar covered one side of a reasonably sized dance floor. Maud headed for the bar and I followed. I heard him ask for someone called Ulli. One of the bar staff ducked under a hatch and led us to one of the conveniently discreet booths along the back wall. There were three guys sitting in the alcove. None looked friendly.

'Ulli?' Maud asked in a remarkably calm voice. I was happy that he wasn't freaking out, but I wanted him out of the way as quickly as possible.

One of the troika rose and shook Maud's hand. He was a big bear of a man. They all looked like they bench-pressed Ferraris, but this guy was leviathan. He was tanned, dressed in an expensive black suit and smart black shirt. His hair had receded to form a prominent widow's peak, a pair of sunglasses perched over his forehead.

'I'm Ulli,' he said, in perfect English. 'Take a seat, gentlemen.'

Time to wave a temporary goodbye to my co-conspirator.

'Wait outside in the car, Maud,' I said, parking myself at one end of the large, purple velvet bench seat that ran in an arc around the booth. Maud scuttled off without a word or a backwards glance.

I was relieved. He was there to put me in front of these guys – and wait until I needed him later. If things went tits up, I didn't want the silly queen caught in the crossfire.

'You must be Mo.'

It was the smallest of the three talking now and he had accepted my dealer name to be bona fide. I nodded assent.

'Peter.'

Peter looked like a male catwalk model in his expensive white linen shirt. His longish hair was slicked back, away from his face. His mouth was shaped in a thin smile, but his gunmetal eyes were cold.

He introduced the third member of the trio.

'This is Bob. His friends call him English Bob. You can just call him Bob for the time being.'

'Pleased to meet you, Mo,' Bob said.

A waiter buzzed by our table and we ordered drinks. All three of them were on Pilsner. I opted for vodka on the rocks.

Peter seemed to be adopting the leadership role.

'So, how long have you been a cop, Mo?'

These guys didn't screw around. They were here to do business. On their terms.

I had expected a grilling to suss my credentials, but the question floored me.

'Sorry,' I said, flustered and confused, 'I don't know what you are talking about.'

As denials go it was pretty lame.

Peter spoke again.

'Of course you don't, Mo, but just in case, you are going to take a trip to the toilet with Bob here.'

Bob was already rising and beckoned for me to follow him. We skirted round the dance floor, Bob in front, cutting a path through the throng, me behind, trying to keep up in the jostling crowd.

I really didn't know what to expect. At least I hadn't been a total mug and Maud was waiting in his car with the cash. We both pushed through the door into the male toilet.

Bob locked the cubicle door behind us.

'Right, sunshine, be a good chap and untuck your shirt and lift it up.'

I wasn't wearing a jacket and complied. Bob checked my chest for a remote transmitter and then the small of my back for a Nagra, the mini tape recorder then favoured by undercover drug enforcement. It was surprising how the clandestine methods of the cops became common knowledge in underworld circles. He seemed satisfied.

'Tuck yourself back in, there's a good lad.'

I was still fumbling my shirt-tails back into my trousers as he unlocked the cubicle door and led me out. We must have looked like more than good friends.

Like I cared. Fear was starting to rise in me. I could feel it like a lump in my throat. I tried to fight it down. This was what I wanted. I needed to be right here with these guys: I craved a big deal, big time. This is what it's like.

Get a grip, I repeated silently as Bob led me back to the other two. Get a grip.

'He's clean.'

'Sorry about that, Mo,' Peter said. 'We can't have any third parties listening in to our discussion. Are you OK? You look a little pale.'

'Yeah, I'm fine.'

I reached for my vodka but quickly snatched my hand back. It was shaking like the business end of a seismograph during an earthquake.

'We only know you as someone Maud vouches for,' Peter said. 'Apart from what he has told us, we don't know the first thing about you. You could be the law. Or maybe you are stupid enough to think that you can walk in here and rip us off.'

'All I want to do is cut a deal,' I said.

I wasn't so cocky now. They had me exactly where they wanted me, and I felt like I was back-pedalling just to keep up. We hadn't even started talking about the merch yet. I made another grab for the vodka and took a deep slug to steady my nerves.

'So, Mo,' Peter said. 'What can we do for you to make your visit to Amsterdam more successful?'

I wondered if Maud had mentioned the previous night's fiasco.

'I'm looking to get sorted for some gear.'

This was better, we were communicating.

It felt like Peter's eyes were boring a hole in my face. His gaze never wavered from mine. Did this guy ever blink, or what?

'Gear? What type of gear are you talking about?'

Peter seemed like a succinct individual. There didn't seem any point in playing pat-a-cake. I decided to keep my answers directly on-point.

'One large of sulphate and 1,000 pills.'

'And what would be our recompense if we were to meet your requirements?'

These guys would drown canaries if there was a Guilder in it for them. This was a master class. Now it was 'think of a number' time.

If my ten grand wasn't enough, I could hardly ask for credit. Counter-clockwise, I could be selling myself short and blow it right here.

They were deliberately asking me to set the price because they correctly understood the dynamic of the deal: need and power.

I decided to put all of my money into the pot. I was here for the gear and was committed to spending the ten grand on it anyway.

'Six grand sterling for the Es and four grand for the speed.'

There was an intense silence while Peter's laser-like gaze held mine before he spoke.

'Those are prices that we would only offer to favoured customers. These are people who buy from us regularly and who don't try to trade us off against the competition. Are you proposing to be a favoured customer, Mo?'

The machine had slipped smoothly up into the next gear without me even noticing.

'I'd need the same order every two weeks, maybe more.'

What the hell was I doing? I hadn't even made a buy off these guys and I was already making promises I wasn't sure I could keep.

'OK, we should be able to help you out. Let's talk about it later. Firstly let's have another drink so we can all get to know each other a bit better.'

Another vodka materialised beside the first. As the evening unfolded, I realised that Peter, Ulli and Bob liked to combine business with pleasure. Now, I can take a drink with the best of them, but these boys could put it away. As we drank, the troika kept grilling me about my business dealings and connections in London. Matching them drink for drink to show I was no milquetoast, I was getting drunker, trying to field their questions, all designed to catch me off guard.

These individuals were plenty scary. They had the physical

presence to intimidate anyone. Factor in the psychological capers they were dishing in my direction and they became seriously frightening. While my mission was to get a fast deal and an ongoing connection, the gleesome threesome were totally focused on building a long-term partnership.

A few pills and the odd kilo of amphetamines here and there meant little to them in the grand scheme of things. If they felt uncertain about me at any point, then they would drop me like a bad habit.

They were all about pushing 100kg per buyer per year through their distribution network. This was purely an introduction for them.

It was up to me to convince them that I was more than a bit-part actor in narco-commerce. I needed to convince all three that I could deliver my end and distribute their gear in volume. I was operating at the pointy end of the narcotics yardstick and these boys were very sharp indeed.

A couple of hours passed in earnest conversation as the booze flowed. Poor old Maud was stuck outside in the car, probably wondering what the hell was going on. See what I mean about narco-time?

I hoped Maud hadn't bottled it and bailed out. As I tottered on the edge of total inebriation, Peter wrapped up the first stage of the pleasantries. 'You know what, Mo. I like you. I think we can do business together. Do you have the money with you?'

'No, but it's close by.'

Ooooops.

They could surely guess from my answer that Maud was holding the cash. If this was a rip-off, I'd just helped it along. My nerves had been numbed a bit by the booze and I surprised myself with my next question.

'So, I've got the money close to hand. What about the items to be purchased?'

Was I slurring my words? I pulled myself together as Peter locked on to me once again.

'We are as cautious as you are, Mo. The merchandise is nearby. Do you want to see it?'

'No time like the present.'

'Ulli, bring the car round to the front.'

It was past ten when we emerged from The Roxy. Their wheels came in the form of a brand new BMW 5-Series, fully loaded with all the toys. Slickerama.

'We need to drive a short distance. You can ride with us.'

I had been expecting this. There was no way I was getting in the car with them. A fleeting premonition of my body being dragged from a canal the following morning flashed through my mind.

Once again, I dug deep and stopped myself getting emotional.

'If it's all the same to you, I'll follow you with Maud.'

'But it's not all the same to us,' Peter said. 'Tell Maud to follow. You will ride in our car.'

His voice was icy. This didn't seem like the time to start arguing: they had me cornered. If they wanted me in the BMW with them, then that's how it was going to be. I crossed the road to where Maud had parked the Peugeot. He wound down the window when I tapped.

'God, you look as white as a sheet, babe. Is everything all right?'

A wave of cannabis smoke washed over me from inside the car. I was too wrapped up with the deal to lay into Maud just now.

'Can you handle the driving?'

'Sure, angel,' he said.

'Follow that Bimmer,' I told him.

I ducked into the back seat of the black saloon next to Peter. Ulli was driving, Bob passenger-side. A couple of minutes later we arrived outside a large, four-storey Dutch-style town house.

Nobody spoke as Maud parked his jalopy opposite. I had been through the likely sequence of events with him a dozen times. He wasn't to move until I gave him a signal to do so.

We climbed the front steps and Peter unlocked the door. The first thing I noticed about the place was that heavy money had been dropped in the decor department. Its interior was modern Scandinavian. Stripped-pine furniture adorned the living room, dominated at the front by two huge brown leather sofas.

Ulli went off to fix some sherberts from a snazzy drinks cabinet, a globe which he opened into two halves. Crystal glasses nestled in a tray under the sphere and clinked expensively every time Ulli removed a bottle from its rotund hiding place.

Peter and I sat down, one on each sofa.

Ulli placed our drinks on the table and sat down next to Peter.

'Where'sh Bob gone?' I asked, half cut.

Peter shushed me by putting his index finger in front of his lips.

We drank in silence for a couple of minutes before Bob returned with a green nylon sports bag.

Peter, clearly the brains of the operation, broke the silence. 'Bob, why don't you show our new friend here that we mean business.'

Bob tossed the bag into my lap where it landed with a dull thud. He sat down next to me and unholstered a .45 automatic from inside his coat. He placed it on the coffee table that stood between the two sofas.

I delved my right hand into the bag; it returned clutching a kilo bag of speed.

I looked inside and there were the pills, the same pale blue pills that I had seen 24 hours before. But now they'd returned with 850 friends.

'Do you want to count them?' Peter had to be joking. Right?

There was another awkward silence, until he laughed.

The other two joined in, so I flashed an inane grin while trying to avoid looking at the gun on the table. That's the weird thing about firearms: whenever there's one in the room, you can't seem to see much else.

'Now, what about your side of the bargain?'

It was my play. I was in a house which was their place of business. Any hope of neutral ground had vanished the moment I stepped in their car. Showtime. If they were going to take my money off me now there was little I could do about it. I rose and so did Bob. He followed me out into the hall and through the front door. He waited there while I crossed the road and retrieved the cash from Maud. God bless him, Maud gave me a thumbs up sign as I crossed back to the house.

Once I was seated again, I placed the cash on the table next to the automatic.

'You don't mind if we check this, do you?'

Peter signalled Ulli to pick up the wad of notes and he peeled off into the hallway.

Now there was silence while the money was counted. I was sure it was all there, as I had counted it out three times before I had left London and twice since.

Ulli returned after five minutes and nodded to Peter.

I heard the switchblade open before I saw English Bob proffering the blade to me, handle first. I took the stiletto and made a quick jab into the bag of sulphate. I withdrew the blade with a small, pinkish pile of powder on the tip. After licking the tip of my right index finger, I dabbed it in the speed and transferred my finger onto the tip of my tongue. I immediately tasted that sour, acidic flavour – the gear was bang on.

'Ulli, get some tape to wrap up Mo's gear.'

Peter was now as keen as myself to conclude proceedings. We exchanged mobile phone numbers over a final vodka and tonic.

I staggered out of the house.

The first thing I asked Maud was whether he had told them, specifically, what merchandise and what quantity I required when he had phoned them.

'Yes. Why?'

So they had pre-planned the right amount of gear to be there.

Only a rank amateur would keep their whole stash at their home. My guess was that they had moved the merch to Peter's house on some preordained signal. There was no way that they would have had the quantities to hand out of stock.

It was heads-or-tails as to whether they had treated me as a one-off case or a total amateur finding his feet in the bulk-buying business. The latter certainly characterised me accurately enough, while the former would have meant a stand-alone deal.

That wasn't what I'd been after.

More by chance than skill, I had landed a real connection. I wasn't about to let it go. I had thrown my hat into the ring with strange narco-merchants, pulled a rabbit out of it and walked away with the goods. I had Peter's mobile phone number ready for my next order. This crucial first deal had been made successfully. I was elated.

Maud drove me back to my hotel and I bade him good night. He was a good bloke, but too much of a liability when it came down to the wire. I had to catch the 7 a.m. KLM shuttle to London. And it was already midnight.

Lying on my hotel bed, clutching 1kg of whizz and 1,000 pills, reality hit.

There had been no sniffer dogs at Customs at London's City Airport on the last two trips I'd made back from the Dam. Which wasn't to say that they wouldn't be there when I landed on this run. I was carrying enough gear to see me sewing mailbags for years.

It was six hours before take-off from Schiphol Airport back to London. I unpacked my purchases of earlier in the day from my holdall and rounded up the clingfilm, large jar of instant coffee and the roll of industrial gaffer tape I'd bought that afternoon.

My priority now was to narrow the odds on a successfully completed mission. I laid out the drugs on the bed. The kilo of speed looked enormous. There was no way I could swagger past HM Customs with that stashed up the Gary.

I'd spoken to a few people in the know in London, including a guy who used to smuggle the odd few ounces of weed over from the Dam for personal use. He'd clued me in on how to avoid unwanted attention from the Customs pooches. One of the only substances known to put dogs off the scent of drugs is instant coffee granules. My method for transportation was simple – wrap the gear in coffee and just walk it though in my luggage. This was high risk, but the vodka was still keeping me brave.

I tore a large swathe off the clingfilm and poured a handful of the coffee granules onto it. I then rolled up the kilo of speed and gaffer-taped the loose edges. This wasn't a new method, but the mistake that many wannabes make is to transfer a tiny amount of the drugs onto each layer as they wrap it.

It only takes a trace amount to send the dogs berserk. Mr Nasty's rule for any wannabe traffickers out there: 'Don't forget to wash your hands.'

You need to do it after wrapping each layer. I put six plastic pieces of insulating insurance between my merch and any zealous hounds sniffing round the terminal.

It took about an hour to wrap it all up, then I crashed. The room was spinning slightly as I drifted off. Had I been sober, I doubt that I would have slept.

I awoke about an hour before the alarm, set for 5 a.m. My head was pounding. I washed down a couple of aspirin with a Coke from the minibar. My nerves jangled. I hadn't even left the hotel.

There was no guarantee that sniffer dogs wouldn't be on patrol at the airport. My early morning arrival was designed to dodge them, but you never know, do you?

I had packed a suit and tie with me so that I would blend in with the business travellers who haunted the early-bird flights. If all went to plan, I would be in work for 9 a.m. with the stuff safely stashed in my flat.

If not . . .

Don't even think about it, I told myself. Prison is not a place known for its fresh air and sweeping vistas.

I shaved, showered and donned my suit and tie. Checking the hotel's full-length mirror, I looked like any other suit on a flying visit to London. I had my cover story worked out in case I was stopped. I'd decided to trade up for the day and would be returning from a banking trip in Amsterdam. I had even had a batch of phoney business cards printed in London in case Customs put the hard word on me during questioning.

I had considered the highly efficient shuttle train from Grand

Central Station to the airport, but the station was usually crawling with cops. I wanted to avoid heat.

As I got into a taxi, the rain bucketed down. It seemed a bad omen. But I was in too far now. Once in the airport departure hall, check-in ran smoothly.

I kept a paranoid eye out for anybody who looked like police or Customs as I checked in my bag as hand luggage. Adrift in narco-time, it seemed like an eternity before the flight was called – less than an hour in the air, then I would have to run the gauntlet. During the flight, I tried to breathe deeply and relax.

The prop-engined plane's rubber wheels bit the tarmac.

I was sweating bullets, but at least my hands had stopped shaking. The adrenalin drenched my system and I disembarked on weak-kneed legs. The couple of Customs guys on duty seemed to be clocking me from the moment I walked into the arrivals hall. My Adam's apple felt like a tennis ball in my throat. I strolled as calmly as I could through the green Nothing-to-Declare doors.

I don't remember much about what happened next.

Customs officers are said to closely watch the necks of passengers as they go through the channels. The giveaway is the jugular vein in the side of your neck. If they see it pumping, particularly if you're travelling alone, it increases the chances of you being stopped and searched.

I focused on trying to calm the flow.

The doors swooshed open to welcome me back to London.

Mission accomplished.

Had I been stopped, I doubt if I would have been able to speak coherently. If questioned, I would have gone down.

My legs were engaged in some weird St Vitus's dance in the cab back to my flat. They were trembling so much that my knees knocked together.

By 9 a.m. prompt that morning, I was sitting behind my Camden Council desk. The consignment was safely stashed in the airing cupboard of my flat. I remember thinking that I'd better get home before six, because the heating came on then: I hadn't been through all this for a smouldering pile of speed and some ex-stacy.

It was Wednesday morning: I was keen to get the gear to market that weekend.

I had decided that we would not dilute this first kilo of Billy. It meant a cut in profits, but would buy customer loyalty: punters expect quality goods for their hard-earned sheks. If they bought a gram of base speed at £10 a throw, then one gets you ten they would come back for more.

Initially, when we began importing from Amsterdam, we only controlled Utopia in Hackney and Majik, a venue nearer Dalston. But combined, these joints could hold more than 4,000 kids on both Friday and Saturday nights.

I wanted our gear out across those dance floors *stat*.

So our punters knew that they were buying the real deal, it was essential to differentiate our speed from the competition's: I wanted our product to be instantly recognisable out in clubland, so I had bought 100 sheets of glossy, double-sided black wrapping paper to visually brand our product – soon, the kids would start asking the floor dealers, our runners, specifically for 'black wraps'.

With any luck, they wouldn't notice a gradual decline in quality as we stepped on it during the next few months. This product was so strong it could keep you awake for days. Even if we cut it by half, it would still tear the top of your head off. But before we could get to any of that, we had to package the consignment I'd just imported.

We convened at Murph's at 6.30 p.m., after retrieving the booty from my place.

Murph's council flat was off the Kingsland Road on the Hackney–Dalston border: bandit country. Rival tribes of feral kids would roam the streets that surrounded the concrete tower blocks on a mission to rob and knob the nights away.

A favourite form of evening entertainment was to set fire to the huge industrial trash bins at the bottom of the communal rubbish chutes running down each stone-clad sky-rise. The kids would wait for Old Bill and Fireman Sam to roll up, then hurl bricks, bottles and garbage at them from the walkways, which sprawled like an elevated labyrinth across the estates. Pikey-points were awarded for accuracy, video-game style, with a special bonus for knocking off a copper's helmet.

The traditional method of wrapping speed involves producing a neat little envelope of paper with the edges inter-folded across the front to keep the goodies safe inside the bindle.

We didn't have electronic scales. And there wasn't time to weigh each gram out and then wrap it. A gram of speed is about the same volume as a levelled-off teaspoon full, so we raided Murph's cutlery drawer and set to work.

Murph's wife was in charge of cutting out the perfect squares of black paper, about three inches wide, and folding them into shape ready to receive their bounty.

Eventually, despite intermittent bickering between Mr and Mrs Murphy, our production line ran smoothly.

Around 1.30 a.m., to the great relief of us all, we finally wrapped the last one.

It had taken us more than six hours to get the whizz ready for sale. Our ad hoc spoon measurement system left us 20g shy of the 1,000g we should have got, but it was near enough. We batched the bindles up into snap-lock bags containing 50 wraps each, then packaged the pills the same way.

By that Sunday night, we were cleaned out. Our profit was three grand for the speed and nine large for the pills: twelve grand for taking the biggest chance of my life. Not bad, but we could do better.

Once we started cutting the speed, our profit rose to about ten grand a kilo. Over time, the retail price of pills came down to nearer £20 each, but we still managed to maintain a 100 per cent margin on the Es at wholesale.

We hadn't yet earned enough of a reputation within clubland at that stage to offer the drugs on a sale-or-return basis. Our method was to wholesale. Murph and Gray would get access to our first two clubs early on in the proceedings, around 10 p.m. They would walk the gear though the door, then pass the pills and whizz to our runners dealing on the nightclub floor. No money would change hands yet: it was up to the runners to sell the gear and ensure they could pay us.

We would charge £15 per pill and £7 per whizz wrap. In those days, pills were going for anywhere up to £25 a pop and speed at £10 per bindle. From about 2 a.m. onwards, Murph would be driving between clubs and circulating around the dance floors to collect our cut of the money.

As we got more organised, we began to wholesale the speed to the runners in ounces, and let them wrap it up. In those early days, we were happy with our percentage as this method of supply minimised our risk. Murph and Gray only held the disco biscuits and Billy Whizz for a maximum of half an hour.

Murph's inimitable style of controlling the runners meant that we made sure that we got paid. Every once in a while, someone would be dumb enough to hold out on us: Murph beat them to a pulp in some piss-soaked back alley behind one of the clubs. Making the odd example out of someone kept business even, and he relished his work.

After the first run to the Dam, I decided never to take that kind of personal risk again. First Murph, then Gary Baptiste, drove the gear back via Calais and Dover in a Ford Cortina Mark II that I had bought at an auction around New Year 1990. The car was modified in a friend's garage. Mechanics spot-welded steel strips behind the front and rear bumpers to hold the consignments. The stuff was re-wrapped into long, sausage-shaped bags to fit. It took us bloody ages to extract the merch from its hiding place when it arrived back in London.

We sprang for a hotel room during the day while the trafficker worked some magic with the coffee and clingfilm. That done, the gear would fit snugly in place within the vehicle's interior structure.

We were to discover numerous other potential hiding places in the Cortina and made dozens of successful runs in our 'drugs dodgem' during the next two years.

Gray used to stick a few cases of French lager in the back to make it look like he was on a booze run. He was stopped several times, but he didn't understand the concept of fear and the car was never searched.

Baptiste soon replaced Gray as the day-tripper, driving down to Dover for the trip to Calais, and then on to Amsterdam to pick up the gear from our new Dutch suppliers.

Baptiste often did both legs solo, unless there was hassle with our Dutch associates which, as they weren't particularly savoury individuals, happened periodically. So, occasionally Murph would tag along.

That Cortina made dozens of trips along the same route in and out of the UK. I credit our success more to Gary B flashing his 100-watt smile at the UK port authorities than to anything else.

Customs could've cracked it eventually, but we weren't going to make it easy for them. In hindsight, we were begging to get busted, but I think it worked so well because we were lucky and kept things as simple as possible.

I would courier the buy-money over on a 6.30 evening flight. I could drop off the cash and be back on the 11.30 red-eye flight that night.

During the next couple of years, I streamlined the relationship with Peter, Ulli and English Bob. We established an element of trust, and it made the runs easier. The troika knew I wouldn't try to rip them off. No doubt they had serious connections in the UK of their own: the best I could have hoped for was a nice clean bullet in the brain and a quick death. I could easily imagine their goons going to work on me with some power tools if I screwed up. Gradually, there was more leeway in terms of when the money arrived and when the drugs were collected. Sometimes I was a day early or late, but this was business and we kept things straight.

We were in business, and business was good.

The orders rose steadily, but not excessively. At one point we were trafficking 5,000 pills and 5kg of speed a week: enough to keep us in the style to which we had rapidly become accustomed.

We thought we were untouchable – we genuinely thought we had cracked it. We reckoned we were the dog's bollocks.

We still bought our token order from the Doherty brothers each week and they seemed to be happy with the situation. The business settled into a routine. We brought the drugs in and sold them almost instantly. We never got over-ambitious by bringing in massive loads, but kept things ticking along nicely. By the beginning of 1992, Baptiste and I had cleaned about £400,000 through our banking scam. But the police were questioning me on ridiculous pretexts every two or three days. Plod would ask a series of connected questions: 'Do you know Irish Ollie?', 'Why do you spend so much time at Ferdenzi's?', 'Nice suit. Must've cost a bit. What is it, do you butter the old dears up and nick their pension books, son?'

Then came the wind-up.

'Makes me wonder how a council clerk can afford a whistle like that. Now then, Mr White, what's this we hear about you and the Adams family?'

It was pressure, and it amped up the paranoia within our group. Should the cops actually catch us in the act, I don't think any of us trusted one another not to rat each other out for a deal. But it wasn't the cops we should have been worrying about.

We tooled up, not to kick off any internecine warfare amongst ourselves or competitors, but because we thought we had to. Our paranoia suggested we needed extra insurance. Our arrogance demanded we bolster our status within the hierarchy of narco-commerce. But tooling up for ultra-violence marked a dangerous transition to becoming serious players within the criminal fraternity, and I did have my concerns about having a heavily armed Murph walking the streets when he was clearly about as sharp as a marble.

My weapon was a Beretta .9mm fully automatic pistol. Compact and, I fancied, quite stylish. Baptiste had a similar piece. Gray chose a Browning automatic, while Murph owned a small arsenal, including a brace of revolvers and a French pump-action shotgun acquired, as was most of our iron, on drug runs to and from Euroland.

Drugs and firearms: what could possibly connect them? The reality of our situation, that's what. We were becoming the complete package as über-gangsters: sharp suits, designer firepower and a complete immersion in the illegality of our business.

As our mini-cartel's operational politics became byzantinely complex and chillingly personal, the gun was a permanent fixture of my life. I never fired it, but occasionally pointed it with intent. If a beating from Murph or our tame doormen hadn't convinced an errant runner or some kid foolish enough to try moving a few pills in one of our clubs then me sticking the Beretta into their mouths sure did the trick. I remember one poor sap being held against the wall of a back alley behind Utopia by Murph as I pointed the .9mm at his right eyeball. He actually pissed himself when I told him I was going to pull the trigger until the clip was empty as retribution for his attempt to fuck with us.

We knew how to spend money, and had reached the level where up-and-coming firms wanted a slice of our action. We had also, without our knowledge, been sussed by the Doherty brothers. My grandiose notions of a multi-million-pound narco-empire proved to be as fanciful as a hothouse full of orchids in the Arctic.

It was a Wednesday night in February 1992 when I was summoned to one of the Brothers' establishments in north London. Pat owned this particular pub himself, but I think he had the licence under his wife's name. All three brothers had served time, problematic when applying for legal registration to serve intoxicating liquor.

I scanned the main bar area. It was rammed with punters supping down pints and making moves for purchases of a different kind.

It was a front.

Nothing too clever, just a watering hole that allowed the Dohertys to pump their product out at street level and, therefore, at maximum margin. One of Pat's hired thugs was at the entrance to the rear bar and he beckoned me over with a simian gesture.

I should have seen it coming, but my arrogance led me to believe that I was on the same peer level as the Dohertys and therefore indestructible.

Strutting over to the bar, radiating coke-fuelled confidence, I omitted to notice that the entire rear area was not only enveloped in shadow but also entirely empty apart from Pat and John Doherty, who were apparently engrossed in conversation over a couple of unfeasibly large whiskies.

Pat turned and gave me a wide grin. Everything else happened so fast that I'm still sketchy on the details. I drew level with Pat at the bar and in a series of fluid movements he slapped me on the back with baroque bonhomie. He slid his left hand down the back of my suit coat, reaching into the back of my trousers to relieve me of my Beretta tucked snugly into the waistband. Almost simultaneously, his right hand, balled into a fist like a lead weight, connected with the bridge of my nose, smashing bone and cartilage and causing the bar and the brothers to fade to black instantly. I don't even remember hitting the floor.

'Who the fuck do you think you are to fuck with us?'

They were the first words I heard as I came to. There was really no answer to that. Even if there was, I couldn't have told Pat Doherty: my mouth was covered by industrial gaffer tape.

I was sitting in a wooden chair with my wrists and ankles taped to its frame. Duct tape holds architecture together, and it was working its magic on me. I could hardly breathe through what was left of my nose. The blood over my top lip was coagulating into a crust.

'Who the fuck do you fucking think you are to fuck with us?' Pat repeated. 'Come on you little fuck, I want a fucking answer.'

I was in the basement of the pub. I had been here a couple of times before when Pat had wanted to show me one of his new toys, usually semi-automatic. Empty aluminium beer kegs lined one side of the concrete-and-brick room and a single, naked light bulb snaked down from the ceiling on a piece of flex cabling right above me.

I could see Pat in front of me and guessed that John must be behind. I could almost feel his presence. Jesus Christ on a funky moped, how did I end up here with these two lunatics?

The answer hit me instantly: I was N2DEEP. I really had stepped out of my league, climbed the ladder just a little too high,

MR NASTY

a little too fast and, because I was perceived as the leader of our flourishing narco-empire, I was going to take the rap.

'You little fuck!'

Pat was almost screaming now. He tore the tape from across my mouth. I didn't have time to react to the flash of pain as he jammed the Beretta between my lips. I could feel the cold steel of my own pistol through the enamel of my teeth. That's the thing with guns. If you don't have one, your own weapon can never be used against you.

As the metal mashed my choppers I wondered if I would leave this room alive.

Pat's method for keeping errant vassals in line involved a pair of pliers and amateur dentistry skills. And sometimes he played with guns.

Pat whipped the Beretta away and I coughed, spitting blood out onto the sawdust-covered floor.

'Don't fucking spit at me, you little fuck.'

Pat really needed to work on his vocabulary.

I could see John now as he had moved over to my right side. I wondered if Mick was there as well. The Unholy Trinity lurking in their own saloon of shadows.

'You really think you are gonna sell gear out there and cut us out? You really think we aren't gonna fucking know what you and your gang of muppets are up to?'

It was John Doherty doing the talking now.

He bitch-slapped me across the left side of my face. My ears were ringing and I could feel blood trickling out of my nose now.

'Christ, guys, we can sort this out.' I don't know how I managed to get the words out. They lacked a certain conviction.

'Too fucking right we can sort this out,' John said. He was the oldest of the three and probably the sanest. I felt a small shiver of relief run up my spine. They were going to cut me a deal.

'You and those fuckwits you run around with are gonna only move our fucking gear from now on. Understand?'

Going back to an exclusive deal with the Dohertys was going

to present systematic, and possibly catastrophic, problems. Even if I did get out of this in one piece, it was bad.

Working directly for the Dohertys likely meant one of three things occurring in your medium-term future: incarceration, death, or both. The Brothers tended to give up selected employees to the cops so the Local Area Drug Squad could maintain its arrest rates. In return, its officers turned a blind eye to the Dohertys' action.

'Cut him loose.'

John had control and was giving the orders. This was better. Not necessarily good, but better. You could at least reason with John. But, then again.

'OK, Al fucking Capone, this is the way it's gonna be. You *will* take 10,000 pills a week from us and you *will* fucking move them. Your cut is down to 20 per cent for your trouble. And you're going to give us a hundred grand within 48 fucking hours for being the snide little prick that you are and giving us the runaround.'

My mind was made up in that instant. I was leaving the drugs business in London as of now. There was no way we could sustain moving that quantity of pills at that margin. Our in-house dealers would have swallowed that as their cut. The Dutch mob wouldn't be happy. And although our money laundering was quite successful, it was impossible to withdraw that much cash from the banks without attracting heat.

Summary: we were royally fucked.

'Get out of my fucking sight and be here with the cash and the buy-money on Friday night.' John kicked the chair as he spoke, toppling me in a heap on the cold floor.

They threw me out of the rear fire escape. I must have looked like a dump truck had hit me, twice.

The fifth taxi I tried to flag down eventually stopped. By the time I got back to mine, I was borderline hysterical. Pat still had my pistol. I felt overexposed and underprotected.

I gulped down three fingers of brandy from a tumbler, but I was still shaking.

MR NASTY

The thought of actually taking the Brothers D up on their kind offer was not worth even one moment's entertainment. It meant I would have been a dead man walking, like most of their goons. I was going to have to run. Fuck the drugs, fuck the money, fuck the car and the flat, just make a bolt for it.

Later, I discovered that Murph's criminal career was put on hold that same night. He went too far in his student-bashing activities and jammed a pint glass into some guy's face. His victim got over 60 stitches: Murph got five years. Exit one enforcer.

I couldn't reach Gray at his flat. I finally got hold of Baptiste at his mum's place. I filled him in. His response was concise.

'Fuck . . .'

He hung up. I knew that he was going to run as well. It was every man for himself.

I packed a bag and £12,000 in cash that I kept in the shoeboxes under the bed, and fled to my brother's place in Islington.

The lease on my flat and the registration for my car were both in a false name, so there was nothing to tie me to either.

For the next 40 or so days and nights after my run in with the Dohertys I became invisible. It was taking me that long to get out of not just London, but the United Kingdom.

My family rallied round. As families do. My eldest brother, with whom I was staying, knew about my illegal activities and told me to stay legit while I was at his place. It was as much for my own safety as protecting his reputation as a barrister. He wasn't exactly ecstatic about my chosen career and the mess I had landed myself in, but he offered to help me get things back on track. The rest of my family knew nothing of what I had been up to and I wanted to keep it that way.

After consistent nagging from one and all to get a 'proper job' instead of idling at Camden Council, I had, thanks to a bucket of bullshit from myself and a good word from my brother, who worked for an associated legal firm, obtained a position as a researcher for a management consultancy. This was now April 1992, and I had moved from my brother's place into a small bedsit in Finsbury Park. Two months into my job as a researcher, the opportunity to work in New York emerged with a client in the talent agency business.

It was a miraculous turnaround.

I jumped at the chance and walked away from the whole shooting match.

The syndicate had imploded.

Gray bailed: I haven't spoken to him since. Murph, banged up in Pentonville Prison, was unlikely to be out and about for a few years. Baptiste hid at his mum's place for a couple of months, then he began extracting cash from some of our myriad accounts. The rest were my donation to the national wealth – made on my behalf in a rather arbitrary, yet mandatory, manner when my itinerant VP burned all the financial documentation. He used the wedge to buy a half-share in the garage where he worked and go legit.

As far as I know – and you'll be astounded to hear I haven't really inquired carefully into this – the Doherty brothers are still operating their business as unusual.

Good luck to them.

I just hope I never see the motherfuckers again as long as I walk this earth.

NEW YORK

'C OR D?'

I arrived in New York in June 1992, feeling like Harry Houdini – with one bound our hero was free. America was not only a new country for me, it represented a new job and a fresh start in life. With hindsight, maybe I should have tried to grasp these concepts a bit more firmly. It was a new opportunity. For the same old Cameron White.

In Manhattan, I was squeaky clean. I arrived promptly for work every morning, wowed to be part of the city's massive energy. I worked diligently in an office of greys, off-whites and tans. Ah, the hegemony of the blandlands: egg-box light fixtures; shiny plants in clean offices; fabric-covered walls; large works of contemporary art that screamed money.

I rolled calls, produced lists and made nice with my colleagues, sharply dressed femmes and men in shirt sleeves, who made self-conscious chatter around the watercooler and small, quick gags when they passed in the halls.

My employers were a successful talent and literary agency on Madison Avenue in the Midtown district near East 64th Street, a short hop from my compact apartment on West 77th Street and Broadway. I had really landed on my feet. My brief stint as a researcher had meant that I was introduced to this particular client whose CEO had noticed some level of potential in me. Maybe it was my inherent ability to construct a deal, or perhaps it was my wideboy charm, but they poached me from the management consultancy and made me a junior agent: from Camden Council to the A list within a couple of months. Brilliant.

Most of my colleagues put in long hours, and the secretaries and personal assistants who pandered to the agents' egos disappeared to Brooklyn and Queens at six o'clock sharp.

That was the hierarchy: they were the Bridge and Tunnel crowd, so I socialised with the other agents most evenings, even if it was just a quick beer to celebrate surviving another day. From the telltale signals gradually dropped into these bonding chats after work, I sussed that my colleagues were indulging in the odd dusting with nasal talc, but they were so discreet that the situation hadn't yet emerged wherein I could put out feelers. Like much else in this high-stakes milieu of limo-sized egos, this was a delicate matter mandating a kid-gloves approach.

As I settled into the gig, I noticed that just after lunch every day, when our office in Los Angeles opened for business, a select stream of agents would sometimes briefly vanish before returning to their desks in a familiar state of preternatural animation.

These guys were informally known within the agency as Los Mescaleros, because after work they sometimes hung out at a tequila bar on 25th Street.

One day, I casually tagged along to the little agents' room behind one of them. Clickety-click-click-click: the plastic credit card's staccato Morse code from within the cubicle confirmed my liveliest suspicions.

The next night I made a point of visiting the tequila bar with Los Mescaleros. We ordered shooters, and after slamming a few I noticed some of the guys had dispensed with the salt and substituted Colombian snuff.

'Look dude, as long as you're not actually caught doing lines off your desk, who cares?' one of the guys explained. 'It gets me through the day, capice? You want in?'

'I'll let you know,' I said.

The gear was biked over to the office every morning. The really on-point agents enhanced their client service by procuring blow-to-go for visiting West Coast talent without New York connections.

'Keep 'em high and they don't ask why,' Matt said. He found coked-out clients less arsey about the financial details that were the straw stirring the agency's drink.

I didn't want to score from within the agency. I'd been a big player in London's narco-land and preferred not to expose myself to the hassles of corporate scores. The internal agency politics were volcanic. Time for a fresh approach.

There was money to be made on the backs of my colleagues by someone with entrepreneurial flair. Mmmmmnn, now who might that be?

If I could tap into and take over from the existing outside dealers with a regular supply, then the dollar waterfall would surely be showering me like a monsoon. I had no worries about treading on the toes of Los Mescaleros' supplier as I found out during one serious tequila session with them that they got their gear from a couple of pretty wimpy bond traders at a Wall Street investment bank. They were paying way over the odds for their cha cha and would be receptive to a new supplier offering better terms. If they had been scoring off a more heavy-duty dealing operation I would have thought more carefully about trying to muscle in on the action, but as things stood I felt pretty sure I could easily replace their current suppliers with no comebacks. I mean, it wasn't as if the guys in the office were wired straight into Bogota. The bond traders were simply ordering a few extra grams of coke from their dealer and selling them on to the guys in my office to cover their own drugs expenditure. Their dealer would probably be a little pissed off once their orders dropped a little, but he would be even more narked if they told him they had actually been dealing his gear on to third parties. They would just have to accept it and keep their mouths shut.

My first thoughts were of myself though and my own drug

needs. Los Mescaleros and other similarly inclined people in the office could wait until I had a supplier in place. I knew I could get them on board any time I wanted as long as the gear was good and the price was right.

I'd kept my nose clean in the city, but despite the skyscraper views, gym membership and proximity to celebrity, my perky lifestyle palled. My existence was so middle-of-the-road that all I could see was a white line.

A little weekend escapism would help me settle down, get me back in the groove. But something separated me from any chance of a chemical minibreak: no connection.

Obviously, I wasn't going to use the office connection from the banking boys downtown, how chewy would that be? Instead, I was going to make my own. I'd come into New York cold, and my only option was to go route one and score from the street.

So, one Friday night, about six weeks after I had arrived in the Big Apple, I cabbed down to Alphabet City with nefarious purposes in mind, and a wedge of bills stuffed down one of my socks, in an attempt at some proactive personal security.

My destination was the little area north of the East Village in downtown New York comprising Avenues A, B, C and D. It encompasses about 20 blocks. I had heard the stories about the Alphabet and knew that for years it had been the city's drugs supermarket, with dealers operating on every street corner offering 'C or D?'.

Coke, Charlie, okey, the white lady, or diamorphine, heroin, smack, scag, horse: the names are numerous, but the drugs and their end results are universal.

I had heard that you didn't venture east of Avenue B without semi-automatic weapons: the smack dealers there had hardcore attitude, and if you weren't packing heat you were underdressed. I decided to try my luck on Avenue A.

The taxi sped off as soon as the driver had whipped the $20 from my hand. At the top corner of the Alphabet, where Avenue A meets East 14th Street, I started to stroll down the sidewalk.

My instant impression was the quiet compared with the traffic and bustle of Midtown during the day. There was an eerie lack of cars driving the streets, and most of those parked by the roadside looked like they had been dumped there some time ago.

Either side of the avenue was banked with shuttered shops and squalid, boarded-up tenement buildings. Graffiti covered every surface, including the sidewalk, as if it had snowed onto the landscape.

I began to discern people huddled against the buildings. It was approaching summer and still surprisingly cold as Manhattan tried to shrug off the dark days of winter. A storm was rolling in from the East River and drops of rain were starting to splatter the sidewalks. Some of the street people appeared dressed in little more than threadbare cast-offs from some moth-eaten charity shop.

A face loomed out of the darkness. It was black, as were all of the faces I could see. The crazy white boy was sticking out like a sore thumb again. The face spoke: 'You want crack?'

I shook my head, and started to move around the man who was now blocking my path. He reached out a hand and pushed me in the chest, sending me back a few steps.

'If you don't want no crack then whaddaya doin' here, bro?'

'Just walking home.'

Not a good comeback, nor even a plausible one, for treading the turf of one of the most drug-infested regions of the whole city at 8 p.m. on a non-school night.

I hurried past the man and heard him muttering expletives to my back. Like I cared.

I adopted the New Yorkers' strut as I progressed down the street: eyes front, no-mess body language and a powerful, purposeful stride eating the pavement like you know where you are going and have the absolute right to get there. It wasn't fooling anybody.

'Hey, bro.'

Another face shuffled from the darkness, moving away from the wall where it had been slouching to again meet me head on in a cross-pavement confrontation. This guy was younger than the first, maybe 16 or 17.

'C or D?'

MR NASTY

'I want some coke.'

'Sure, bro. I've got some $20 rocks with me. Let's walk.'

'I don't want crack. I just want some coke. To snort,' I added for emphasis.

'Got no coke, only rocks. Ain't no coke on the streets, Homes. Come with me. We can light one up and you can get high before you buy.'

I wasn't having this situation run away from me.

'Look, I just want to get hooked up with some coke. I'll make it worth your while.'

'How much worth my while?'

'Fifty bucks worth your while.'

'OK, walk with me, walk with me . . . bro, have you got the fifty now?'

Mr Nasty's rule on street dealing: never flash the money until you've seen the goods.

'I've got it. You'll get it if you hook me up.'

The kid acknowledged the state of affairs with a nod, then jerked his head for me to follow him.

We walked for 30 yards and then took a hard left into East 10th Street, just skirting the perimeter of Tomkins Square Park, a notorious drug-dealing haunt at the time. We crossed Avenue B and walked through to Avenue C. Danger signals were flashing through my mind, but I persisted.

My new friend introduced himself.

'I'm Scooter.'

'Mo,' I lied for the thousandth time, weakly grasping his proffered hand. Scooter led me round onto C and then up the steps of a totally dilapidated tenement, its brown stone walls bristling with graffitied tags. We tramped up three flights of creaking wooden steps surrounded by paint flaking from the walls and eventually stopped in front of a steel reinforced door with a slot cut in its front. Scooter knocked.

'Just be cool, Homes, and we'll both get what we want.'

The crude shutter mechanism slid back and two bulbous eyeballs peered out from the gloom.

'Pauly, it's Scooter. We need handing some blow.'

With a click like a rifle shot the shutter returned to its place. There was a pause for a few seconds. I heard several bolts being drawn back. The steel door opened a crack and my new friend, Scooter, pushed his way into the apartment. I followed, right back into the game. We entered a hallway devoid of furniture, pictures, anything. It was rank, redolent with the stench of damp and decay. The floorboards creaked with every step.

Scooter led me into a lounge where the master of the door was resuming his position on some cushions scattered on the floor. In front of him was a low wooden coffee table covered with a heavy user's debris: syringes, metal spoons, a large glass bong. Its sides were greasy and opaque from whatever had last been smoked in it. Littered among all this paraphernalia were dozens of scraps of paper, some with numbers scrawled on them.

'Who da white boy you bringing in here, Scooter? I ain't here to talk to no strangers.'

'It's cool, Pauly, this is Mo. Mo the Blow. He's looking for some fine white lady to party with tonight.'

'How big a party you want, Mo the Blow?'

I still felt residual caution and aimed low.

'Just a couple of grams.'

Pauly regarded me. He must have been about 40, although his drug-ravaged frame seemed tissue thin and he looked a lot older. His dark ebony skin was stretched drum-tight across his face, bathed in a sheen of sweat; his eyes protruded from his skull like a bullfrog's.

He reached a slender arm under one of the cushions on which he perched and nodded for Scooter and me to sit.

Sit? Sit where?

Apart from Pauly's private cushion pile by the coffee table, there wasn't any furniture. An antediluvian portable TV on the floor in the opposite corner of the room displayed a screen of silent static.

Scooter hunkered down on the carpet and I did likewise. I could feel the floor sticking to my jeans. I made a mental note to burn all my clothing when I got home. If I got home.

Pauly retrieved a polythene bag from under the cushion and, with a sweep of his other hand, cleared a small space in front of him on the coffee table. He produced from his stash a fist full of small snap-lock bags the same size as those used for nickel-and-dime weed deals.

'You want $20 rocks or straight blow?'

'Straight blow.'

Pauly cocked his head to one side as he sifted through the bags and selected two. He placed both in the space cleared on the table. Each looked to contain about a gram of white crystalline coke powder, tinted with a sour yellow tinge.

'That's $200, Mo the Blow. Cash on delivery.'

Pauly seemed to find it amusing every time he called me by my newly minted moniker and erupted into a series of wheezy chortles. I had $200 in my back pocket and another 5 century notes stuffed down my sock with a couple of $50 notes in the billfold as travelling money. I removed the cash from my back pocket and placed it on the table in front of me.

'I want to try before I buy.'

At the risk of sounding like a broken record, remember: taste and try before you buy.

Here it was risky, but I wasn't going through this to get screwed by some twisted drug gargoyle.

'Why'd ya bring me this fool, Scooter? Shit, don't nobody work on trust these days? Here, white boy, dip yourself in here.'

He tossed one of the bags over to me and I carefully opened it up. I licked my right index finger and dabbed it into the contents, before rubbing my dust-coated digit across the front of my top gum. The numbness spread through my mouth with reassuring rapidity. The gear was OK. Not great, but good for a street deal, and at $100 a gram it was time to stock up.

'What do you think of that fine toot, Mr Mo the Blow?'

Pauly was chuckling to himself again.

'Seems good. Gimme another four of these.'

Pauly stopped laughing.

'That'd be cool, bro, just as long as I see the cash to pay for the stash.'

I reached into my sock and pulled out the rest of the money. I reeled out another $400 and put them on the table with the other two. I could hear Scooter beside me sucking on his teeth as he realised he could have mugged me on the way in.

Pauly reached into the larger bag again and sorted out another 4g. This time he handed them to me instead of merely flinging them in my direction. I must have been his deal of the day.

I pocketed the gear as Pauly reached over and gathered up the bills. Deal done, it was time to get the hell out of Dodge. I rose to my feet, Pauly did likewise.

'What about my $50?'

Scooter had remained on the floor and was evidently angling to make a purchase of his own. I peeled off the relevant note from my now depleted billfold and dropped it into Scooter's lap.

'Be seein' ya, Mo the Blow.'

'Yeah, later, Scooter.'

Pauly was heading to the hallway and I followed. I was getting twitchy as he started to unlock the door again to let me out. Maybe it was just the coke.

'You just be remembering old Pauly when you havin' that party. Just don't be remembering me to anybody else ya hear?'

'Don't worry, Pauly, this is a private arrangement.'

I was down the stairs and out of the building before the first bolt had been slid back into place.

Mission accomplished. I knew I would return.

I contemplated my purchase.

Cocaine is an organic drug. It is derived from the coca plant native to the Andes in South America. It was first isolated as a narcotic in the mid-nineteenth century, but its effects weren't medically recognised until the 1880s.

In 1883, Dr Theodor Aschenbrandt, a German Army physician, prescribed cocaine to Bavarian soldiers to reduce fatigue during training. The following year, Sigmund Freud published *Uber Coca*, a paean to the drug that helped popularise its use throughout Europe. Cocaine was distilled into powder, tinctures, wines and beverages.

In 1886, John Pemberton of Atlanta, Georgia, began to market Coca-Cola, a syrup synthesised from coca leaves and African kola nuts.

Cocaine use was widespread and, by 1902, the US harboured an estimated 200,000 addicts: tabloid hysteria panicked legislators into passing the Harrison Narcotic Act, which criminalised the drug.

Cocaine usage declined steadily until the 1960s. In the decade that followed, its popularity soared once more, as the newly formed South American drug cartels deluged the US with tonnes of white powder.

Cocaine hydrochlorate was glamorised as a recreational drug and was wrongly and widely believed to be non-addictive. By 1982, there were over ten million users in North America.

Crack is a free-based form of cocaine made by 'cooking' cocaine powder, water and baking soda until it forms a solid, which can be broken down and sold in individual rocks. It first appeared in major US cities around 1985 and spread like a forest fire. It is typically smoked but can be crushed for snorting or injection. The high is one of the most intense that can be induced by narcotics. It only lasts a few minutes, and its euphoric nature means that crack is highly addictive after being taken only occasionally.

Cocaine was expensive, but crack could be bought for as little as $10 a hit. It swiftly cemented its skeletal foothold within blue-collar neighbourhoods and poorer urban communities. Around 18 months after it had hit the streets in volume, the crack wave and its concomitant ultra-violence engaged the US authorities' attention. Congress imposed mandatory sentencing laws which dramatically increased the penalties for possessing or trafficking crack, now perceived as a more serious civic threat than its powdered cousin, cocaine: the ratio between sentences for crack and powder cocaine offences was set at 100:1. So a low-level crack dealer like Scooter would be subject to a harsher penalty, if caught, than a higher-level powder cocaine dealer.

There are two schools of thought as to how crack derives its name. Some say that the tiny rocks of cooked-down coke look like the pieces of plaster that fall out of the cracks in the ceiling in Harlem tenement houses. More likely is the fact that crack cocaine actually cracks and sizzles when it is ignited.

It was certainly popular in Alphabet City.

My nocturnal visits there to see Pauly increased until I was stocking up with four or five grams every weekend. I had left London with my shoebox money and a suitcase full of clothes. Three months after arriving in New York, most of my disposable income was propping up the South American economy.

When Charlie gets hold of you, there is little left to live off. While crack is terrifyingly addictive, both mentally and physically, powder cocaine really attacks the psyche. Your psychological dependence on the drug can quickly get out of control once it sucks you in. My fractured finances needed a break: I'd have to trade up and buy in bulk. I would save myself cash on the coke I was buying, which up to now had been for my personal use, and I could also approach Los Mescaleros and offer to start supplying them to cover my outgoings. With this in mind, I visited Pauly one hot Friday night in September 1992. I had a proposition for him.

An element of trust develops between dealer and client. Initial mutual suspicion is supplanted by the realities of commerce: the dealer has the goods; the client has the cash to pay for them. My dealer needed my business. I was regular, bought in quite high volume and paid on the nail. He was a solid supplier and didn't draw heat. But I needed to work round our cosy reciprocal arrangement to bypass Pauly's dealing tier and move up the chain. And there was a vitiating factor, which would help me do an end-run round this whacko.

Pauly was a user. Not just a chipper, with a lightweight recreational habit, but a full-blown junk hound. Smack, coke, crack, crystal meth, PCP . . . Pauly soaked it all up. Heavy users are predictably short-term thinkers: how they can finance their habit for the next 24 hours. The big picture and the long-term view are not concepts that junkies understand too well. Hence my pitch to Pauly.

It was about 10 p.m. when the now familiar shutter cracked back and Pauly gave me the eyeball. After the unlocking ritual, he led the way into his minimalist lounge.

'Mr Mo the Blow. What'll you have? I've got some mighty fine meth which'll wire you tighter than a watch spring. We can blow out on the pipe and I will get you high, boy.'

I was not in the mood for Pauly's spaced-out junk hyperbole: I cut to the chase.

'Listen Pauly, I need to score some weight, an ounce, maybe two.'

'Sure, no problem, but I don't keep that kind of stash here, man. I'll have to order it in for you.'

'Yeah, well, I'm gonna need this kind of weight regularly and need a connection that can supply me in Midtown.'

I could see the instant objection in Pauly's eyes: I was cutting him out of the loop.

'Word up, Mo. I am your connection. Wha's the matter? You getting nervous about coming down here and playing with the cannibals?'

'Pauly, I will still use you, but I figure that we can help each other out here. You give me a connection and it will look good for you. And I'll pay you a finder's fee.'

Pauly considered his options. He was potentially going to lose me as a customer anyway and might be able to salvage something from the wreckage by garnering a pay-off for services rendered.

'How much for handing over my connection, white boy? Remember that ol' Pauly would be sticking his schlong in the meat grinder if anything went wrong. These brothers are not to be fucked with. No sir, not to be fucked with.'

He was trying to shake me down for as much as he could get. I had given it some thought and had decided to be generous in my appreciation of his efforts.

'Five hundred for the connection.'

Pauly whistled out through his teeth. I had hit the right notes with him here.

'OK, but this is the only time I am gonna do this. These people don't take kindly to their name being used in vain. Catch my drift?'

'As clear as crystal meth on a sunny winter's morning, Pauly. I'll keep it clean and put the word in for you.'

'You got the big five? Gimme it and I'll fix you up.'

Pauly was in the groove now. He could see the prospect of $500 in his back pocket and maybe the chance to trade on me to keep in his supplier's good books. They were obviously types who didn't bother with street deals for chump change.

I felt sure that the next rung up the ladder would be more attuned to dealing an ounce at a time. I took out the $500 from my black Levi 501 jeans and handed it to him. He fanned the bills out a few inches from his face.

'My, my, they call me Mr Green. OK, boy, I'se got to make a few calls. You sit here and be chill.'

Pauly unravelled himself from his cushion pile and clomped out of the door. There was a payphone I had noticed in the hall. It was obviously used by the tenement's dope dealers, so remained unvandalised.

Pauly was gone about ten minutes. I sat there contemplating what I was about to do.

Trading up to a supplier rather than a street dealer merited careful consideration. I had to assure my new connection that I was on the level and could buy in weight regularly. There was also no room for error from now on. Deviation from the rules would mean physical harm. I had already accepted these new parameters and was ready to play on the bigger field.

Pauly slouched back in and resumed his Buddha-like position before me.

'OK, bro, we is set for later. My man will be outside the Hotel Elysée in one hour. You know where that's at? You'd better have the money with you. One and a half large for the weight.'

Pauly grinned at me. I masked my smile. It could wait until later, once the business had been conducted successfully.

MR NASTY

I reached out to him with my hand.

Pauly knew it was goodbye and it felt strangely awkward. I had become used to Friday night visits to this drug fiend, and now the dealer–client bond was being broken. His word must have stood for something, as he wasn't coming with me into this new territory.

As he closed the door and I was set to scurry down the stairs, he said one word to me.

'Luck.'

I cabbed back to my apartment off Broadway and counted out $1,500 on my bed. It took about 20 minutes to walk to the Elysée, a small hotel on East 54th Street and Madison Avenue.

I was glad to be dealing in Midtown. I could almost hear the cracking sound of the sliver-thin ice I was skating on every time I scored down in the zoo of Alphabet City. I was lucky that I had not been liberated from my cash by one of its hot-wired inhabitants.

I must have waited for about 15 minutes watching the after-theatre supper crowd coming and going from the foyer. At 11.15 p.m., a late-model Oldsmobile pulled up to the kerb and the electric window slid down.

'Mo?'

I nodded and made to walk round to the passenger side only to see that that seat was taken. I hopped in the back, my heart fluttering in my throat, and we sped away into the stream of incessant traffic.

Two elements were in play from the giddy-up: we were heading uptown along Madison, and I had company. The two front seats were occupied and there was a third passenger next to my currently warm body.

I wanted to get the deal rolling.

'I've got the cash,' I said.

'Just be cool, Homes,' the driver said, a clear signal for me to sit tight and zip my lip.

We took a right into Fifth Avenue and were now skirting

Central Park. We were still heading uptown. I started to take stock of my immediate surroundings.

The two guys in front were both black, the third, next to me, was white. All of them were dressed like New York hip-hoppers: gold chains hung like wreaths around their necks, and the ubiquitous Ray-Ban Wayfarers were worn by all. The white guy next to me was turned halfway towards me. His left arm extended across the top of the back seat behind me, like it was his seat and I was just sitting in it. No turning back now.

The Metropolitan Museum of Art was on our left as we travelled into the Upper East Side. We passed through Yorkville, still hugging the park, then moved up into Spanish Harlem. At East 111th Street we took a right and cruised for a few blocks before reaching Jefferson Park. The streets were much quieter than Midtown. An occasional yellow cab cruised the kerbs. We pulled up opposite Jefferson and the driver killed the engine.

'Check him out.'

My backseat neighbour leaned across and started to pat me down, searching for wires, weapons, God knows what. After a minute he seemed satisfied.

'He's OK.'

Then the driver spoke.

'Pauly tells us you wanna grab an ounce of Ye Yo.'

'Yeah, that's right.'

The area was much quieter than I had first realised. The perfect place for a rip-off. I felt tenser than a pet on fireworks night.

'You'se have the money?'

OK, here we go. I reached into my back pocket and pulled out the wad of bills and handed it to my right to be counted. The dumb-ass took a couple of minutes to sort through it. How hard could it be to count to 15?

Every sinew of my being now just wanted to book out of this car. I was suffering dealer's downers: thoughts flash through your mind suggesting that whatever could possibly go wrong probably will.

After a narco-eternity of fumbling and muttered cussing,

Einstein seemed happy with the money count and nodded to the driver who turned in his seat to face me. This guy could only have been about 19 years old. His head was shaved bald down both sides and his grinning mouth was filled with gold teeth. He extended a hand.

'I'm Justice.'

I was too wound up to catch the funny side to this and shook as his masked eyes sought to stare me down from behind his shades.

'Vic, give the man his blow.'

The guy in the front passenger seat opened the glove compartment and withdrew a small bag filled with white powder.

'Twenty-eight grams on the button, my friend.'

He handed it to me. It could have been soap powder for all I knew, but this was definitely not the time to ask for a taste.

'You must be cool for Pauly to vouch for you personally, man,' Justice said. 'Tell me, are you cool?'

He reached down under his seat then turned to face me again. But this time he was pointing a snub-nosed, nickel-plated .38 about six inches from my face. The gun barrel flashed in the street lights' sodium glow.

I gave a silent prayer to any guardian angels who might be flying by.

'I'm cool,' I said. 'I just wanna cop this blow and walk away.'

I could feel the fear, the bile rising in my throat.

'Y'see, Mo, we are happy to do business with you, but you have to know not to show us any disrespect. We can't be having that.'

'I wouldn't do that, Justice,' I said, cranked up really high.

I reckoned that by calling him by name he might see me not as his next victim, but as a human being, an individual like himself.

I figured wrong.

Justice jabbed the piece at me until it touched the tip of my nose. I could feel the cold metal; smell that seductive aroma of gun oil.

'You'se had better believe it, skinny boy. 'Cos if you ever, ever, fuck with us, we is gonna turn you into a sieve. Understand?'

I nodded. This was just a show of force. I was not going to die tonight in the back of this car. I was going to make it.

'Give him the number.'

The passenger-side occupant handed me a piece of paper with a NY phone number on it.

'Whenever you need anything you dial that number and ask for Justice. And don't be handing it over to no cops or I'm gonna drill you.'

He jabbed at me with the pistol again. I nodded my receipt of the number, confirmation that I had taken his advice to heart.

'Now get out of my car.'

The Olds was moving before I had both feet on the sidewalk, tyres screeching their treads off. I watched the brake lights fade across the asphalt and then wink out as they took a left. My heart was pounding a manic rhythm in my chest.

I sat down on my haunches and sucked in the crisp air, lungful after lungful. I was hyperventilating and had a bad case of the shakes, yet, bizarrely, I was lifted by that adrenalin rush, the elation that only comes when the deal is done.

I stood up as a cab rolled by and hailed it to the kerb. It took about 15 minutes to ride back across town to Broadway. I took the stairs two at a time, not bothering with the dodgy elevator. It was only when I was standing in my apartment with my back against the door that I started to breathe a little easier.

I walked through to the tiny kitchenette and took a thin paring knife out of the cutlery drawer. The package I had been handed in the car was about two inches long, one inch wide and about an inch deep. The plastic was wrapped around on itself and taped closed at both ends. Carefully, I slid the tip of the knife through the cellophane and extracted a tiny, heaped mound of powder and tipped it on to the blade. I then transferred the powder onto my tongue and started to rub it around my gums with my finger.

Jackpot!

This was primo.

I had a new connection and my blow was now costing me

about $50 a gram. Not only had the quality improved noticeably, but the price had halved.

More bang for fewer bucks.

I had the juice.

I got game.

Now the Dohertys and the tallyman and the no-marks were all in the rear-view mirror of another car in a different place, another space, an ocean and half a world away.

My personal use of controlled substances had been pretty much continuous for the preceding four or five years. I had made the transition from smoking dope to dropping E and acid on a regular basis as London's clubland exploded. Cocaine had at first been a luxury for me, but, as my disposable income rose dramatically, I soon found myself snorting Charlie almost every evening and was prone to really caning the gear if I was out for the night. More worryingly, I had sampled heroin a few times in the year before I arrived in New York and found that I liked its narcotic effect. I occasionally smoked a bit of smack if I had been on a coke bender and had convinced myself that it was a smooth way to come down and get some sleep after a night on the town. I wasn't a scag fiend by any stretch of the imagination, but there really wasn't any drug that I wasn't prepared to try: my acceptance of heroin as a drug that I was quite prepared to use was to come back and haunt me as my problems with addiction spiralled out of control over the next few years. By moving up to scoring my cocaine by the ounce I was really entering a dangerous phase in my drug use: that pivotal change whereby your consumption shifts from being recreational to becoming necessary for you to function properly on a day-to-day basis. Looking back, it was that one deal that signalled the beginning of the mayhem and misery that was to become a part of my existence as drugs began to take control of my life. I was really kidding myself that I was buying more coke in order to start dealing again. I was buying more coke because my own appetite for the drug was beginning to overtake me.

My new-found supplier proved productive during the next few

weeks. I was scoring much more than I would need for weekly use and decided to spread the sweeties around.

I had made a couple of connections with Los Mescaleros who took a few grams for themselves, and more for friends and associates at $100 a gram. This is typically how small-scale users finance their habit. A small circle of like-minded individuals poses minimal personal risk but allows for bulk buying.

I was moving more than half an ounce to people I knew, so I scored from Justice once a week. I needed to maintain this regularity to keep him delivering the goods. Any less and it wouldn't be worth his car's while. However, I was careful not to overextend my activities to a wider audience. Only one person has to slip up and tip a bad hand to Officer Dibble for the whole house of cards to come tumbling down.

To be honest, Justice and his car of cronies worried me. It wasn't just his pistol-waving caper during our first meeting, but because they were all young, dumb and full of come. Justice was too brash; he was heading for a fall and was liable to give up everybody he knew to the law as part of a gargantuan plea-bargain.

I was aware that survival in New York's narco-world meant being prepared for any eventuality. Including being tooled up. I raised this with Justice after he picked me up outside the Elysée one night.

'So you want to get your ghetto pass? No problem,' he assured me. 'Meet me here tomorrow. Same time, same place, same face.'

'Cool,' I said. 'You got the shit?'

'No way, not today, Homes,' he said.

'There's a problem?'

'Twenty-four hours from now,' he confided, 'there's gonna be some high-end cha cha hitting the street. You chill, we'll talk.'

More nervous than usual, I waited outside the hotel that rain-drenched Thursday night.

Justice pulled up on cue. Surprisingly solo.

'Get in, Mo.'

We pulled out and took a left. We were moving downtown.

'Where are we heading?'

'We have to stop off at a party. There's a dude there who can fix you up with everything you need.'

Justice cracked his maniac grin. It discouraged discussion. I had got to sniff him out during the preceding few weeks: he was a heavy crack user. So he was as predictable as a pregnant nun. Given that Justice was about to become a willing accomplice in arming one of his new customers suggested that he wasn't exactly thinking straight.

We cruised through Midtown and cut across to First Avenue where Madison fades out. Soon after crossing Houston into the Lower East Side, we stopped. The border with the East Village was starting to get gentrified and we hadn't yet arrived in the bandit country down towards East Broadway.

The street was lined with trees and brownstone tenement buildings. Most of the properties had been renovated: no graffiti, and the fire escapes smelt of fresh paint.

Justice turned in his seat to face me.

'We'se gonna meet some very connected people in here, Mo. You just follow my lead and keep your mouth shut.'

'No problem. I'm just here for the piece.'

Justice gave me a serious look before opening the door and getting out. I did likewise and followed him up the steps of the building directly opposite the car. He pushed the buzzer to one of the apartments and a harsh voice came over the intercom.

'Who'se buzzin'?'

'It's Justice.'

The door clicked and we were in. I could feel the music as soon as we were in the hallway. The methodically lazy bassline was rocking the house, shaking its walls. We climbed the stairs to the second floor where the door to one of the apartments was open, waiting for us – along with a reception committee.

Two huge black Rastafarians stood barring our way. They were both wearing black suits with T-shirts underneath and had more 'dope ropes' around their necks than the Fort Knox gift shop.

'You carryin', Justice?'

Justice shook his head. He looked jumpy. The two dreads

moved aside and I scanned the room. It was jam-packo-rama. They were a mixed crowd: on one hand, your suited Midtown professionals, and on the other, a sprinkling of uptown brothers and downtown scenesters.

The joint had been tastefully decorated in light pastel tones and there'd clearly been some heavy investment in the home. Someone had got up a makeshift bar on trestle tables along the far wall. The music was thumping through two oversized Wharfdale speakers on either side.

Justice moved over to the bar and I followed. I noticed a low coffee table. A huge punchbowl on it was filled with cha cha bindles, judging by the way that people were dipping into it.

A matchstick-thin blonde catwalk model crouched at one end, hoovering up lines with apparent abandon. Most people were using every available surface to rack up some toot. In the centre of the room, a few couples swayed to the music in stupor-charged bliss.

I only realised that I was staring when Justice nudged my arm and handed me a bottle of beer. I swigged, then spotted probably the largest man I had ever seen. He must have been about 6ft 6in. in his bare feet. The pineapple of full dreadlocks on his head added a few extra inches as well. He wore a blue, pinstriped double-breasted suit, his chest bare underneath, a giant gold crucifix hanging around his neck. It was his eyes that caught my attention. They seemed to bug out of his face as if on stalks, a classic tell indicating a monga cokehead. Worryingly, as he nodded and chatted to his guests, he was moving towards us.

The giant drew level in front of us. I had to tilt my head back to look at his face.

'Respect to Justice. Who ya bringing to my crib?'

He was assured and smooth.

'This is Mo, the guy I told you about on the phone.'

Our host extended a hand that crushed mine within its grip.

'I'm Burrell. You're welcome in my home, Mo.'

His accent had a heavy Jamaican undertone, and he grinned as he spoke, exposing a mouthful of gold.

Burrell looked like he ate nickels for breakfast and spat them out as razor blades.

'Justice tells me that you want to get fixed for some iron,' he said.

'That's right,' I murmured above the party noizak.

'You want some heavy-duty shit or a Saturday night special, Mo? We cater to everybody's tastes here.'

Burrell had an unnerving habit of continually looking you up and down while he spoke, as if he was constantly changing his opinion of you.

'More of the Saturday night special, I think.'

'You say this bwoy is level, Justice?'

'Yeah, Burrell, this guy is cool.'

The huge dreadhead gave me a final appraising once-over before motioning to a door in the corner of the room.

'If Justice vouch for you, then you be cool. I'd prefer it if we conducted business somewhere more out of the way.'

The two goombahs from the door were now standing behind Burrell and all three of them moved.

'Come, come.'

Justice gave me an imploring look as if to beg me not to fuck this up. The adrenalin flowed freely as we entered a bedroom with a divan the size of a minor international airport at its centre. Black silk drapes hung from the ceiling, matching the sheets on the bed. The walls were slate grey and a huge projection television set dominated the floor, which was carpeted with pile you could lose your toes in. One of Burrell's goons closed the door behind us.

There were just the five of us in the room: me, the man, his peon and two front bumpers. Unless you're there for sex, it doesn't get much more intimate at this level. Discreet: should something go wrong, fewer eyes to see, fewer tongues to tell.

Burrell moved to a black bedside cabinet and opened the drawer to remove a silver Colt .45 automatic. He dropped the clip and showed it to me. It was fully loaded.

'Me thinkin' dat you'se no killer. Who ya wanna pop with dis ting, mon?' His Jamaican accent was now pumping in a patois style, as if he had turned off his party face to take care of business.

'Nobody. I just want it for insurance.'

Burrell studied me again before glancing at Justice.

'This man here tell me that you been buying weights from him. What you do for a living?'

'I work for a bank,' I lied. I sure as hell wasn't going to tell this psycho what I really did for a living or where I worked.

'You'se banking bwoys sure like your gear. There's be plenty of me customers out there in the same line of work as you. So, tell me, Mo, what you be thinkin' about our friend Justice here?'

The question floored me a little.

'He's cool.'

'No, Mo. Let me tell you dat this bwoy is a fool. Isn't that right, Justice?'

Justice just nodded.

'You'se see this Jam fool here, Mo. He'se thinkin' himself a big man now. You'se gonna show me how big a man you are, Justice? Tsch, you'se be dealing to the nickel and dimers and you'se be knowing your place or me'se gonna cut you bwoy. Me'se gonna cut you in two.'

Burrell moved in front of Justice, pushed the clip back into the Colt and held it under his chin.

'I told you not to be dealing no weights to nobody. If there's gear to be moved to brethren like Mo, then it's Burrell who be doin' the moving.'

Justice looked terrified. Understandably so. I too was having a 100-watt bayonet bulb moment as I realised I was in an impossible situation: my custom was being traded over to Burrell.

'You'se gonna be dancin' with me now, Mo. You'se understand me.' I had no choice. I nodded. Burrell took the gun away from Justice's face and then passed it to me, handle first.

'Feel the weight of that, Mo, 100 per cent American made, 100 per cent clean.'

I took the gun and felt it slide easily into the palm of my hand.

'Me gonna give you a weight for fifteen and a number to call on. The iron's gonna cost you another five.'

Two grand for the coke and the Colt? Under the circumstances, it seemed churlish to negotiate.

'Now, pay my brother here.'

Burrell indicated to one of his henchmen and I settled up.

'Justice, you'se got to be going now. Mo, you can stay and party.'

Justice looked relieved to exit, stage left, and I slid the pistol into the waistband of my trousers so it fitted snugly against the small of my back. The Rasta who had taken the money from me moved across and opened the bedroom door as a signal for us to rejoin the party.

Justice had vanished and I wished that I could do the same. It was clear, however, that Burrell wanted his newest customer to hang around for a while. He rested one giant, paw-like hand on my shoulder and steered me towards a small group of people who were snorting coke off one of the sideboards. He made an introduction and left me to make awkward small talk.

The group consisted of a couple of bond traders and some guy who owned a bar up on East 44th Street. They were all Burrell's clients and were enjoying their Andean snowstorm. I could feel the gun under my jacket and it was starting to make me edgy.

After about 15 minutes, the talk was so small it could have slid under the door as easily as a strip of chewing gum. I decided to do likewise. But suddenly, Burrell was in front of me.

'Leaving us, Mo?'

'Yeah, I've got to be somewhere.'

Somewhere? Anywhere but in here with this bugle-blitzed freakshow.

'Be safe, Mo, and you call Burrell tomorrow, you'se hear me?'

He handed me a business card. It simply had 'Burrell' printed above a mobile phone number.

I took it, smiled, and made like Yugoslavia and split.

Well, I wouldn't be seeing Justice anymore; that much was

clear. The issue was whether I would be able to stop Burrell from getting his hooks into me. I had seen it happen countless times before and had even used the tactic myself when distributing Ecstasy in London. The key is to get a fish on the line, in this case me, and then pump as much gear through them as possible.

Burrell wanted me to call him the next day. That meant that I was going to have to make another buy off him pretty soon. I could always have taken the option of not calling him, but then I would be without a connection for personal use. I wasn't sure how much Justice had told him about me. Justice knew where I lived after dropping me back at my apartment block one night. I couldn't take the risk. I would have to make that call.

I didn't sleep much that night and it wasn't down to cha-cha-charlie. Dealing with Burrell was going be like dancing on dynamite. My custom had been traded without my consent, but there was nothing that I could do about it. Justice was a low-level distributor who was more prone to bravado than direct action. Burrell was a different species.

I made Burrell as a Yardie. They get their name from the backyards of Jamaica's capital, Kingston, which spawned them. They operate in posses and advance with lashings of the old ultra-violence. Yardies have no qualms about eliminating the competition, members of their own posse or random bystanders. They're well-armed and dangerous.

The Caribbean has long been a staging post for cocaine shipped north of the Andes. Carlos Lehder, a kingpin in the Medellin cartel, actually bought an island, Norman's Cay, from the Bahamian government and used it as a bridgehead for flying coke into the US.

The Yardies were often subcontracted by the Latino cartels to use their mules to take the drugs to their final destination. It was a short step for them to start running their own fully fledged distribution network, buying kilos at wholesale prices from South American suppliers and maximising their margin. Together with the Dominicans, they were the major players in the New York crack trade at street level at that time in the early '90s.

By morning, I decided that I had no choice but to call Burrell and attempt to convince him that I was a peon who dealt part time only to friends, and not really worth an important man like him bothering about.

I punched up the numbers from a payphone outside my office. Burrell picked up on the first ring. The conversation was terse.

'Be at my apartment, seven o'clock.'

'Tonight?'

'Tonight.'

I was home by six, rounding up my fundage. I knew that he would insist on me making another buy.

That's how it works in narco-world. I had been to the bank and had also moved nearly an ounce of blow in the previous week. I had $5,000 to play with. I was praying that he only wanted to move an ounce at a time through me because I was still sitting on the ounce I'd scored from him the night before.

My only comfort was feeling the weight of the Colt .45 as I slid it into my waistband.

I needed at least a shot at bailing out of a firefight if the shit came down.

I was at Burrell's at seven prompt and was buzzed into the building. Burrell was sprawled across a sofa. The matchstick model from last night lay comatose in one of the armchairs that had been moved onto the former dance floor. The two heavies I had seen 24 hours before were again standing by the door to greet me.

'Whassup bwoy?'

I took a seat in a padded leather chair opposite him.

'Me gonna move you some mighty fine coke, bwoy. You ready for this?'

From which I surmised he was asking me if I had brought cash with me. I decided to pre-empt him.

'I'll take another weight for fifteen.'

'No, no, no, you listen to me, bwoy. How much you have on you? Empty your pockets out on this table here and let me see the colour of your money.'

How sick-o-logical. I had the whole five grand in my trouser pocket. I hadn't divided it up. There was nothing for it so I reached to get the money.

At that moment I felt an arm wrap around my neck, pulling me back into the chair.

'Easy, mon. Me gonna have my man check you out first just to see if you don't come here for some nasty business.'

Burrell's goon let go of my neck and bade me stand. He quickly found the gun and removed it from my trousers.

'Why you'se coming in my home all ironed up? You thinking I'se gonna hurt ya? Me only gonna clip you'se if you don't wanna be part of the family. Now pass over that money and don't be thinkin' of messin' with Burrell.'

I tossed the money onto the coffee table. Burrell plucked it up and counted it.

'Hey Mo, five large. You'se be buying 100g with this kind of cash.'

I sat back down. Burrell signalled to one of his flunkeys who slipped into the bedroom. I was going to have to move heaps of hampers from the Pampas if I was getting another 100g on top of the ounce I already owned. It was spectacularly stupid to have brought all the cash, but now it was too late for self-recrimination.

Burrell sat up straight. His casually menacing stare hinted at the violence that boiled and burned deep inside.

'Your friends at the bank are gonna be mighty pleased with you, Mo. You gonna give them some fine white lady to go out to play with.'

I nodded. I was in deep now. All my spare cash was going into this unwanted deal and I assumed that he would be expecting me to make another buy pretty soon. I didn't have to wait long to find out.

'Today is Friday. It should be no problem to move this gear over the weekend. What you say to that, Mo?'

'I can't move anything over the weekend. The bank is closed. I won't be able to put anything together until next week.'

I was stalling.

'You'se got until Wednesday then. I be expectin' you here at seven o'clock and don't think you can be fuckin' with me. Justice been told me all about you, Mo.'

I shuddered. He had got me just where he wanted me. I was now part of Burrell's distribution network and there was nothing that I could do about it. Just then, the bedroom door opened and his Rasta henchmen returned carrying a plastic bag with the coke in it. The Rasta handed it to me with a sneer.

'You'se had better get busy with it, Mo,' Burrell said. 'Remember that I'se be seeing you on Wednesday.'

Evidently my cue to leave.

'You be taking that pea shooter with you and don't be coming here packing again.'

I picked up the Colt and ankled, my head spinning as I cabbed back uptown.

How could I move all that gear in a few days?

Monday was pay day, so I would have some cash to play with, but I had unwittingly raised the stakes now. Burrell would be expecting me to weigh in with another $5,000 in the middle of next week.

That weekend I was busier than a Palestinian undertaker. Entering Alphabet City's street dealing fraternity was a non-starter. Come for the scuzz, stay for my murder? No way, Ray. So I phoned around my connections and by Sunday night had managed to move 20g. But it was only because I slashed my price down from $100 to $70 a gram. Even with this fire-sale 33 per cent discount, I had only moved about 30g by Tuesday night.

There was a limit to how much my associates would be able to take from me. They were now already stocked up with as much Bolivian marching powder as they needed to walk them though the following week. With my paycheck I had managed to scrape together another $5,000 – I was down to my last few dollars.

Wednesday night and I was outside Burrell's. I had left the Colt at home: provoking this maniac didn't strike me as smart play. I was about to press the buzzer when I heard a voice behind me.

'Hey, bwoy.'

I span round to see Burrell staring at me through the open window of a new model black Cadillac Seville.

'Get in, Mo,' he said. 'We'se going for a ride.'

I wavered. I havered. I did the actuarial life expectancy calculation. Then I walked over to get in the back seat with Burrell.

'No fool, you'se can ride up front with Delroy.'

I eased into the front passenger seat and turned to face Burrell.

'Let's take care of our business first. It's gonna be you holding the gear while we drive.'

The hired goombah I now knew as Delroy handed me another bag full of coke.

'That's another five thou, bwoy.'

I handed over the cash to the driver.

Jumping Jehozaphat, I now had nearly 200g of coke. It would take me at least a month to shift it.

'I'm having trouble moving all this gear,' I pleaded. 'I'll need some time to get things sorted out. Justice was giving me a weight a week and I was only just getting through that much.'

'Me not interested in your problems, Mo. I'se be expectin' you on Sunday at seven to pick up again, ye hear me?'

I decided not to press my point; it was like singing an aria to a lip-reader. A monga marketing blitz loomed if I was to make the payment on Sunday.

We pulled out and headed towards the East Village. The Friday night traffic was hellacious: most of the streets were gridlocked in an angry cacophony of shouty horns. We must have been driving for about 45 minutes before we levelled into 125th Street. Smack bang in the centre of beautiful uptown Harlem. Late evening. Honky, don't let the sun set on you here.

'Just cruise, Delroy,' Burrell commanded.

We had made this journey in silence, but I could now sense our back-seat passenger brooding as we drove. Something was going down. I had no choice but to ride it out.

We took a left turn at Manhattan Avenue, circled the block and then doubled back along 125th. The street was crowded with commuters scurrying home, local yokels doing their folksy things, and street people who were hanging out, hanging in or hanging on, lounging against the small mom-and-pop stores and liquor marts that lined the sidewalks.

'There he is, pull over, pull over.'

We slammed on the anchors and Delroy jumped out of the car. He moved like a huge, dreadlocked big cat and grabbed a fella who was leaning against a phone booth on the corner of Lexington Avenue. There was a brief tug of war and then they were both back in the car with us.

'OK, Delroy, drive.'

We took off back into the traffic.

'Listen fool,' Burrell screamed in the face of our new passenger, 'where's my motherfucking money?'

The dude's designer tracksuit suggested he was a cut above the regular street clockers. He wore his hair in long dreadlocks like Burrell. I guessed he was probably a lower level member of his posse.

Burrell obviously favoured the up-close-and-personal approach. A kingpin would normally delegate keeping the troops in line to an underling. Like Murph, Burrell was a man who enjoyed instilling fear into others at first hand. He was getting off on his powerplay.

Maybe this poor wretch was in too deep with the boss. It crossed my mind that my own situation could swiftly descend into this same harsh realm if I didn't start successfully moving some big-style quantities of blow. Burrell was making his point. This was a demonstration of his power. He was piling on the pressure.

'Where's my fuckin' money? You'se be one special fool to be stealin' from Burrell.'

'I haven't got it, mon.' The street dealer talked fast. 'I'se been picked up by the pol-eese. They keep me for two days. I swear to you.'

'You'se think I'se stupid,' Burrell bellowed in the peon's face. He whipped out an automatic pistol and pushed it into his victim's chest. 'Me send you to Babylon for stealin' from me.'

Our guest squealed.

'Me blow you away fool. Who are you'se to fuck with Burrell?'

'I'se not got the money. I'se swear to it mon.'

'Liar.'

Burrell brought the handle of the gun down flush onto the guy's nose in one swift, explosive movement. I heard the bone and cartilage splinter. His face erupted into a cascade of blood. I watched. My guts churned.

As a dealer I've been around the block, but I knew that I was in deep with Burrell and that pretty soon it might be me on the receiving end of his rage.

'Shit, Burrell. Me no cheat you. I'se swear to it.'

His hands clutched what remained of his face. The blood flowed freely from his shattered nose, the car filling with its pungent, coppery smell.

'Me give you another day and then you'se will pay me what you owe. Otherwise me send your sorry soul to hell. Pull over.'

We pulled up to the kerb.

'Get your Jam fool arse out of the car. Me no gonna have to come up here to find you hidin' from me. You'se be meeting Delroy at the club tomorrow night and you'se be bringin' the money with you, or me take down you and your family. Me gonna lay waste to your kids an all of them that you'se know.'

The errant dealer got out of the car, cupping one hand around his busted snoot.

'Fool to be fuckin' with me,' Burrell muttered as we cut into First Avenue and started to head back downtown. The man was totally pumped now and kept murmuring and mumbling under his breath as we rode back. Eventually he spoke to me.

'Where's you getting out? You'se ain't comin' back with me carryin' all that powder on you.'

'Just drop me here.'

Bailing out of the car right now suited me fine. A high-voltage vibe of testosterone and adrenalin crackled from Burrell. Violence and menace bubbled within his body, a bad voodoo doll casting a spell I wanted no part of. I could feel his eyes burning a hole in the back of my neck. We stopped on the corner of First and East 80th Street. Burrell leaned forward between the two front seats.

'You listen to me now. You'se is gonna move your gear and see me again on Sunday night. Me no want to hear any of your excuses that you can't be movin' my coke. Now go.'

Pull the handle and press escape. I slammed the Caddy door and started putting one foot in front of the other. Burrell's ride sped away. He had things to see and people to do.

Me too. I was really in play now. I had a shitload of coke and five days from scratch to come up with another five large. This was assuming that Burrell was going to stick with the usual amount. Maybe he'd up the ante? I'd just seen his method of dealing with those who couldn't come up with the cash for him.

I was fucking up, big time.

My mind reeled as I walked all the way down to PJ Clark's near East 54th. I had calmed down by the time I was sipping a bourbon and soda at the long mahogany bar. The place was crowded with Midtown suits, but I felt utterly alone.

I had really done it this time. Only yesterday it seemed that I was dealing with Mr Easy Peasey in the form of Pauly. Now the hunter was the prey and I was being used as a coke conduit by a tribe of Jamaican psychopaths.

I downed another drink, paid my tab and walked up to Broadway.

I needed time to think: no way could I unload all the devil's dandruff I had stashed at my apartment. Everybody I knew was hitting and holding after my previous few days of narco-commerce.

I had taken the last of my money out of the bank to pay Burrell for the new batch. I had about $500 in emergency money back at home, but that wasn't going to get me far. Even if I had decided to run, I had nowhere to go. I couldn't go back to London, as there was probably a contract out on me generated by the wrath of the Doherty brothers. I needed a bit more time out of the UK to let things cool down there.

It was a long, slow walk back to my apartment, not so much the stride of pride as the peregrination of rumination. And I still hadn't come up with a solution.

I uncapped some whisky when I got in and tried to storm my own brains. One thing was for sure, I had to lay off the product for now. I would need to be firing on all synapses to get out of this one.

I spent most of the next 48 hours in a daze. I had toyed with the idea of hitting the clubs to flog some Ye Yo, but the last thing I needed was to get busted. Dealing when you're desperate is always asking for trouble: it breeds carelessness.

Friday morning dawned. Charlie wasn't moving; I was still only $500 up. Nothing for it: time for a fire sale. So I spent much of the morning clandestinely talking to my agency connections, offering them gear at cost, $50 a gram. It was short-term expediency; I'd saturated the market, nobody in my pool would pay $70 a gram now.

By Friday night I had raised another $1,200 but it looked like the ceiling. And I would have to spend the whole of the evening cabbing around Manhattan dropping the coke off to buyers.

I was now delivering to people I didn't know, and so was stepping into the danger zone as far as attracting potential heat from the NYPD went. When you touch one element in an equation of risk, all the other bits wiggle to balance it all out again.

Mr Nasty knows: strangers mean danger.

My corruption of Los Mescaleros and their compadres had been radical and rapid. Before, toot had been discreet. Now, the entire office was wired into the narco-highway. Even the receptionists were scoring off me.

I drew up a list of regular customers and realised that they were all tapped out. I would have to find secondary targets.

Kowalski came to mind.

Leon Kowalski was a junior intern at the agency. He had heard that there was coke about, and word had filtered through to me that he was looking to make a buy. To my knowledge, Kowalski didn't dabble in drugs at all. My dealership was enticing the hearts

MR NASTY

and wallets of drug virgins. Sure, he had put himself on offer, but at the time scruples sounded like a TV movie project I'd file in the shredder.

I called Kowalski on Saturday morning.

'Leon, it's Cameron. How're you doing?'

I had to drop my drug pseudonym, Mo, when dealing with colleagues. They were off-street; they knew me.

I was starting to feel exposed. Despite trying to stay clean, the humungous lines of blow I had been snorting fuelled the paranoia. But my dealer's reflexes took over.

'Listen, Leon, I've heard that you might be in the market to buy something to help your weekend go with a bang. I may just be able to help.'

'We're talking about coke, right?'

He couldn't hide the enthusiasm in his voice. I had him. All I had to do was reel the fish in.

'Sure, Leon. I may be able to help you out if that's your particular preference. Look Leon, I don't just deal to anyone, you know? Just a small circle of close friends who know better than to go mouthing off about where they get their supplies from. Understand?'

'No problem, Cameron. You can trust me.'

Trust me. Every time someone says 'Trust me' I count my fingers.

'That's good to hear, Leon,' I continued. 'I don't just deal a couple of grams here and there though. Reality is it's got to be by the ounce or not at all.'

'An ounce . . .?'

'Hey, if you can't handle it, no problemo, dude.'

'How much will that cost me?'

'Two grand. Straight up.'

I was hustling the sap but, hey, I was being hustled. I rationalised the transaction by perceiving myself as a clearing house: people stressed me, I laid off that stress, pushed it around the pool. Like Leon probably knew that an ounce was a significant amount of jazz salts for a first-time buyer? Yeah, right.

There was a pause on the other end of the line.

Then Leon spoke again.

'When can I get the coke?'

'Just get into a cab and get over here right now. No time like the present, my supplies are going real fast.'

My guess is that he was out of the door and hailing a cab before the receiver hit the cradle: 20 minutes later he was on my doorstep. I beckoned him in and led him through to my living room where I had already measured out an ounce onto my glass-topped coffee table – an essential item for every discerning cocaine freak.

Leon sat opposite me as I cut him out a couple of lines from the side of the pile.

'You do this type of gear a lot, Leon?'

'Oh, sure. All the time.'

He was as green as broccoli, obviously lying, and I allowed myself a snarky smirk. Another mark was about to fall under my spell.

'Have you got the money on you?'

Leon handed me over a wad of bills. I didn't bother counting it. Leon seemed kitten scared – I knew he wouldn't screw me. I rolled up one of the bills and handed it to him. He bent down over the table, unsure of what to do next. This was embarrassing.

'Hold one side of your nose with your finger and put the bill up your open nostril. Then just sniff it back.'

Leon did so and rose from the table spluttering like the first timer he was.

'Now do the same with the other nostril.'

As he bent down I watched in horror as his head snapped back and his coke-clogged schnoz splattered out one almighty sneeze. It was a Woody Allen moment. The ounce wafted out across the table, most of it spraying onto the carpet.

'Jesus Christ, you moron. What the fuck do you think you're doing?'

Leon looked aghast by what he had done as I started scraping the remaining coke together on the table once more.

'Well, you've paid for it now so what you've blown into the wind is gone now. You're just going to have to take what's left and leave the rest in the shag pile.'

I piled up the remaining half ounce of blow and used a teaspoon to scoop it into a small plastic bag. Leon was still frantically trying to sniff back the coke and the fool didn't even argue with me. This was the problem with dealing with people – the customer service element of narco-deals. It was a part of the job I had never had much time for.

The rest of the weekend dragged by and I was unable to move much more product. I had a little over three and a half grand to my name by the time the clock ticked round to Sunday evening.

Time to bite the bullet.

Not turning up for my appointment with Burrell was not an option: I had seen first-hand his likely response should he have to trouble himself with coming to find me. I pocketed my cash and then, as an automatic response, picked up the Colt.

No way that I was going in there unarmed. Yeah, he had warned me not to pack, but by this stage, all bets were off. I didn't envisage Burrell being too thrilled by my pleas of poverty, so perhaps best bring along the old equaliser.

I hailed a cab and made the tortuous journey down to the Lower East Side. I smoked an express cigarette before pressing the buzzer once again and entering Burrell's lair. The door to the apartment was open as I reached the second-floor landing.

'Me like one thing about you, Mo. You'se punctual at least.' I was back within my secret life where people knew me simply as Mo.

I sat down opposite Burrell. There was another Rastafarian who I hadn't seen before sitting next to him on the sofa. The man already had the bag out waiting for me.

'I haven't been able to move all of the gear yet,' I said. 'I can only take a weight this time.'

Wasting time is like wearing round-toed shoes, pointless. Best get this over with.

'Me no deal no weight. Tsch, you be foolin' with me. You'se

gonna take another five grand's worth and not be complainin' to me that you can't be moving no gear to your fancy banking friends.'

'I've got three and a half large on me. That's it.'

Burrell paused and then leant forward in his seat, fixing me with his cold death stare.

'You'se not hearin' me, Mo. You be thinkin' that I'se some kind of chicken-shit coke dealer. Me'se big-time, bwoy. Me'se cut you up and feed you to the fish in the Hudson River. You'se s'posed to be a tall bwoy out there dealing to them that has the money to buy big. You'se think I'se gonna deal a fuckin' weight at a time? We'se in the major league, Mo. Kilo after kilo of blow all the way from Jamaica. Me show you not to fuck with me. Me show you the man that Burrell is. Get up, you'se comin' with us now.'

Burrell rose to his feet. His colleague did likewise.

'C'mon, you'se is comin' with us. Me show you who you'se messin' with. Me show you'se my power.'

He was in rant mode now, spittle coagulating on his lower lip.

In that instant, as they stood waiting for me to get up and accompany them, I flashed on grabbing my Colt.

'Hey,' Burrell's new best friend growled.

I might be able to plug Burrell, or his lackey: but not both. And who knows who else could be lurking around the place?

It was a sucker's bet.

The moment passed, and I sucked it up and followed them both out of the door and downstairs. The Cadillac was parked up and we got in, me in front again as Burrell stretched his considerable frame across the back. No talking in the car now.

So much narco-action happens in cars that, during the 1990s, hip-hoppers would refer in their lyrics to 'a car', describing a crew on a mission. Usually to score, play some girlies, cruise the hood, whatever game is playing.

Narco-cars, narco-time, narco-planet.

Inside this car, I realised it was pointless me trying to plead with Burrell. Appealing to his better instincts would be like knitting water.

I was bricking it.

'This is it,' I thought and reviewed the tragic fiasco of my life. I was convinced that this car would drive me to the river and someone inside would put a bullet in the back of my head. Burrell was right. I was a fool. I had sealed my fate as soon as I had decided to trade up from Pauly. Mr Hubris meet Mr Nemesis, it seems you're going to be working together very soon.

With the benefit of my 20/20 hindsight goggle-bins, I could now see that for a city boy to be scoring weights was a sure-fire, dead-cert way of attracting all the wrong kind of attention and overdrawing, in a fatal style, at the karma bank. My game would be terminated with extreme funk not by the NYPD cops but by those who dispensed a more summary narco-justice: no need for due process or sissy arrest warrants – sentence first, river burial to follow.

My descent had been swift. William Burroughs said: 'I can feel the heat closing in.' I was visually rehearsing where the ropes and tape would go, how much of a Revenger's Tragedy the Act III, Scene III of my life would be.

The Caddy's engine ran smoothly as we cruised down towards the Bowery and took a right into Park Row cutting back up towards East Broadway. The car made a hard right into Montgomery Street and pulled up about halfway down its length. We were in a lower Manhattan industrial area by the East River.

The street was lined with warehouses, locked down at the front. It was about 7.30 now and the place was deserted. Burrell opened the door and got out.

'Move ya sorry self, Mo.'

I got out of the car, as did the driver, and followed Burrell as he walked up to a shutter door set a few feet back from the sidewalk. He looked up and down the empty street before rapping on the metal grill. There was a pause. An electric motor whined as the shutter crept upwards. Burrell stooped underneath it before it was level with his head. I followed him in.

We entered a large warehouse space filled with crates. Burrell led the way, his cohort followed behind me, the meat in their sandwich. We skirted around the crates and moved up a flight of metal steps at the side of the main floor area. At the top was another cavernous storage area. There was a Formica table to our left, on which was an Uzi machine gun and several clips. The two goons I had met previously at Burrell's place were waiting. One was carrying an automatic pistol and the other packed a fully automatic machine gun. The Mac 10.

'I'm gonna show you, Mo, who you'se be dealin' with now. You'se is in the presence of a great man. Me gonna supply all of this city and you choose to try and fuck with me. You'se be tellin' me that you can't move 100g for Burrell. Me show you now.'

Burrell moved over to the table and put a clip into the Uzi.

'Ain't nobody round here to hear your screamin', bwoy.'

I was doing the nodding dog routine. Smiling and nodding, nodding and smiling, playing for time off a clock I didn't have.

'Remember that. Show me what you've got, bwoy. Put dat ting on the table and be cool.'

Burrell had fully lapsed into Jamaican patois now. His eyes bulged in the hazy, neon-lit semi-darkness like huge, bloodshot, squishy white marbles. I could distinctly make out the veins pulsing and popping under the skin by his temples.

He must have had a heavy night. I wondered, in a disinterested, parenthetical sort of way, just how much bugle Mr Burrell packed up his nasal cavities of an evening.

I felt the cold steel of the Mac 10 automatic jab into the side of my neck, but couldn't see which one of Burrell's cowboys was cattle-prodding me.

Snap decision. Better do as the man said. An easy choice under the circumstances. I drew the Colt from under my jacket and put it on the table as Burrell had asked.

The barrel of the Mac 10 was ice cold against my neck as the Jamaican reared up to his full, imposing height in front of me.

How in the Jesus H. lapdancing Christ had I managed to get myself into this? I was isolated in a Lower East Side warehouse with a homicidal posse of synapse-fried dreadheads.

I tried to forgive myself as the previous six months flashed through my mind with startling clarity; six months I now wished that I could take back and make over. What a tragic fool I was.

'Me no like you, Mo, but me no gonna kill you'se this time. See, you'se belong to Burrell. All of your friends an' family belong to Burrell. You'se is going to be part of this family until I decide otherwise, ye hear me?'

Burrell dropped the Uzi back onto the table.

'Me be hanging on to your piece now. Me not be wanting you getting' no ideas about creepin' up on Burrell from behind.'

That was that. He was keeping my gun. I was totally vulnerable, not that I would have had any chance of taking these guys on head-to-head.

'Take this fool outside and let him walk home. You'se be callin' me in two days' time with the five grand. I don't wanna be hearin' no excuses from you, Mo, or I'se be bringin' you back down here an' playin' with my toys again.'

For a moment, my jelly legs wouldn't work. I was thinking I'd done well because I hadn't messed myself. I focused on putting one foot in front of the other, travelling towards the stairs in Delroy's footsteps.

I didn't wait for the shutter to fully unfurl, dipping underneath when it was at waist height. Then I ran.

I ran for block after block before finally slumping against a shop front opposite St Mark's in the Bowery. I was fighting for breath. They were fucking psychopaths.

Now I had no chance. No choice. Scraping together the $5,000 and surviving beyond Tuesday night looked like a long shot.

I still had the three and a half grand and could make a run for it. But where would I go? I needed thinking time. I hailed a passing yellow cab and headed for home. The odds were Burrell probably knew where I lived. I couldn't take the chance that he didn't. I was pretty sure he didn't know where I worked as Justice hadn't known, so couldn't have told him and I certainly hadn't spilt the beans.

It was time to move.

Now.

I started packing right away. I didn't have much stuff and hadn't supplied legitimate referees when I secured the apartment. The real estate agent had been anxious to let the place, and had been lax in following through on the check-ups.

I boxed up my few possessions and then grabbed the stash of coke. I didn't want to take any chances of one of Burrell's posse coming to find me before our next rendezvous, so I stayed in a $50-a-night hotel down on West 44th Street, before calling in sick at work the next day.

I waited until midday before venturing back to my apartment. The concierge wasn't in the foyer, so I grabbed my stuff and brought it down to the sidewalk outside in a couple of trips. Then I headed back to the hotel. I stayed there for a week while I found another apartment. I remained off sick, complaining of flu. I was terrified of leaving the hotel room in case Burrell would be cruising by.

Eventually, through a *Village Voice* classified, I found another shoebox to inhabit, on East 76th Street over by John Jay Park. But even as I moved, using a U-Haul like a pioneer pressing the Western frontier, the fear was still inside me.

I ditched the coke: 200g – $10,000 worth – in the East River. I was on tilt. I couldn't take chances. I'd decided to exit stage left from Narcobiz Inc.

My agency colleagues would just have to find their own gear from now on. For the next three months, I kept my nose clean. I travelled straight home from work, still terrified that I might see the black Seville drawing up to the sidewalk and the barrel of an Uzi sliding out of the rear window. Gradually, I started to relax. Keeping off the gear helped. I even started to get things together at work.

Everything was getting back onto an even keel until one Monday morning in December 1992. I was called into the meeting room. Crisply, I was informed that my sojourn in New York was at an end. I was being seconded to the Los Angeles office.

I had been working with the guys out in LA more and more, sorting out protracted contract wrangles for multiple film projects they had with East Coast-based talent.

Evidently, my hard work and straight-arrow lifestyle was paying off. Which was A-OK by me. Most of the action happened out West, and I wanted to be in the place where the movies were actually made rather than just reading about the power deals in *Variety*.

Great. I could stand a tan.

LOS ANGELES

RISING STARS
AND FALLEN ANGELS

Gonzalo Rodriguez, 'Gacha' to his associates, formed part of a loose coalition of South American kingpin traffickers known as the Medellin cartel. The US Drug Enforcement Authority (DEA) first coined the term 'cartel'. Reality was that it was a loose coalition of narco-businessmen who periodically traded with each other. Other members included the dealmaker, Carlos Lehder, the Ochoa brothers and the ruthless Pablo Escobar.

Cocaine's fortunes had waned stateside until George Jung, later immortalised by Johnny Depp in the film *Blow*, entered the arena in the late 1970s. Following his 1974 imprisonment for dealing cannabis, Jung met his first Colombian connections behind bars and, three years later, shipped in his first big coke consignment – 250kg out of the Bahamas. Jung rapidly bolstered the Latino drug lords' North American distribution.

Gonzalo 'Gacha' Rodriguez owned production labs across Latin America and had part shares in others with the Ochoa brothers and Escobar. Lehder was purely involved in the trafficking aspect of the business. Jung concentrated on end-of-line distribution, filtering the cash generated in the US back over the border to Latin America.

MR NASTY

133

'Gacha' had the whole Mexican frontier to play with and used illegal 'wetback' immigrants to mule over cocaine in volume. His distribution network spread virally up the West Coast of the US, with California as its commercial epicentre.

By the '80s, cocaine saturated the North American market and an incessant flow of laundered money washed back to the cartel. Gacha was the initial mastermind behind deluging Los Angeles with Colombia's numero uno export.

So in coke-fuelled 1993, Los Angeles was possibly the worst place I could have pitched up after my rapid exit from New York.

It was January and I had found myself a modest apartment on La Brea Avenue, just off Santa Monica Boulevard, a stone's throw from my new office on West Sunset Boulevard. Not that I walked to work.

LA's vibe is different from NY's street hustle. If you walked anywhere in LA you were some kind of mutant. The city's freeways sprawl across the topography: wheels are essential to survive and thrive in the City of Angels.

My work was a hotbed of shark-like deals and Machiavellian backstabbing. Just the way I liked it. I was immediately brought in on several large movie deals. My speciality was renegotiating artists' contracts when, once filming had started, they chucked their toys out of the pram. One moment I'd be arranging for some errant thespian to get a bigger trailer to enhance those relaxing moments between takes; the next, I'd be completely reworking a project's financing structure with the studio.

The job brought me into contact with A-list celebrities, but the wow factor fades fast: bodies by Nautilus, brains by Mattel. When you see at first hand how lame and peculiar many of these individuals are, you start to realise what a crap-shoot it all is.

My agency was the power broker in Hollywood. It made things happen, but everyone had 747-size egos.

Cocaine was omnipresent, from the office toilets to the bars and clubs on Sunset and Vine. It was high purity and cheap, fuelling Monday morning power breakfasts in Marin County and

Friday night dinner parties along the Pacific Coast Highway.

But I was a late starter in LA's happy hour in hell, running on empty for a couple of months while I settled in this new terrain.

I remember the first time I was summoned from my office, in the building's basement, to the third-floor lair of Rick Bernstein. Bernstein was a Young Turk with the agency. He had a Hollywood client list to kill for and a slash-and-burn attitude.

On my entrance into the small office that served as his antechamber, I was greeted by three of his assistants in immaculately tailored power-suits and telephone headsets. They rose in unison and trooped out of the door after one had signalled for me to enter Bernstein's lair.

His matt-black-and-chrome business hub was humungous. The great man sat behind a large oak desk at its far end, rattling instructions down the phone.

'Get the flowers to Posey right now . . . tell Quentin's people the Manson musical's a soft go at Fox, but no way is OJ attached . . .'

I took a seat in front of him and surveyed the framed movie posters and gold discs on the walls. Bernstein looked about 25 years old. He wore the agent's uniform of Italian silk suit and an understated, conservative tie.

'. . . a hard no on the Trump kid abduction idea . . . Hey, is Arthur Miller still alive? He's a playwright. If he is, have Todd brief me on Shannon Doherty, we need to know her marriage-biddability. And this Schindler's Top 10 List, send the Jewish Defamation League a fax . . .'

It was his hair. It had been lacquered into a gravity-defying concrete bouffant that towered inches above his forehead. My eyes were continually drawn to it. In LA, the higher the hair, the closer to God.

Rick had been instrumental in my move from New York. Maybe he recognised my tireless devotion to 10 per centery. Or perhaps he had heard rumours of my sideline in dealing blow.

Bernstein hung up with a final 'Ciao' and regarded me quizzically with his brooding eyes.

'So, what's happening, Streak?'

A funny hat and a nickname for everyone. Getting a nickname meant you were in. It was happening fast: I wanted to slow play it.

'I'm being kept pretty busy, Mr Bernstein.'

'Please just call me Rick. All my friends do, and most of my enemies as well. Where do you think you fit in to the equation?'

'I'd like to think that I was one of the former.'

'Good call, Streak.'

We shot the breeze for a few minutes. I gave him some edited highlights on my action in the New York office. He listened intently, his gaze never wavering from my eyes. It was like trying to stare down a baby cobra. Then he hit me one from leftfield.

'OK, Streak, what's your definition of a good deal for the agency?'

I pondered briefly, sensing some hidden agenda at work. I had been forewarned that Rick had a ruthless core philosophy. Play it slow, I reminded myself. Be diplomatic. Cast bland bread on the water, see what comes back.

'I think a good deal is,' I said slowly, 'where we enter into an arrangement on behalf of the talent with a studio and conclude it in a fashion which is beneficial to all parties. We get the deal done, and then walk away with all parties ready to do business again in the future.'

Beeeeg mistake.

'You've got a lot to learn, Streak. Let me tell you what a good deal is. You enter into an arrangement whereby you fuck over everybody concerned and screw the last dollar out of the situation. Fuck the talent and fuck the studios. We are the agency and we decide who does what and what goes where. We walk away as the winner: everybody else has to just grit their teeth in a shit-eating grin and go with our flow.'

I sat there stunned. He had hit me with his signature rapid-fire delivery. I had listened to the hushed tones in which the junior agents spoke about him. Now he was in full flow.

'. . . that shithead's being sued by his own career for defamation of character . . .' he said of the husband of one of our star clients, a network comedian with a number one franchise and weight issues. The man had parlayed wifey's fame into his own TV show which was winning share and ratings.

'. . . but there's a rumour he's been legally dead for ten years and the guy you see on TV is just a glove puppet . . .'

'No!' he suddenly barked into the phone, 'you tell Don Simpson to fuck off and stick his fucking piece of shit up his faggy ass.'

Rick was a caricature of a Hollywood agent, but this is what they're like. Thousand dollar suits and alligator-skin shoes. A home on each coast, priority reservations at Two Bunch Palms and mistresses falling out of their closets. Screaming and scheming, hostile takeovers, cheap shots and convenient alliances. 'Hello,' he lied. Stab them in the front, it saves time.

This guy had made it to his pole position through naked aggression and a devious, self-serving malevolence that would have made Machiavelli blush. Bernstein was at the top. And he was going to make sure that he stayed there.

'I've got to get over to Paramount now, but why don't you come over to the house later and we can go for a drive.'

He gave me a look that would have stripped paint. A look that said if I ever fucked with him, nobody would ever find my body. Not in one piece, not in this lifetime. At least that was what he wanted me to think.

'Get Celia Brady's cell on line one and have Lex bring my ride round to the front . . .'

The audience was over. I shuffled out of his office thinking that if I'd had a forelock I wouldn't have known whether to tug it or pull it out with the rest of my hair so I could make a rope and strangle him. I was going to be spending the evening with Slick Rick: who knew what he had in mind? Concentration that afternoon proved difficult.

Bernstein lived on Motor Drive in Hollywood. Quite smart: manicured lawns, backyard tennis courts, and pools around which to schmooze, schmingle and manoeuvre.

Rick's property's imposing frontage provided the shady façade of heavy money.

I rang the bell, shifting from foot to foot like a tart waiting for confession. I was expecting a butler in full morning dress to answer the door in sedate tones. But Rick did it himself.

He wore jeans and a polo shirt. With his fast-breaking smile showcasing $20,000 of bridgework and his eerie orange perma-glow skin, he looked like an embryonic George Hamilton.

That's the entire trajectory of a Hollywood career: Who's George Hamilton? Get me George Hamilton. Get me a George Hamilton type. Get me a young George Hamilton. Who's George Hamilton?

'Evening, Streak, I hope you've got your speed hat on. Come in.'

If I thought the outside of his pad was palatial, the inside was something else.

You rarely saw this much white marble outside a museum. Two sets of symmetrical staircases curved up from the hallway to the first floor. The decor screamed money with all the taste and subtlety of a trailer-park lottery winner.

My host led me through to a lavish living room at the rear and then out onto the poolside veranda. We were not alone.

A couple of tanorexic girls with copper-tone flesh and thin thighs lounged on sunbeds by the pool. They looked to be about 17 years old. Maybe more. Probably less. So Rick likes his bananas green, I thought. Sandwiched between them was a bloated whale of a man, all greased-back hair and a porn star moustache. He was leaning forward, concentrating intently as he chopped up lines on a white side table.

'Streak, this is Benito. King Benny to those with the nod.'

I shook his hand, my gaze drawn to the small mountain of gak he was racking out.

Benito clocked the look in my eyes.

'I think your friend here wants to have some fun, Rick.'

His accent was heavily Spanglish. He motioned to the table. Rick bent down and snorted about half a gram up each nostril through a silver Tiffany straw.

He straightened up and passed me the tube whilst sucking the coke noisily into the back of his throat. I leant forward and hoovered a couple of the pre-cut, pencil-thick lines. The gear hit my brain in seconds. This stuff was max purity, top quality and fresh off the mule.

'C'mon, Streak, we can party later. I want to show you something first.'

Rick moved away from the rear lawn towards a garage at the far reach of his domain. He opened a rear door. Parked nearest to us were a customised Jeep and Rick's Jaguar, but that wasn't what grabbed my attention. At the far end were two matching Ferrari Testarossas, their scarlet paintwork gleaming under fluorescent lights.

Rick tossed a set of keys to me. 'Get in, Streak.'

He walked over to the nearest Ferrari while I clambered into its twin. The garage door slid upwards in an arc above us as he fired the ignition.

'Start your engines.'

He was already pulling out as I got my flame-red monster into first gear. I could feel the power shooting up from the throttle pedal and nearly stalled as the leaden clutch bit. We moved line astern into Motor Drive and cruised through the palm-lined boulevards. We drove for about ten minutes until we hit Ventura Freeway, then Rick pulled to one side so that I was forced to overtake him. Within seconds he was looming large in my mirrors, headlights flashing and speed increasing. I nudged the car up to 60mph, but he was still tailgating. The speedometer jumped to 70-plus; he pushed behind me. Always trying, always gaining.

The freeway was crowded, but it didn't seem to deter him as he cruised behind my rear bumper. We were clocking 80mph now. Suddenly he was alongside me.

He floored the pedal and just managed to evade a Buick and slot in inches away from the bonnet of my car. I'd caught a glimpse of his face as he'd passed me. His noggin was pushed back into the headrest and he was grinning. This guy had bought a condo in Flip City.

We continued down Ventura, the speedo clicking above 100mph. Bernstein threw a radical left onto the San Diego Freeway. I only just made the bend, in a radial-melting turn, but Rick didn't even slow down.

His car swerved from side to side as we ate up the bitumen ahead.

We cut onto Santa Monica Freeway, heading towards the beachfront. The chang was still coursing through my bloodstream, revving me up. The needle was wavering around 110mph when . . . Rick's brake lights kicked in.

We slowed down as we whistled by Palisades Park on our right. Suddenly, the ocean was in front of us and we were on the Pacific Coast Highway. Rick peeled into a car park, which fronted onto the beach. I pulled in beside him and got out of the car.

'Not too sloppy, Streak.'

Rick was out of his car, greeting me with a slap on the back. My hands shook. This episode of our adventure was evidently finito. This guy had a deathwish and obviously didn't care who he was going to take with him.

Work hard, play hard, fuck hard: OK. But die hard? That was a movie. 'Come on. I haven't shown you the best bit yet.'

Rick walked over to his car and I followed. He leaned in and flipped open the glove box. Nestled inside, on top of a road atlas, was a Desert Eagle.

Forget the Magnum, the Desert Eagle is the most powerful handgun money can buy. It's produced for Israeli Special Forces and can punch a hole in you the size of a football. This guy was driving around with it like it was a fashion accessory. He was as mad as a meat axe.

'Let's get back to the ranch.'

He climbed back into the Ferrari and fired up the engine. The drive back was sedate, perhaps because we had a police cruiser tailing us, waiting for us to make a move.

I was breathing like a badly beaten second favourite at Hollywood Park as I slumped back into one of the sun chairs by the pool. The juvie chikas had vanished, but Benito and the blanca morta were still there.

Rick fixed bourbon and cokes in highball glasses as the silver straw was handed to me once again.

And again.

And again.

We must have ploughed through about half an ounce during the next couple of hours. Rick was stratospherically high, becoming increasingly animated and agitated as he elucidated, with snoozesome braggadocio, the deadly details of his many done deals.

Cruise this. Grant that. Yah yah blah blah wah wah wah: cut to black, roll credits and goodnight.

At ten o'clock Benito stood up to leave and I seized the opportunity to exit, quickly.

Rick sprawled on his sun lounger. The bourbon had taken its toll. He was wrecked.

'So long, Streak. Be seein' you later,' he slurred.

Benito and I walked through the house to the front door. He paused in the hallway and his eyes locked onto mine.

'I'm going to give you a number,' he said. 'If you want to get fixed up for anything, anything at all, then call me.'

He handed me a card and then held the door open for me. Putting Bernstein's fondness for re-enacting Death Race 2000 aside, it was the easiest connection I had ever made: King Benny was Rick's supplier.

I was back on the roller-coaster again.

I kept out of Rick Bernstein's way the following week, which wasn't difficult as I was ensconced in a micro-office down in the sub-basement of hell. But the following Friday he collared me as I was walking back from lunch after a macrobiotic salad-fest with colleagues also at the plankton end of this particular food chain.

'Streak. How's it hangin'?'

'Straight down the middle, Rick. How are things with you?'

'Fine and dandy, Streak, just fine and dandy. Listen, I have some people coming over to the house tonight for a few drinks. Why don't you come along?' Before I could pitch my excuse to him he had already made his assumptive close on the matter.

'Great, I'll see you at about eightish.'

With which he was off, slithering through the foyer towards the elevator that would transport him to his lair of lies, lunch and lines.

Terrific. I faced the prospect of another evening in the company of this wannabe Bond villain and his certifiable friends. There was no way that I was going in cold. I would have to give King Benny a ring and see if I could get sorted out with some pharmaceuticals to make the evening more bearable. More than likely, Benito would be attending, but I didn't want to take the chance of running on empty for this soirée.

I called as soon as I got back to my office.

Benito picked up on the third ring.

'Yeah?'

'Benito, it's Cameron. We met at Rick's place the other day, and you said for me to give you a call if I needed anything.'

'Sure, I remember you. What can I do for you?'

His accent had a heavy Latino tone, but his English was perfect. I decided to jump in as King Benny didn't seem like a timewaster.

'I'm looking for some Ye Yo. Can you help me out?'

'Sure, sure. How much do you want? I can do you a kilo or a half kilo. It depends on how much you wanna party.'

Mother of Mary in the Mall, I had made the man as heavy duty, but hadn't sussed he knocked out gear in bricks. Time to look like the amateur that I was.

'Actually, Benito, I was only looking for half an ounce.'

I sucked in my breath as I said it, waiting for the oncoming tsunami of abuse. There was a brief pause and then Benito spoke.

'I can do you half an ounce. Are you sure you can handle it?'

Great. A sarcastic drug dealer. I reiterated that half an ounce would be perfect. He told me to swing by his place of business at five o'clock that afternoon.

I whiled away the intervening hours with routine business

activities, but my mind was set on the score. I was juiced on a natural energy high as I readied myself to get back into the saddle.

I ankled the office at 4.30 and retrieved my car from the back of the building. Benito had told me to meet him at a pool hall at the Santa Monica end of Pico, one of Los Angeles's main drags. Traffic was still light and I pulled up outside just before 5 p.m. I had a thousand bucks on me and was pretty sure that this would be enough. I got out of the car and surveyed the building.

I was parked outside a double-storey, stand-alone construction with a glass front, which had the windows completely blacked out. A neon sign above the door simply read 'Pool'. Does what it says on the tin, right? I sucked up my courage and entered.

From the outside it had seemed deceptively small. Inside was a huge sprawl of pool tables, covered with a rainbow of baize felts, ranging from standard green through agent orange to woo woo blue.

Most of the players using the tables looked Latino. I clocked the red bandannas on the noggins of many wielding their cues. Mr Nasty's rule: never play pool with a guy who brings his own stick.

I had been in LA long enough to establish that the city was a theatre of continual gang warfare. There were hundreds of small gangs, baby enterprises of petty crime in action 24/7. Turf was the issue: trespass sans permission and you could end up dead, Fred. Most of these warring factions were in some way affiliated to the two dominant gang forces, the Bloods and the Crips. Members of each were recognisable by their colours: blue for the Crips, red for the Bloods. This was some sort of Bloods clubhouse. And everyone was giving me the death-ray look.

I moved across to the bar that ran along one side of the room. I leaned in, and caught the eye of one of the two duty barmen. He studiously ignored me and carried on wiping the glass he was holding.

'Señor?'

The barman raised a wary eye to meet my gaze, reluctantly put down his glass and strolled over to me.

'Si.'

'I'm looking for Benito. I was told to meet him here.'

'Who wants him? You a friend of his or something?'

This was not good. Without delicate handling it could get sensationally worse. Keep it simple stupid, I told myself and smiled.

Smile, smile, smile. It's the LA way, pal.

'I'm Cameron. He's expecting me.'

Señor Sullen stood and looked me up and down from behind the bar before turning and picking up a phone. He spoke Spanish into the receiver and I caught my name being mentioned before he hung up, looking at me again for a few seconds, like I was something he'd noticed on his shoe sole that shouldn't have been there.

The barman turned and strutted to the far end of his domain. I stood there, feeling as relaxed as a rabbi in Mecca during haj. Click went the balls, glug went the gangbangers' beer. Tough it out, I thought, it's the American way.

You know how when you're a kid, and you're waiting for something you've really, really been looking forward to, time seems to slow down to a slug crawl? Well, I had a full-on Christmas Eve minute that lasted a lifetime. Narco-time again.

A figure pushed its way through the crowd that had imperceptibly begun to congregate around me. He was about 5ft 5in. He looked mean.

'You'se here for King Benny?'

I nodded. Showtime. Residual gak paranoia kicked in: was this a set-up?

'OK,' he said, 'you'se come with me.'

He led the way through the predatory mob at the bar, and I followed him to the back of the hall. We took some stairs, which I hadn't noticed, in silence. From there I followed him into a hallway which traversed the back of the second floor. My guide pushed open the door nearest to us and held it open for me.

I found myself in a reasonably well-furnished office. Venetian blinds covered the windows, blocking out the late-afternoon Californian sunshine's glare. Wasn't it Billy Wilder who said that if it wasn't for blinds, it would be curtains for all of us? A large wooden desk sat in front of the windows and there were two stuffed black leather sofas in the centre of the room facing each other. Benito reclined on one. My escort occupied the other.

'Come and sit.'

Benito appeared friendly, but the whole Justice–Burrell thing had shown me how fast a good situation could become mui chewy.

'Guess you've met some of the family already, huh?'

Did he mean the private army downstairs? I nodded and flashed my ivories. We're all friends here. Aren't we?

'So you want half an ounce. That shouldn't be a problem, but tell me, how comes a friend of Rick ain't looking to cop a kilo? I figured you'se guys to be millionaires or something, with your fancy office and souped-up wagons. Rick usually calls me for more than half a weight.'

Yariba, Bernstein was certainly doing the right thing for the Peso Boliviano. He placed his orders by the kilo? Flip City just annexed a romper room.

'Rick's the bossman. He makes all the money,' I explained. 'I just run his errands.' Benito laughed and then tossed me a small snap-lock bag with the blow inside. 'That'll be $800 my friend.'

I peeled out the wedge and handed him the green. Benito took it, stood up, then walked to a fridge set against the wall of the office. He grabbed a couple of green beer bottles, opening them deftly on the side of the desk with a sharp bang of his palm on each lid.

'So, is this going to be a regular thing?' he asked, ''cos I can't be doing no ounces here and there myself.'

He passed me the bottle of beer and I took a deep slug on it. Wiping my mouth with the back of my hand I replied, 'Sure thing, Benito. Just let me know how you want to deal from here on in.'

'I'll give you the number for Manolo here.' He nodded towards the guy seated next to me.

'He will be looking after you from now on. It isn't good for me

MR NASTY

to be doing this kind of business directly. You understand? There is a lot of heat around at the moment. The cops are coming down hard on all of the gangs. Plenty of my people have been busted for bullshit charges and slung in the hole.'

'I understand.'

I had no comprehension of his situation. King Benny was obviously heavily wired into the Bloods and used them as his foot soldiers. That made sense. Why would someone like him risk getting busted for a few grams of Ye Yo when he had plenty of expendable gangbangers who would do his low-level dealing for him? Maximum coverage, minimum risk. The gang codes forbade anybody ratting out another member, so King Benito was sitting pretty in the catbird seat.

'That's mighty fine coke. Fresh in from across the border. My cousin brings it in.'

'Who's your cousin?' I asked.

'Most people call him Gacha.'

Ooooops. This guy was a cousin of Gonzalo Rodriguez. King Benny moved up a notch on my board. While he wasn't the telephone exchange, Benito was certainly connected.

My nerves started to adge up. If Benny baby was as high up the food chain as he was representing himself to me, then he was also in the business of taking the hard line with anyone who crossed him.

Token taken: don't cross this man, I thought.

'Anyways,' he said, 'you'se just enjoy your buy and call Manolo when you are ready to make your next move.'

Manolo got to his feet before leading me out of the office, down the stairs and back out through the pool hall. A few of the natives glanced in my direction but most just carried on with their games. I was somebody who knew Benito and no longer engaged their interest.

On the drive back to my apartment I got caught in heavy traffic on a steep hill with fluorescently lit shrubs and freeway signage. It happens in LA of a Friday evening: the town's company ants want their weekend. Freeways fill with steel, fumes and chrome.

It was nearly seven before I got home. Just time enough for a quick shower and a sampling opportunity. First, I poured three fingers of vodka over ice and sat down at my dining-room table. Then, carefully, I opened the snap-lock bag and tapped out a small pile onto its veneer surface.

Clichés, why do they become clichés? Because they're true. So, yes, I used my platinum Amex card to chop the crystalline mass into finer powder before dividing it into four lines. I bent down with a rolled $50 bill and scooted a couple of lines before taking a slug of the vodka to hasten the coke's transmission into my bloodstream.

Bang!

It hit me like a flash and tremors shook through me, rising swiftly from my feet to the top of my head. The front of my entire face instantly numbed. This fish was fresh off the pier.

Maybe it had come from Gacha as represented. I would certainly be making another buy from Manolo in the near future. But, of course, I knew from my Amsterdam days about sucking in a new customer with grade A merchandise, then subsequently palming them off with stepped down, cut-up product once they were regular punters.

OK, so the quality would vary in the future, I told myself, but for now I should enjoy this prime-time powder.

Snorting up the other two monga lines before ducking into the bathroom for my shower, I noticed it was already 7.30. I'd have to jam if I wasn't to be late hitting Rick's. My sense was that Bernstein was a man who demanded punctuality. I was still too scared of him to pull a stunt like making a grand diva entrance hours behind schedule.

Yet it was about 8.30 by the time I pulled up outside his Motor Drive residence. Narco-time, you know? I had banged a couple more cheeky lines before leaving home and so was feeling all gain, no pain, all over again as I dropped my car keys into the palm of the suspiciously studly and, one suspected, hired-by-the-hour valet parking attendant. I pushed the doorbell, a Puerto Rican maid, probably another of tonight's freelancers, promptly ushered me in. She led me through to the back lounge.

The joint was jumping like a Haitian pole vaulter. This crowd looked both hoity and toity. Here was the A list and associated vile acolytes; there were fit blondes and goth D-gals in frilly black lace dresses, flirting with lantern-jawed, gym-buffed mookies representing California's native gene-pool. Wall to wall bright young things engrossed in wheeler-dealer conversations: people glanced up as I walked through to see if I was someone they should know.

'Cameron!'

'Carrie!'

We mwahed-mwahed.

'Those irritating dental pains cleared up yet?' I quipped.

She admonished me with a laugh that flowed into the murmur of good gossip; I took my moments with Ronald Reagan's ballet dancing son and some black chick rumoured to be running a psychic phoneline shakedown. Glasses clink-clinked, fuelled with chilled champagne supplied by discreet flunkeys.

Was the help blind?

For Rick's sake, I hoped so, because I'd walked into a South American snowstorm here: Chuckie Chucklebuck was large and in charge. There was no attempt to hide the naughty narcotic's consumption from view. Guests were racking out lines everywhere. Some graphic designer was snorting off a cheerleader's tits. I could see why Rick felt it expedient to buy kilos and how he'd become involved with King Benny.

'They have this big house in the canyon with a screening room. My friend Bridget went there the other night and saw this car-crash movie he's made with these Armenians . . .' someone said.

Personally, I've always been cautious about the where and when of my narco-exposure. If I am making a score or in the presence of a dealer then I have no qualms about taking a sample. Unless they're tooled up. But at this level . . .?

Whatever, I do balk at taking a toot in front of people I don't know, particularly if they are likely to be characters that I may be doing legitimate business with in the future.

You never know, you know? So I moved my righteous fat ass to a bathroom on the ground floor of Rick's sumptuous crib.

When Hollywood realtors are selling a property, the number of bathrooms, you'll be astounded to learn, is often crucial. One of Joan Collins's properties boasted something like 21. Be clear, I'm not saying her or her pals are coke freaks. What I am saying is that, in a high-maintenance, appearance-obsessed society, people need their bathroom privacy. And, in Bernstein's bathroom, all mirrors and gold taps, I quickly chopped out a couple of fat lines on the black marble surface by the sink, ingested same, then rejoined the merry throng, grabbing a flute of champagne on my way back to the main room mayhem.

Despite the amount of chang, or maybe because of it, the party was actually pretty dull. Most of the crowd were agency related, all shiny hair and bright smiles, trying to be another smart, polite person that everyone liked.

I sussed that Rick had an apartheid boundary in his life between his work and play zones. I wondered if I'd crossed the line.

I noticed that he had a very young-looking girl on his arm, about the same age as the duo I had noticed by the pool on my first visit. The watercooler gossip was that Bernstein liked young chikas and didn't mind paying a top-dollar rate to enjoy their company of an evening.

He revolted me. Professionally he had me in his thrall, but there was something quite vulgar about the way he threw his money around. Given my antecedents it may sound a bit rich, but, although his house may have been big and opulently furnished, it was also pretty tasteless. It was like some LA screaming queen's vision of what their mom back in the burbs thought good taste should be.

Rick's tuner was between stations: to have obtained all the trappings of wealth at such a young age suggested, to my cynical and jealous mind, that burn-out was on the cards.

Things loomed large in that season's scripts streaming into the agency:

The teens huddle together for comfort in the shower stall. Ebony, wide-eyed and scared, finds her nipples have hardened like clothes pegs under the uncontrollable flow of cold water. By the stairwell, a zombie figure looms behind the cistern.

The amount of bugle Bernstein was getting through should have been his *réveil*. This prompted me to briefly ponder my own situation. I was roughly the same age as Rick; we were both young, wedged up and yupwardly mobile. We both had our secret vices and liked to party hard. We were well paid but, to be honest, prone to chemical lapses. I had convinced myself that I would calm down soon, before my mind cracked. Yet I could see some of the signs already. I was already finding it increasingly difficult to operate without my Peruvian llamas' pyjamas. I wouldn't have even turned up at the party if I hadn't scored off King Benny. Maybe there wasn't much difference between Rick Bernstein and myself.

I tried to persuade myself that no matter how near the bottom of the barrel I sank, I wouldn't end up like Rick – Rick with his Ferraris, his immediate circle of narco-biddable party pals and jailbait call gals. You could've stuck an apple in his mouth and the picture would have been complete.

I made happy talk with some of his guests. Most were LA hustlers, junior studio execs and fledgling indie producers. 'You know about sharing?' a D-girl called Pigrat was saying. 'Well, we want an 8.9 Nielsen share.'

'Oh the poverty of your ambitions!' replied a game show talent booker. No one was paying her any attention below her balcony. She could've done Shakespeare off it for all anyone cared.

Eventually I tired of making an effort, and of Rick's garish bathroom decor as I took hit after hit of the coke. I said a few goodbyes and ducked out around 11 p.m.

Driving home I made a conscious decision to steer clear of Rick Bernstein. He was just too slippery to hang close to.

Once home I took a quick nosedive into my now seriously

depleted half-ounce before snorting a couple of drops of vitamin E fluid up each nostril.

Cocaine is a caustic substance to the sensitive membrane inside the nose. Take too much and you can burn a Daniella Westbrook-style hole right through the middle of your hooter. The vitamin E helped repair some of the damage. I also took a lot of vitamin B12 at this time, cutting the end of the tubes with a blade to snort the red liquid within. It seemed like a good idea at the time.

I laid off the Ye Yo at the office. I was busy and just got snorty at night, especially if I had to go out. Most of my action was work-related: film parties, wrap parties, pre-production parties. They sound glamorous, but chip away beneath the surface in LA and you find . . . more surface.

The parties became monumentally more tedious. They weren't really parties: they were events – a party is a social affair attended by friends, family, colleagues; an event is a quasi-social commercial shindig to publicise something, someone or some product. Attending them, I had to don the agency badge and silver-tongue my way through each evening. Everyone had their hand out and wanted something: a speaking part, a better script, another life. The coke dulled the pain of living my shallow existence to a certain extent, but soon I had exhausted my supply.

Time to hook up with Manolo.

I called him on a Friday afternoon when I knew that I could escape from the office for a couple of hours without attracting attention. At first he had a little difficulty remembering me, and his faltering Spanglish posed a slight problem with communication. I reminded him I was the gringo in the suit from the pool hall, and we agreed on an ounce for fifteen hundred smackeroos.

Manolo told me to meet him in a car park about a mile further on from the pool hall on Pico and to come alone. Actually, I wasn't thinking of bringing a posse with me, but, looking back, maybe I should have.

I left the office at three and cruised down Pico. I drove past the car park, which seemed pretty full, and parked about 100 yards further down the road before doubling back on foot.

I wandered around for a couple of minutes before spotting Manolo in a battered blue Ford pick-up truck. I opened the door and slid in next to him.

'You'se got the money?'

Manolo already had the ounce in his hand and was obviously keen to complete business. No sooner had I got the money out of my pocket than I heard the brief whirl of a police siren. I turned and looked out of the dusty rear window to see a black and white, its blue lights flashing, pulling in behind us.

What freaking nightclub are we in now?

All seriousness aside, shit, this was a bust. Manolo hadn't wasted any time and was already out of the driver's door and sprinting across the car park. I did likewise and bolted from the truck. I ran in the opposite direction to Manolo, figuring in my manic-panic that we would split the two cops up if they had to go after us separately.

Good call!

One officer went after Manolo and the other pursued me. I ran to the edge of the car park and vaulted a low wooden fence. I turned briefly and saw that the cop had his gun drawn and was running me down hard. But he'd put the hours in at Krispy Kreme Doughnuts, and was carrying excess baggage.

Jumping over the other side of the fence put me in the back garden of a block of condominiums. I sped across the gravel and leapt another fence on the other side.

'Freeze!'

No way, Jay.

I kept running, my legs working furiously, my heart pounding.

I sprinted across another backyard before climbing a six-foot chain-link fence with adrenalin-fuelled energy I didn't know I possessed. Looking back, the fence proved to be too much for the cop and he simply leant against it breathing hard. This didn't deter me from my flight. I wanted to put as much distance between the bust and me as possible.

I kept running for the next five minutes, leaping fences and skirting round swimming pools in my desperate bid for freedom. Eventually my lungs seemed like they were ready to burst: payback for too much airway-congesting coke and 20-a-day nici-sticks.

I didn't know what had happened to Manolo, but if he had been caught I felt safe enough. He didn't know anything significant about me to tell the cops. And he would have had more sense than to drop King Benny in it. If John Q. Law charged him with possession of the ounce, then he was looking at some time inside as he probably already had a rap sheet. Dropping the dime on his boss would have meant one thing: a shiv in the back while standing in the lunch line in the lock-up, showering with the brothers or metalworking in shop.

I sat on my haunches breathing deeply while trying to get my bearings. I was in the middle of a residential area, and decided to cut off at a 90° angle in case the cops had driven round in front of me where they could lie in wait.

I lumbered over more suburban backyard fences. Eventually I emerged on a roadway with several shops on it and, more importantly, a phonebooth.

I was still panting as I phoned for a taxi and told it to pick up from outside Danny's Ice Creams. During the ride back to the office, I calmed down. Close call, but I was OK. The cops must have seen me wandering around the parking lot and decided to zoom in when they saw me getting into Manolo's pick-up. It made sense, a guy in an $800 suit sitting in a compromising position with an easily identifiable gang member. Seeing it from their point of view, it would certainly warrant closer inspection.

I couldn't concentrate on work when I got back and booked out at 5 p.m.

Thank God I had left my car away from the scene. I waited for a few hours and then cabbed down to retrieve it. There was no sign of any LAPD and I drove nervously home, just glad to have gotten away with it. But I still had two problems. No coke and, now, no connection. I considered calling King Benny, but felt that it was probably wiser to let the dust settle.

I managed to last all of three days before my rapacious appetite for Señorita Blanca overtook any nagging doubts and I phoned Benito. The news was not good. Manolo hadn't been so lucky and was currently incarcerated upstate awaiting a bail hearing.

Benito seemed to take it on the chin and told me that he would be prepared to do business with me personally for a while, but I had to see him at the pool hall. No problem, I could face a staring contest with 100 or so Latino gang mercenaries if it meant getting my hands on the goods.

We arranged to meet that afternoon and things went smoothly. I scored the ounce and drove home. No dramas. No problems.

Life fell into a routine for a few months after that. I managed to stay out of Rick Bernstein's way. I scored off King Benny every two to three weeks.

I was earning good money, but recycled most of it through my schnoz. I thought about putting some dough-ray-me aside and maybe going for a big score, a half-kilo. But I took a view that I wasn't in Bernstein's league just yet and could live with myself if I never got there at all. Meanwhile I was scoring monga coke that switched me on like Blackpool's illuminations. But it was also starting to fry my synapses.

Subtle threads of paranoia crept into my cerebral make-up. Ever since the Manolo incident, I was extra-vigilant lest there were plain-clothes cops on my plot.

I began to dread visiting the pool hall, half expecting a fully loaded SWAT team to smash through the windows in a storm of flying glass.

This is when the fear gets to you. Cocaine induces paranoia, and with the amount I was tooting it began to spread through me like a tropical disease. I had been lucky to escape the bust, but how long would my luck hold? And yet, I couldn't stop myself.

It's said that, unless it's freebased (smoked) or crack, blanca morta isn't physically addictive. But psychologically it was midnight and I was wearing shades.

Once more narcotics impinged on, and had again become an integral part of, my life. Every waking hour revolved around either scoring or snorting what I had bought. Heavy users finds that it invariably dominates and defines all other facets of their existence. I was banging my way through four or five grams a day and was completely hooked now. I wouldn't get out of bed unless there were a couple of lines ready by the nightlight. I was twitchy and itchy: crank bugs crawled under my skin and I was in psychological freefall.

I was losing the plot, no exception.

I tried to stop myself converting any mention of monetary sums at the office, within whatever context, into multiples of grams of coke. My sleeping pattern was taking a hammering too. I was drinking pints of vodka to edge off the day's Ye Yo high for a few hours of shut eye.

My work began to suffer. I was making stupid mistakes and nearly landed in serious shit over a couple of deals that my coca-induced carelessness sent south. Like Rick Bernstein, I felt that the coke was turning me into a livewire, able to handle anything the business threw at me. Truth is that I had started to hate myself. I had begun to loathe myself and my life as the despair and desperation of my drug dependency impacted on my psyche with increasing force.

My job involved dealing with sycophantic executive twunts and tinsel-licking spoiled-brat movie stars. My mission, oh hallelujah, was to screw the last brass cent out of everyone here or thereabouts. My social life was geared around what went on in the office, and I simply couldn't inflict my private punishment park on any prospective long-term partner, so led the single life. Even I wasn't quite that selfish yet. How could I be in two places at once when I was nowhere?

I had never felt so alone. Instead of dulling the pain, Charlie Chang amped up my problems. Babe, I just couldn't help myself. It seemed like I never could, never would. Despair marked me like the black rubber tyres of 4 a.m. reversing over my face.

The despair of an addict.

It was all becoming too much, yet not enough, for me. I had genuinely decided to pack it in for a while, but only (yeah, yeah I know: tell it to Narcotics Anonymous) after striking one last deal with Benito. I had convinced myself that this was to be my last throw of the dice in LA's drug casino.

Did I know the dice were loaded? Did you? Like you care?

Thought not.

Neither did I. The devil danced on my shoulder. I couldn't resist upping my order to two ounces to keep me in tea for three: cha cha cha for just a little while longer . . . while I, ahem, resolved this thing.

As I entered the pool hall all seemed silky smooth. The sullen barman phoned upstairs as per usual. I was led up to the office as per usual. As per usual?

'I don't have what you want with me,' Benny said. 'We'll have to drive on over to a friend's crib to pick it up.'

'Sure, no problem.'

I felt less than delighted. But in LA, if you want to get ahead, go along.

Benny and I took the stairs down to the parking lot behind the hall, where we got into someone's shiny new silver Lexus. Business must have been good for Benito. I wondered if he was importing consignments from Mexico and all points south with the help of his cousin, Gacha. It made sense, as he had a huge army of street-level distributors: the Bloods who frequented his pool hall and their connections. Junior gangbangers were probably responsible for the nickel-and-dime street corner clocking, while the higher echelons of the gang got more involved in bulk distribution. I knew better than to ask.

If King Benny was hooked up with traffickers from across the border then he was heavy and wouldn't take too kindly to me questioning him about his business arrangements. Why would ya?

We cruised down Pico Boulevard for a couple of miles before taking a hard left into a run-down residential area. Benny circled around a few blocks before stopping outside a dilapidated, stucco-fronted, single-storey house set back from the road. There was an old Plymouth, its wheels removed, up on blocks of concrete in the front drive. The lawn hadn't seen the business end of a blade in years.

We got out of the Lexus. Benito led the way up a narrow gravel path to the front door. He rapped loudly. After a few moments, the curtain covering the back of the door was pulled aside and a Hispanic face peered out into the sunlight. The man nodded at Benito, opened up and ushered us inside.

The interior of the house looked like a bombsite. There was no carpet; just bare wooden floorboards. The plasterboard was crumbling. The walls were riddled with holes and Spanish slogans sprayed graffiti-style.

Our host led us through into the sparingly furnished main room. About a dozen men and women sat on plastic chairs or on the floor. The air hung heavy with the sickly sweet smell of marijuana.

Most present clutched glass pipes or homemade plastic bongs. One man, wearing a skanky vest and cut-off jeans, ignited the contents of his pipe's bowl. The crackle was unmistakable. This was a fully fledged crack house.

It was like this 24/7: addicts bought their rocks on the premises and stayed to smoke away the days and nights.

The smoker in the skanky vest and denim shorts glanced up to where I stood in the doorway. He stared at me with glazed eyes. If he was surprised at seeing a suited-and-booted Caucasian lone gun in the house he didn't show it. Stupefied, he raised the pipe to his lips once more.

Benito gestured for me to follow him, and we moved towards the back of the house, which opened out into a large kitchen area. The work surfaces were covered with detritus. Unwashed plates and glasses overflowed from the sink. The stench of rotting food emanated from the trash can, which had long ago abandoned the impossible task of containing the garbage that spilled from its lid onto the filthy tiled floor.

At one end there was a table, cleared to display a set of electronic scales.

Benito and I sat down opposite two Latinos, one wearing Bloods' colours. In any operation as big as King Benny's, there are low-rent street-level connections like this.

Twenty-dollar rocks sold to all comers. It's the tier at which the most violence happens. I couldn't see any weapons, but I felt sure that these two soldiers must be armed to properly protect Benito's merchandise.

Rip-offs are rife at this level and that front door would have given way with one kick. You didn't need to be a neurosurgeon to realise that the local gendarmerie would know about crack houses on their turf.

I was anxious to get the deal done and blow this popsicle joint. But Benito seemed in *mañana* mode.

He exchanged greetings in Spanish with the Blood. Formalities concluded, the other hombre began bumping his gums as he produced a large polythene bag of chang, which he carefully tilted towards the scales. He poured the white powder, carefully weighing out precisely 56g, clocked on the numerical LED display: 2oz on the nail.

His colleague had reached under the table and produced a homemade crack pipe: a two-pint soda bottle, from which the hollowed-out shell of a plastic ballpen was jammed down at an acute angle halfway down the plastic. Some kind of putty-type substance, at the join where the pen met the bottle, acted as an airtight seal. Aluminium tinfoil had been spread over the open neck of the bottle and pressed down in the middle to form a small bowl. I could see tiny pinprick holes in the tinfoil.

The smoker produced a small foil-wrapped rock of crack from his pocket. He placed the white rock in the centre of the foil bowl and raised the pipe to his lips. Taking a lighter he angled it down and sparked up the rock, taking a deep breath as the smoke was sucked down the length of the bottle and up the pen into his eager mouth.

He held the smoke for about ten seconds and then exhaled noisily.

Benny handed me the 2oz. I passed the required $3,000 over

the table to the crack smoker. The trio did the Spanish bumpy gum thang. I just sat there wishing I were somewhere else.

After ten minutes or so, Benito eventually seemed satisfied that business was running smoothly, made his farewells and we walked back down the hallway.

'Sorry about the detour, my friend. These guys are holding a shipment for me, and I thought we might as well go to the source, as I don't personally have more than an ounce at a time in my office.'

'No problemo, Benny,' I assured him.

Secretly, I was glad that this would be my last buy from him. I was getting too close to the action at grass-roots level and that's where mistakes get made. I had escaped one bust already and preferred not to attract any unwanted heat. I was going to do this load, then start a new life.

We climbed into the Lexus and Benito keyed the ignition.

The car came out of nowhere, screeching to a halt just in front of us. It was a dark blue Chevy Nova with a battered, paint-flecked hood and tinted windows. A figure leaned out of the window and pointed a pistol straight at us. Immediately Benito slammed the gears into reverse and floored the accelerator. The tires spun, burning rubber, sending up a plume of smoke. At that instant the windshield cracked into a spider web of safety glass. We sped backwards. Benito slumped back in his seat and let go of the steering wheel.

We careened off the kerb and the car turned towards the other side of the road. I could still hear shots being fired in quick succession as a hole was punched in the glass just inches to the right of my head.

We hit the other kerb and bumped over it, travelling backwards over the front lawn of a house and smashing into a front wall. The car stopped: I heard the screech of the other vehicle as it pulled off and hurtled in front of us down the road.

I sat dazed for a few moments before reaching up to my face and dabbing a smear of blood away with my right hand. The shattering glass had left me with a cut on my forehead. But I hadn't been punctured by any of the flying lead.

Benito had not been so lucky. A pattern of blood spread, wet on his shirt, near his right shoulder. It didn't look fatal. But he was gasping for breath. He clutched his right arm with his unimpeded left hand. The blood kept soaking into his shirt.

This was the first time that someone had fired at me. I fought down the bile. I sat rigidly in my seat trying to catch my breath. My chest felt like a huge boa constrictor had wrapped its coils around me and was squeezing hard.

The blood from the cut in my forehead was starting to trickle into my right eye. I winced as it stung. This was my blood.

'Fucking shit, I could have been killed,' a voice said.

Mine.

I was on tilt. This wasn't in the script. All I wanted to do was to score some blow and then make tracks. Not this. Not now. Dear God. I was staring at Benito. The blood was still spreading. 'Grip, gotta get a grip,' I said.

Benito was saying something in Spanish but I couldn't understand him. It took several seconds before the distant police siren registered. In that frozen moment I saw LAPD officers and me, a prominent Los Angeles film agent, sat next to a known drugs baron in a bullet-ridden ride.

Adrenalin surged. Instinctively, I opened the door. I staggered slightly as I got out of the Lexus, my legs squishy gel.

I vamoosed.

Benito was calling out something in Spanish. I ignored it and started to barrel down the street. The police wagon hadn't turned into the road yet, but I could hear the noise of the siren closing. If I could make it to the street corner I would vanish from its line of sight.

I pounded along the sidewalk, my tie blowing over my shoulder as my arms pumped like pistons. Just as the black and white hit the scene I swerved around the corner.

I didn't look back. I kept on running.

Where was I?

I guessed my legs pounded a sidewalk parallel to Pico. Lungs pumping, I ran a couple of blocks. I banked left, to navigate back onto Pico. Once on the main drag, my body was still in overdrive. People stared. I forced my legs forward, bigger strides, pushing the pace.

Fully freaked, I kept running back in the direction of the pool hall towards my parked car. That was when I heard more sirens.

I slowed to a walk, my lungs on fire, my limbs aching, sweat-splashed clothes drenching my body in a cold, clammy wash.

Two black and whites zoomed past, flashing lights and sirens blaring towards the crime scene.

I was back at my car in 20 minutes.

There was no one outside of the pool hall. News of Benito's encounter at the wrong end of a slug had not filtered back yet.

Good.

I got into my ride and gunned the engine, pulling out into the traffic.

Mother Teresa in a miniskirt, this was radical. My mind raced. I tried to put into context what had happened. The shooters could have been the Bloods' enemies, the Crips. Maybe it had just been an opportunistic drive-by. Anyone in a Lexus had to be high up gangland's pecking order, a scalp worth taking, maybe money worth making.

I pondered darker scenarios. It could have been a rival dealer who had instigated the hit, maybe Gacha himself, displeased by some transgression of his cousin's behaviour.

Like bringing some flyboy gringo into the hood.

For all I knew at the time, the traffickers south of the border had zero scruples about taking out members of their own family. If this was the case, they would be gunning for anyone associated with Benito, however tenuous the link was. Such is the power of the cocaine kingpins.

This wasn't some bad TV movie of the week; it was real and I had played myself right into some random act of street violence. Paranoia overload loomed large in my mental rear view. Then I saw it, flying directly above me, its rotors whirring.

The helicopter seemed to be tracking me as it flew over me to my left. It could have been a traffic 'copter for all I knew, but my paranoia was edging onto the redline now.

All the action had distracted me from something that I'd forgotten, but that now came to mind with nerve-slashing clarity.

I was still carrying the 2oz of chang.

I nudged the car up to 70mph, weaving through the light traffic. Was it my imagination, or was the chopper keeping pace with me? I glimpsed the entrance to a Wal-Mart on my right. Abruptly I turned into it, cueing emergency stops and a fusillade of horns. I sped across the forecourt into the sanctuary of a two-storey car park. Its gloom enveloped me. I pulled into an empty space.

It took about half an hour before my heart slowed its pile-driving jackhammer beating. I was miles away from the scene but still didn't feel safe. But I knew that I couldn't stay here forever.

I eased the car backwards, then nosed it out into the sunlight. I drove at a steady 40mph back up Pico all the way back to my apartment.

All shook up, I called the office and whispered lies of migraine. The evening was locked in, scanning cable news channels, searching for a report on the shooting.

Nothing. Nada. Zip. Zilch. Zero.

Maybe King Benny was such a big fish that the cops were keeping it under wraps. I sat and drank vodka until the room started to spin. I still had the coke, but was all thrilled out.

The sunshine streamed through the window onto the sofa. It was 6.30 a.m. I showered and shaved. Arriving early at work, I got busy with a festival of admin and organisation, colour-coding the post-it notes and creating coherent To Do lists, subdivided into 'Urgent' and 'Less Urgent', with certain items in bold.

Nine sharp, the phone rang.

'Rick wants to see you, can you come up please.'

The connection clicked dead. I trooped upstairs and past his three assistants. Rick was standing in front of his desk, leaning his weight against it, his hands clasped in front of him.

MR NASTY

He looked edgy.

'Siddown.'

I took a leather armchair opposite him.

'I hear there was some trouble yesterday.'

Bad news travels fast. I wondered how he knew I'd been in the car. Maybe King Benny had made it.

'Did anybody see you?'

'No, I bailed before the cops got there.'

'Well, Benito won't put you in the frame, there's no need for it. But I don't want any heat coming in this direction. You understand?'

I did, implicitly. Rick was covering his back. He looked shifty and began pacing the carpet in front of his desk.

'I think it would be a good idea if you cooled off for a while and didn't get in touch with any of Benito's friends. I don't want any kind of repercussion occurring.'

'I was thinking of taking a break anyway, Rick.'

'Good, good. See that you do.'

He turned and sat down behind his desk and gazed at his diary. I scurried out back to my office.

The next few days were quiet.

That weekend I exited LA to spend a few days in San Francisco. A short stay by the Bay would keep me far away from any twitchy-fingered gangbangers.

My paranoia was so amped up that I suspected that I was a target on Gacha's hit list. Probably nowhere near the truth, but my job and fondness for the jazz salts had bred solipsism and a righteous sense of self-importance.

Sipping a latte under a sun umbrella at a café on North Beach, I decided caution should be my watchword.

Back in my own bed, I slept better on Sunday night. I arrived at the office at 8.30 a.m. Monday morning with my double-columned, *italic*-fetished To Do list. The agency was getting wired for the web and two supermarket tabloids had outed our glove-puppet comedian as a former gay porn star.

As Jack Nicholson says: 'Another day, another half-million dollars.'

MR NASTY

Only I wasn't making five hundred large a day. And outside the agency sat two LAPD squad cars. As I walked across the car park, I noticed several unfamiliar vehicles that I made as unmarked police wagons. A uniformed cop stood in front of the doorway with his arms folded. I passed by him and climbed down the stairs to my office like there was nothing unusual in any of this.

Inside I churned like a Dutch milkmaid with Tourette's: were they here for me? How could they possibly have traced me? Should I call a lawyer or tough it out?

I sat in subdued silence, interrupted when my office door flew open and Julian Gold, one of the other junior agents, burst in.

'Have you heard?'

'Heard what?'

'They're taking Rick Bernstein downtown. Apparently there was an incident at his house over the weekend involving a young girl.'

'An incident?' I said.

Jesus Christ on a chain gang! Rick was probably going down for statutory rape of green bananas. Somehow, I couldn't see him doing eight to ten in the State Penitentiary. Bernstein would try to plea bargain his way out of as much of the rap as possible – which meant he might well give me up as witness to an attempted homicide, and fleeing the scene of a crime: plus I would face some awkward questions as to what I was doing in the car with Benito in the first place. I shooed Julian out of my office. I didn't have much time and would have to act fast. I tried to clear the paranoia from my mind and think rationally. My only chance was to put as much distance between myself, Rick, Benny, the whole catastrophic mess as possible.

I would have to get out of LA.

Now.

Thirty minutes later I was standing in front of the agency boss, Louis Katz, and tendering my resignation. 'And when were you thinking of leaving us?'

'In about ten minutes,' I said, turning swiftly on my heel and walking out.

I no longer cared what bridges I was burning. I just had the overwhelming urge to purge. God knows what Rick was spilling to the cops at that very moment.

There was another factor: King Benny probably wouldn't take too kindly to me having run off and left him to take the rap.

I was playing scenarios through my paranoid internal projector: Mexican death squads hunting me down and executing me for the betrayal of their paymaster; Bernstein putting me at the centre of a Los Angeles underage narcotics/sex dealing ring.

I drove back to my apartment and started packing. I could take my clothes, but would have to leave the rest of my possessions, including the car, behind.

I went through to the bathroom and flushed the 2oz of coke down the toilet.

I was on tilt, but the LAPD would probably be called there once I defaulted on my rent and I didn't want any incriminating evidence left around, even if I was thousands of miles away.

I had done it again. Gone was the chance of leading a straight life as an upstanding citizen. I cursed myself for getting involved with coke gangsters and sexually deviant power brokers. Yet again fate had slipped some lead in the boxing glove, but could I really complain?

My quest for drugs had brought me to this point, and I had instigated the chain of events that had led me here. I felt a profound sense of disappointment with myself. I had blown it. Most people would have given their right arm to have landed the opportunity that I had now squandered.

What now? Back to London with my tail between my legs? It didn't bear thinking about. I could have had it all, but the drugs had brought me right back down to street level with the hustlers, the zomboids and the killers.

I knew for certain that I would have to move on from this point in time and this state of mind. I promised myself that my drug career was now, officially, at an end.

But would it be a promise I could keep?

Somehow I doubted it. By the time I was in the taxi to the

airport I was already convincing myself that a little light recreational substance abuse was all right. But that's exactly what it was, abuse.

I was killing myself slowly with drugs and alcohol and seemed powerless to stop. I would be clean until I blew off some self-esteem and I got back onboard, riding the wave again. This time though, I was determined to manifest my destiny on my own terms. If drugs were to be a part of my life, I would control them and not vice versa.

I was going to take back my life, drugs or no drugs.

I was on a flight out of LAX that evening, still dreaming the dream. Dream on. Let's say America no longer held the magic for me that it once did.

MR NASTY

BANGKOK

SMOKE

I woke from my light doze and groggily looked around me. The 747 was packed with the usual suspects: cute couples with wholesome young families; bright-eyed students on life-enriching backpacker adventures; and sex tourists. They're easy to spot. Middle-aged men, chugging cans of beer as they studiously ignore those around them. They sit, hollow-eyed, in climatically correct, tropical-weight trousers and short-sleeved shirts, their spare-tyre stomach fat straining their seatbelts.

And there was me.

Since leaving Los Angeles, I had knuckled down and built a career. The LA shenanigans had scared me straight: I had held down a day job as an information technology manager for three years. My family had welcomed me with open arms and, thankfully, few questions. I had managed to keep my rampant drug use a secret from my parents and they seemed pleased that I had adopted the routine of the nine-to-five grind.

We were cruising through to the end of 1996 and drugs were still a part of my life, but restricted to an occasional Ecstasy tab to party away Saturday night. I'd lulled myself into a rutty situation and felt staler than a hot cross bun in mid-August. Work was OK, but the idea of a defined career still appalled me.

I needed to escape the seething metropolis for a couple of weeks and I was looking for a major high to make me feel like I was living again rather than just existing.

The flight had been delayed for a couple of hours on the tarmac at Heathrow, and I was worried that I would miss my connection at Bangkok. I looked at my watch. Nine hours down, two to go.

I caught the eye of a pretty Thai Airways stewardess and asked for a vodka and tonic. She gave me the benign smile the Thai people have perfected and fixed my drink in the galley. Glass in hand, I settled back into the seat and started counting down the minutes until we landed.

It was the first time I'd been to Southeast Asia. I'd read up on the subject, and the prevalence and availability of drugs there had caught my eye. After careful thought, I chose Thailand. The drug scene was risky; the sentence for trafficking heroin was death. Or if you got lucky with the best justice money could buy, life imprisonment in the arse-rupturing prison known as the Bangkok Hilton.

There seemed to be a thriving Ecstasy scene in the small islands that littered the Thai coastline. And the weed in this part of Asia was probably the best in the world. So, as we finally touched down in Bangkok, I felt a mixture of trepidation and excitement.

Fortunately, my connecting flight had also been delayed, so I boarded with half an hour to spare.

Just a 60-minute short hop and I'd be in Patong, the chosen locale for the first 10 days of my chemical vacation. The brochure described the coastal resort as a bustling mix of beaches, Thai culture and vibrant nightlife. But I hadn't travelled several thousand miles to merely lie by a pool sipping Mai Tais.

I was looking for some action.

My hotel in Patong was a half-hour drive from the regional airport. Thirty minutes packed in a minivan with bawling infants, dumb-breasted mamas and seedy old men.

At the resort, I was booked through and shown to my room. I dumped my bags and set off to explore.

Mid-afternoon activity seemed to centre around the main road running along half a mile of curving, golden sand. Most of the buildings appeared modern: shops, souvenir stalls and myriad market traders offering a plethora of cut-price fakery from Prada tops through Gucci bags to replica machine guns.

At first sight, Patong was a bit of a let down. What had I expected? Hordes of smiling oriental faces proffering me pipes of pure opium? Beach vendors toting disco biscuits in blister wraps? I walked back to my hotel to catch some rays. I would wait until nightfall, then go down for the lowdown.

The heat and humidity hit me again the moment I stepped from my air-conditioned room. It was April, early evening and it must have been about 30°. I wandered down Patong's main drag, my cotton shirt clinging to my back as the sweat rolled off me. I heard the thumping strains of dance music and headed towards its source, The Banana Bar. Its interior was dimly lit with intermittent neon flashes throwing shapes and colours over drab beige walls.

Compared with London's club scene, the decor was underwhelming, but at least the place was crowded. I ordered a vodka and orange from the bar and leaned back against it, drinking in my surroundings.

It was early, about 7.30, but at first blush it didn't look promising. Western tourists predominated: podgy legs sprawled from tropical shorts, sunburnt arms, red raw like lobster claws, poked from vividly coloured T-shirts.

They were mainly drinking beer or cocktails, complete with a tropical umbrella. Dark-eyed pill-thrilled nutters clutching plastic bottles of water were nowhere in sight. Little point in wasting time here. It was a club, but sans clubbers.

I reprised The Banana Bar experience at the other establishments along the beach front: a Latino cocktail joint; an authentically fake Irish pub, transplanted into the dark heart of Asia, serving ice-cold Guinness; a knock-off Johnny Rocket's.

I was beginning to wonder if I had made a mistake coming here. I was also beginning to wonder if I wasn't getting slightly

MR NASTY

pished. Although limiting myself to one drink in each boîte, the liquor and the lag combined to make me weave slightly as I detoured from the main drag and headed towards the town centre.

About 50m from the beach, locals thronged busy side streets lined with bars and eateries. The bars had a common feature: young Thai girls perched on stools, sassily underdressed in halter tops, hot pants or miniskirts.

Rick Bernstein would have been in his element. Saddo Western sex tourists prowled the roadways searching for young flesh. I'd stumbled into the red-light district.

One of Mr Nasty's golden rules in successfully making a score: always ask a hooker where the drugs are. If they don't know, then ten gets you twenty they'll know someone who does.

So I selected a random bar, sat down and ordered beer.

Within 60 seconds a Thai girl sidled up and sat on the adjacent bar stool.

'You want company?'

She reached out to stroke my face. I smiled wanly.

She looked about 15 years old, her straight black hair framing an incredibly pretty face.

'You buy me drink?'

I nodded and she ordered a bottle of beer. She raised it suggestively to her lips before taking a short swig and winking at me.

'Me Mai. What your name?'

'Cameron.'

'Camera?' She burst into a fit of giggles.

Me no Leica, but I let it go. I wasn't here to tutor B-gals in the niceties of English elocution.

I leaned in, beckoning her closer with a conspiratorial gesture. She lowered her head and listened intently, perhaps anticipating an invitation back to my hotel room or an offer to accompany her to some convenient place of business.

'Do you know where I can get some pills?'

'Pills?'

'Yeah, pills, you know, Ecstasy.'

She pulled back immediately.

'No Ecstasy. Is very dangerous. Police are all around.'

She subtly emphasised the point by drawing her finger across her neck in the gesture of a cut throat.

'I know, but do you know where I can get some Ecstasy? I will pay you.'

'Me no help you. Me get in trouble.'

She hopped down from the stool and retreated to nest on a chair beside the bar's back wall. Her stare was several degrees below room temperature.

Washout.

I tried the next bar. And then the next. The response was the same: 'Me no help you. Be careful. Too much dangerous.'

By 11.30 I was plastered and decided to call it a night. Mildly discouraged, I staggered back to the hotel.

I had hit most of the girlie bars in town, surrounded by sweaty, balding vultures who spruced up their vacation by hitting on chicks young enough to be their granddaughters.

All I wanted to perk up mine was a freaking pill.

The next day dawned with a monster hangover. I'd been mixing vodka, whisky and beer the night before and, after breakfast, I put in some poolside overtime at the zzz factory while my headache subsided in the baking sun.

Since pills weren't in my medicine bag, I decided to score some grass. I could spend a stoned afternoon listening to tunes on my CD player while topping up the tan. But where would I get the weed?

Picking the brains of the prostitutes seemed to be a non-starter. So I decided to try the next option in Mr Nasty's rulebook: a taxi driver.

Taxi drivers know their turf. They're used to dealing with strangers. And they understand cash. Just one problem: there weren't any taxis in Patong. Tourists ran around town in those sweaty minivans, or by flying solo on the backs of motor scooters. The scooter drivers worked the pavements hustling for business. That would have to do.

Back in my room, I changed into a clean shirt before heading back into town. I spied a scooter driver touting for business and sidled up to him. Miming smoking a cigarette by putting two fingers to my lips and puffing, I tried the soft word on him.

'You know where I can get smoke? Weed? Marijuana?'

His response was swift. Without a word, he got on his bike and sped away from the kerb.

Brilliant. Even the local minicabbers were giving me the air.

Jesus Christ in a minaret, all I wanted was a quiet smoke.

For the next 90 minutes, I hit up most of the scooter drivers along Patong's main street. The response to my request was starting to get monotonous: 'Too dangerous. Me take you to see nice girl instead.'

In frustration, I gravitated towards the town centre, and there I spotted him.

He was lying astride his scooter, his sun hat pulled down over his eyes. He wasn't hustling the few tourists who passed through this part of town. He was just draped over his bike, soaking up the sunshine. I walked over to the road and nudged his arm. He slowly tilted his head back to see me and flashed me a warm Thai smile.

'Where you wanna go, friend?'

I went through the pantomime of smoking a pretend joint, and asked him if he could help me score.

'You police?'

'No. I just want to get hold of some grass. I'll pay you for your trouble.'

He regarded me quizzically for a few seconds before sitting up.

'We go. But out of Patong. Not very far.'

He nodded to the seat behind him and I clambered on, wrapping my arms around his waist. We lurched onto the road and were soon weaving through the traffic. I closed my eyes at times, certain that we were going to be flattened by an oncoming lorry or bus. Lane discipline and speed limits were novel concepts here.

The scooter's engine whined like an angry mosquito. Soon we

were leaving the outskirts of Patong and heading up a steep hill that marked the town boundary. Halfway up, we pulled in to the side of the road. Half a dozen other scooter riders lounged on their machines under the shade of a cluster of palm trees.

'How much you want – 1,000 Baht, 5,000 Baht, 10,000 Baht?'

I hadn't a scooby-doo how much bang I'd get for my Baht, so I opted for mid-town. 'Five thousand Baht.'

The driver dismounted and joined the group.

They conversed in Thai for a few seconds before one of the others handed my driver a mobile phone. He tapped a number into it, paused, and then talked. That done, he said: 'You go now. He will take you.'

He pointed to the rider who had given him the mobile phone. Evidently this was not the place to seal the deal. I paid my driver off with 500 Baht and climbed aboard the new driver's moped.

We rode in silence, apart from the hum of the engine, for about ten minutes. Gradually the roadside buildings, little more than huts with palm thatched roofs, gave way to open, rolling fields where Thai ploughmen urged on oxen teams tilling the soil. The landscape was a rich, verdant green, and the wind off the road felt good on my face.

We were slowing down. At the side of the road, another scooter was waiting: I was told to change bikes again. We sped off, a good 10km out of town. And very much, I sensed, on my own. I could be robbed and left by the roadside; nobody might find me for hours. Banishing such negativity, I tried to kick back and enjoy the scenery.

After a further five minutes, we came to an open plain. I looked to my right and saw the sea stretching out towards the horizon. The sunlight coruscated off the rippling waves.

It was beautiful. We cut a right off the main road and bumped down a hard, sun-baked earth track, rutted on each side by the passage of four-wheel-drive vehicles.

Finally the engine cut out and we stopped. In the comparative quiet of the afternoon sun's fierce heat, the cluster of white-walled buildings assumed the chimerical quality of a mirage.

We stood in an open circle of red earth with buildings surrounding us. A pergola with a palm leaf roof stretched from the village buildings on my right towards the beach. A group of Thais squatted in its shade, smoking cigarettes. Behind them, under a tarpaulin, lay the bulky outline of a big speedboat, its prow resting on a wheeled towing-trolley.

'You come,' my driver said.

We drifted over to the men and, following his lead, I squatted down on my haunches.

He spoke to one of the group, who stood and strolled over to the hut nearest to us. He disappeared inside.

'You have money?'

I nodded and my driver seemed satisfied. He didn't ask me to flash the cash. After all, I couldn't run off. Where would I go? I didn't know where I was. I had also noticed that one of the men within the semicircle before me cradled an antediluvian rifle in his arms.

After waiting for a few minutes, the Thai emerged from the hut carrying a cloth bundle. He came over to us and sat down next to me.

What I saw next amazed me. He unwrapped the bundle and nestled in its centre were several briquettes of solid weed. They ranged from oblongs that were slightly smaller than a matchbox to larger bricks equivalent in size to a cigarette pack. All had been compacted into blocks, then shrink-wrapped in cellophane ready to travel.

'Five thousand Baht?' the bringer of the bundle asked.

I passed him five 1,000-Baht notes, and he handed me a mid-sized block of grass from the batch. I held it in my hand marvelling at how professionally it was presented.

'You stay, you smoke?'

I needed no invitation on a silver salver, and nodded. One of the men produced a wooden pipe from his pocket and began tamping down some weed into it. Raising it to his lips he struck a match before inhaling. He was still holding the smoke inside him as he passed me the pipe. I took a couple of tokes on it and felt the dope wash into my bloodstream, relaxing every muscle, glazing my eyes into the classic stoner's stare.

This stuff was aces. Everything I'd heard about Thai weed was true.

As we sat and smoked for an hour it gradually dawned on me what I had stumbled across. This was a marijuana staging post.

I couldn't be sure if it was processed and packaged here, but this was certainly where it was shipped out. The gear probably travelled in the speedboat under the tarp and was then loaded onto a waiting ship offshore. From there it would be dispatched to a larger port before leaving the country.

I couldn't believe how laid back this group of Thai guys were about things. The mere possession of drugs in this country carried stiff penalties. Yet here they were passing the peace pipe in public with a tonto white round eyes.

My driver got to his feet and stretched his legs.

'You come now. We go.'

I waved farewell to my new-found friends, and returned to Patong. My head spun after smoking the weed and, at times, I thought I was going to topple off the bike. I was glad that the rider hadn't smoked any Bob Hope as we hit town and rejoined the chaotic, frenzied traffic. He dropped me on the seafront and I gave him a 1,000 Baht note. He smiled and took off.

I stopped at one of the market stalls and bought a small wooden pipe for a couple of hundred Baht along with some hippyshit beads, then retired to my hotel room.

I eventually managed to organise myself poolside, then zonked out. The weed numbed the frontal lobe of my brain. The bar staff flitted from sunlounger to sunlounger with drinks. I would've loved to order one, but was too stoned to speak. Slowly, as the sun began to move towards the horizon, I straightened myself out.

There was little point in reprising the previous night's futility. But I had heard some of the tourists by the pool talking about a place they had been to called The Shark Club. This wasn't one of the dives that I'd taken in to date, so I decided to give it a go. After a bracing cold shower, I headed out into the hot night air.

Following the directions given to me by the hotel's receptionist, I peeled off from the centre of town on the other side of the red-light district from the beach. A huge square building, painted bright pink, sported the neon outline of a shark. I paid my 200 Baht, and a Thai bouncer stamped my hand with an ultraviolet mark.

Inside, there was a good crowd for so early in the evening, but most were working girls or tourists lurking by the numerous bars on each of the club's three levels.

The music was earache: bad Euro '80s sub-disco. A couple of girls in sequinned mini-dresses danced round their handbags in the centre of the room on the ground floor.

I would have a better chance of scoring in the Vatican. I didn't even bother with a drink and legged it out of the main entrance back onto the street.

I wandered aimlessly, mulling over whether to buy chicken or shrimp from one of the roadside vendors' canopied carts, when I spied a rainbow-coloured banner fluttering from a pole.

The rainbow flag is a symbol of the gay community, and the flag was obviously a signal to Western visitors. I had found the gay district: one narrow street crowded with bars and small drinking clubs.

It was early, so young boys lounged languidly on chairs outside the bars. No one tried to hustle me, unlike their female counterparts the night before. This was laid back. If I was going to buy some E, maybe this was the place.

The gay crowd have always been early-adopters of new drugs. Compared with Straightsville, gay nighteries are usually a pharmacological cornucopia: amyl nitrate, speed, Ecstasy . . .

The dope was still making me feel laconic, so I took my time strolling up and down the street before selecting a spot. At least the music was better than in The Shark Club. Technobeats pulsated from the sound system behind the bar and filled the space with a deafening roar. One of the young catamites came in from the front of the bar, where he'd been sitting with his chums. He sat on the chair next to me like the B-gals the night before.

Buying sexual companionship in Thailand was easy. Scoring drugs was hard.

'Hi. My name is Mok. What's your name?'

'Mo,' I lied, extending a hand, which Mok shook lukewarmly.

I had spontaneously used my real name with the first girl last night, but decided it was too risky.

'You American, Mo?'

'No I'm English. I'm just here on holiday.'

'One day I go to England. Perhaps you take me?'

'Perhaps . . .'

I stalled. I leant towards him to make sure I was heard above the dance music.

'You know where I can get some pills? Ecstasy?'

Mok recoiled from me and began shaking his head.

'Too early to get pills. Very dangerous if police catch you.'

Too early? So, there were pills in Patong.

'Yes, but I need to get some now.'

Mok looked me up and down. My long hair and the hippyshit beads, wrapped around each wrist and draped around my neck, made me look more like a stoner than a cop. Mok seemed satisfied that I wasn't heat.

'Me go ask. You stay here. It cost you 1,500 Baht.'

'What. Each?'

He nodded.

'Each pill costs fifteen hundred.'

He moved off and conferred with the crowd of rentboys outside. Halfway through their discussion, an argument flared. From what I could gather, and the stares thrown in my direction by the others, someone didn't trust me. The confab broke up, and Mok walked back to where I was sitting.

'Not here. You come. You come.'

I rose and followed him out of the bar. One of the other boys stood up and Mok introduced us.

'This is Sonny. He will take us to place where you can buy. We must be careful. You come.'

Spirits rising, I followed the two boys as they led me to the end of the street and took a right. We walked for a few minutes, the duo constantly looking around in an exaggerated display of self-protection. We stopped outside a glass-fronted shop. It was a pharmacy.

I couldn't believe it was this simple. We were standing outside a dodgy-looking backstreet chemist ready to score some E! Mok opened the door and signalled for me to follow.

A professional young Thai man wearing a white coat appeared from a side door to stand behind the counter. Mok spoke to him in Thai and the man nodded before withdrawing through the door once more. After a brief delay he returned and handed me a blister-wrap containing a small, blue diamond-shaped tablet. I turned it over and saw the word 'Pfizer' embossed on the back.

'No, I want Ecstasy, not Viagra,' I hissed into Mok's ear.

'Good pill. You buy. We stay up all night.'

He grinned at me. He was trying to hustle me after all. I was angry.

'Me no buy Viagra,' I said, mimicking his stilted English. 'Me only want Ecstasy.'

'But pills very dangerous,' he replied.

'I know, but I need them. Do you know where I can buy some?'

Mok stared at me in silence. I felt exasperated.

'Ecstasy? Pills? Where can I get some?'

'OK, you come with me.'

When we stepped out of the shop the other boy had vanished. Mok led the way as we headed back to the street where I had met him. I slumped back in my chair in the bar and ordered a bottle of beer.

'You wait here. I come back soon.'

Soon: I knew how that played in narco-time. Mok darted out through the open front of the bar and vanished. I took a long draw on the ice-cold bottle of beer. None of the other boy-hos approached me. It was hands off; I was Mok's main squeeze for the evening.

The temptation to jack it in as a bad job was overwhelming.

But the faint possibility that I might actually score kept my derrière rooted to the sticky vinyl seat. I waited, sipping another beer.

An hour slowly rolled by. Draining the bottle I finally stood up to leave. And then Mok was suddenly beside me.

'I have pills,' he chattered excitedly.

'You have Ecstasy?'

'No I have pills, yaba.'

I knew what he was talking about.

Pronounced 'yarbah' and known as 'crazy medicine' in Southeast Asia, this wasn't what I had in mind. But it would do.

Originally manufactured by the Nazis to help keep their troops awake, yaba has become increasingly popular in this part of Asia. Some claim that it is now bigger than heroin in Thailand.

Yaba is a derivative of synthetic amphetamines like speed, and can be manufactured more quickly and easily than traditional forms of the drug. It is mostly methamphetamine, running 80 per cent pure. Much of the cut is cast-off from heroin production. Yaba usually comes in pill form, often red or orange, sometimes green. With its potent mix of visuals and intense highs, some narco-commentators predict it may soon become popular on the global club scene.

Although yaba is still very rare outside Southeast Asia, government reports suggest that foreign countries are being targeted by yaba producers from within the Golden Triangle – the drug-producing areas which straddle the borders of Thailand, Burma (Myanmar) and Laos.

Yaba's main ingredients – salt, household cleaning products, distilled cold medicines and lithium from camera batteries – can all be bought legally. The drug is easily knocked out at home with a couple of casserole dishes and a hob.

The rewards for manufacturers can be huge, as much as a 1,000 per cent mark-up. Since the equipment needed is portable, labs can be moved rapidly, making it difficult for police to track them down.

I'd never encountered it before, but yaba was supposed to

create intense hallucinogenic effects that could keep you awake for days, although some had reported that the visuals only come as a result of sleep deprivation during binge sessions. There was also a downside. Yaba is habit-forming and can be addictive. In Thailand during the late 1990s, the number of students entering rehab to deal with yaba dependency rose by nearly 1,000 per cent. And regular use has been linked to lung and kidney disorders, hallucinations and paranoia.

One common hallucination is 'crank bugs': users believe insects are crawling under their skin, and go loopy trying to debug themselves. Those coming off the drug are also susceptible to severe depression and suicidal urges.

Was any of that going to deter me?

'How much, Mok?'

'One pill is 200 Baht. I have four pills. That's 800 Baht.'

I could do the maths, and four yaba tabs at 200 each was lusher than hustling for a 1,500 Baht Ecstasy tablet that never appeared.

Mok held out his hand, palm up. There were four small orange tablets nestled there, calling my name. Mok was no doubt making a margin on the merch, so I didn't feel the need to bung him.

I paid him and, in time-honoured fashion, I made my excuses and left.

Back at the hotel, I lay on the bed and scrutinised the pills. Each was bright orange, about 5mm in diameter. I grabbed a beer from the minibar and washed down a couple. I lay back down on the bed and put my headphones on, waiting to get stupid.

It came on slowly at first. After about half an hour I felt pins and needles on the palms of my hands and the soles of my feet. This sensation slowly spread before ebbing a touch. Then, after about 45 minutes, the rush kicked in.

It felt like there was electricity pulsing through my veins. The speed hit was intense. My pulse rate was rising like an express elevator and my heart pounded in my chest.

I rose from the bed. I was dizzy. It soon passed.

I jumped in the shower and then, filled with vim, vigour and vitality, headed off into the night.

I hit the bars along the seafront. The yaba seemed to counteract the effects of alcohol. I was necking vodka like a Russian peasant. At one in the morning I had been on the tablets for only four hours and was still wide awake.

The bars were starting to close frighteningly early so I shimmied back to The Shark Club. The hand stamp from earlier that evening was still valid, and I made my way through the heaving dance floors.

I danced like a clockwork clown to the cheesy disco beats. I was 'lost in muzak': legs stomping, arms flailing, head nodding like a loon.

The Shark Club closed at two o'clock. But I did not. The yaba kept me awake until dawn, when I abandoned all pretence at sleep as energy coursed through me. Then I crashed.

I spent the day poolside, practically comatose. My thirst raged, and even the succession of long, tall glasses of fruit juice couldn't stop my throat feeling like a dried prune. Best lay off the yaba for a day or two. And next time, I thought, best take one tablet at a time.

Another golden nugget from Mr Nasty's rulebook, kids: start with a small dose of a new drug to get the feel of it – as you find your feet, you can increase your intake as you go. It's easier than blowing your wad and answering awkward questions after having your stomach pumped. Or answering nothing, on account of being dead.

Meanwhile, I still had two pills left, enough to last me until I left Patong. Days passed smoking weed in my room, lazing by the pool perfecting my tan. At night, I'd bar hop along the beachfront with new-found drinking pals.

The week passed quickly and pleasantly. All too soon it was time to pack for the next leg of my holiday: Bangkok. This was where I hoped to make my big score and spend four days of narco-induced bliss before flying home.

Things were not to run as smoothly as I hoped.

During the twelfth century, Arab traders introduced *papaver somniferum* (the Eurasian poppy) to Asia from the Mediterranean, where it had been cultivated for its medicinal properties. This is the flower that gives us opium and then, once the refining process is complete, heroin.

Poppies grow on cool plateaux over 500 feet above sea level. The plants develop rapidly and propagate easily. Growers plant at the end of the wet season: September and October in Asia. When the petals fall off, they scrape the poppy's bulbous seed calyx with sharp blades. These cuts create a white sap that oozes from the plant. Farmers leave it in the sun for a day or two to harden into gum. Then they collect it and pack it tightly into banana leaves.

The crude opium is transported from the hills by pony, or armed convoys, to middlemen who sell it on from Afghanistan or the Golden Triangle to narco-merchants.

Few escape opium's enticing lure. Even those who cultivate it.

All too often, the hill-tribe growers swiftly become addicts themselves. Up to 30 per cent of Southeast Asia's Hmong tribe is hooked on opium. And 80 per cent of northern Laos's income is derived from opium.

Small nickel bags, locally known as parakeets, can be used as currency. When you unfold the paper wrap to get the drugs, it appears that there are two triangular wings on each side of the bindle, giving it a bird-like appearance.

Only a smidgen less than 70 per cent of the world's heroin, and 60 per cent of heroin seized by US law enforcement, is exported from the Golden Triangle. It is not really a geographic triangle, but a loosely US-defined area that covers eastern Myanmar, northern Laos and scattered parts of northern Thailand. The common elements are remoteness and inaccessibility, lack of law enforcement, and the right altitude and climate to permit poppy cultivation.

Thailand's position in the Golden Triangle is more geographic than economic. It is a net importer of hard drugs and a major transit route on to the First World. About 50 per cent of the opium that enters Thailand from Myanmar heads for the US.

The Thai opium crop is 25 metric tonnes a year. It is under

constant threat from government eradication programmes, and tough border controls to keep its northern neighbour, the rogue regime of Myanmar, at bay. But somehow the mule trains get through the rough terrain, and insurgents prevent the Thai Army from effectively policing or sealing off the area.

Most of Myanmar's opium is transported in pony caravans along simple trails into China's Yunnan province, and eventually to the drug syndicates in Hong Kong. Alternatively, it moves south through Chiang Mai in northern Thailand down to Bangkok.

Once the pony caravans reach minor towns, the heroin is then trucked to major cities, from where it is shipped or flown to Europe, the United States or Mexico.

A third route is from Moulmein in southern Myanmar to Bangkok and, surprisingly, into Malaysia and Singapore. These two countries widely publicise their imposition of a mandatory death penalty for drug smuggling, while simultaneously serving as major centres for the export of drugs. Not something you'll be reading about in their holiday brochures.

The Triangle is dominated by warring rival factions: heavily resourced private armies run by warlords. Heroin is a misery drug produced by totalitarian dictatorships: Myanmar, Pakistan, Afghanistan. Join the dots and make your own connections.

It remains impossible for law enforcement agencies to penetrate the region without a full-scale armed incursion, something they remain reluctant to do. So the heroin trade continues.

There have been a series of treaties, the odd regime change and some minor operational successes to staunch the flow, but smack trafficking is still endemic in the region. I was heading to the business's dark mercantile heart. Bangkok.

My attitude to smack may strike you as ambivalent.

Considering my general predilection for narcotics, I both fear heroin and crave its warm embrace.

I had chipped – been a very casual user – from time to time, but had never volunteered for the wholesale oblivion sustained use entails. My prior use of the drug had mostly been to ease the comedown after a heavy night on coke and E when I was still a pill-monster in London. I had enjoyed the occasional smoke of pretty low-grade smack on the odd occasion, but was keen to try a purer experience of the narcotic.

I have seen the devastation that heroin can cause. An addict's craving for smack to stave off the horrific symptoms of withdrawal is terrifying to behold. Growing up in Hackney had exposed me to more than my fair share of heroin addicts. Many of my school friends had ended up as scag casualties and I had witnessed first hand their tumble into a pathetic, sub-human existence. Yet, despite my well-reasoned respect for the narcotic, I still intended to score in Bangkok. My attitude was quite simply that I would bliss out on smack while I was on holiday – I had no intention of trying to take any gear home with me or sustaining a habit when I was back in London. The object of this exercise was to cram as much personal pleasure into the week I had left in Thailand as possible. To be honest, I had become so bored with my life I was looking for a quick thrill and taking my drug experimentation to the limit by using heroin would provide me with that rush. My coke-ravaged experiences in New York and LA had done little to deter me from my continual drug use, but had set me on course for the ultimate high. Coke and whizz just weren't doing it for me anymore and I needed to check out of reality, if only for a short while. I felt that I knew the dangers involved and was prepared to accept them. For all the outward appearances of being a normal member of society I was still a drug-monster under the surface. To give up drugs you've really got to want to stop and that just wasn't on my agenda at the time. I needed to up the ante as it seemed the only way to shake myself out of a severe case of the humdrums.

This would prove to be the riskiest phase of my trip. Trafficking meant the death penalty; simple possession could draw a lengthy prison sentence – yet the lure of high-purity narcotics at a knockdown price got the better of me.

Once more, I was on a mission.

I took a room at The Pavilion Palace Hotel, a comfortable place on Patpong Road, for four nights.

Patpong was once Southeast Asia's most notorious red-light district. Not any more.

Most of Patpong's sex scene has shifted to the Soi Cowboy and Nana Plaza areas of Bangkok. Now it's just hustlers, scalpers and knock-off designer tat.

I strolled down Patpong Road on my first evening in the sprawling city and clocked some nightspots. Impossibly skinny young Thai men shouted across the pavement at me: 'You come, live sex show, you meet nice girl, she show you good time. Best girls in Bangkok, you take a look?' Most of these places were too upmarket for my purpose, if you can call a Bangkok sex bar upmarket.

Eventually I found what I was looking for: The Pink Bar.

There was nobody outside touting for business, but I could hear the strains of the omnipresent go-go dancers' backing track thumping through the doorway. It took less than ten seconds for the house mama-san to appear.

'You pay me 200, 200 Baht.'

Evidently the price of admission, and probably recoverable should you decide to avail yourself of a girl's services. I paid and walked through to a raised circular dais at one end of the room where some torpid Thai girls lounged. Each wore a bikini that had a numbered circular badge affixed to her skimpy cloth briefs to simplify the selection process.

There was a sprinkling of Western tourists: the usual mix of tragic, seedy-looking men who paid for sex because it was the only way they would get laid. Two weeks of sin in the fleshpots of Asia. Why, it troubled my virtuous soul.

I steeled myself, and ordered a beer. The moment I sat down, the procession of girls began. They walked up to me in turn, wondering if I wanted them tó sit with me. I politely declined. They soon got the message: I was a lousy mark.

This wasn't working, so I drained my beer and went sideways. Back on Patpong Road, I considered trying one of the three-wheeled tuk tuk drivers for a steer. But it was too risky. This wasn't scoring a bit of puff out in the sticks. Smack was what I was after, but I had no intention of rotting away the rest of my young life in the Bangkok Hilton.

I checked some other sex dives but none felt right, so I ended up drinking the evening away in The Comfort Home bar. It served suds, not hookers. The endless bottles of beer bored me. I trekked round the market, saw a large oriental rug that had a weave which spoke to me, and bought it for a few thousand Baht.

Back at The Pavilion Palace, a porter took the carpet from me and followed me up to my room. He put my parcel down and, as he was turning to leave, an idea struck me. Who else would know where everything happened in a city apart from the working girls and the taxi drivers?

The hotel porter.

I peeled off a 1,000 Baht note from my billfold and handed it to him. His eyes widened.

'Thank you,' he said, turning towards the door.

Now or never.

'Just a minute. I want to ask you something.'

He turned to face me once more, and I moved to close the door to block his escape.

'I'm looking for heroin. Can you help me?'

'No. Me no find any. Heroin very bad in Patpong.'

This guy could help me. He was about 17 years old and had that rabbit-in-headlamps look in his eyes.

'Please. I will pay you good money if you can help me find heroin.'

'Me no help you. Me lose my job at hotel. Me go to prison.'

'Please.'

I was begging now. He hesitated, and looked at the Thai currency he still held in his hand.

'My brother may help. I see him when I finish work here. You wait. I come for you.'

Result! I'd had bad luck in the girlie bars, and this looked like my next best shot at getting hold of some gear. My early evening boozing had taken its toll, and I dozed off on my bed.

A quiet but persistent knocking on the door awakened me.

I opened up to the porter. He shut the door behind him carefully. He looked around as if there might be cops hiding in some cranny within the room.

'My brother, he will help you,' he said in a hushed whisper. 'You come to Taurus disco. Nine o'clock.'

'How much heroin can I buy from your brother?'

'Me not know. You talk to him tonight.'

He looked as comfortable as a monk in a massage parlour, so I let him go. Perusing my Bangkok guidebook, I found an entry for the Taurus disco: it was on Sukhumvit Soi, one of the newer red-light districts which had snaffled Patpong's sex business. I settled down to wait the few hours before the meeting.

Narco-time dragged: a midget running a marathon. I remembered a joint near the Hotel Elysée in NY where I used to wait for Justice – half its clientele looked like actors, hoping they'd be discovered; the other half were druggies, hoping they wouldn't be.

I checked my watch again: it felt like an hour had passed, but it was barely ten minutes. The more you want to cop, the slower narco-time crawls. All my senses were in overdrive and my increasing excitement didn't come from the desperation of addiction but more from the expectancy of making a score. It's the need–power equation: I was trying to balance it, but it wouldn't add up, and the wait seemed like an eternity. Until, promptly at 8.30, I walked to the meet.

I was in the disco by 9 p.m., standing in the ground floor bar swigging from a long-necked beer bottle.

I downed three more during the next hour as I waited and watched the club fill.

There were no hookers in this place, and the Westerners seemed younger than in Patpong's sleazoid bars. The music sucked big time. I toyed with cutting my losses and trying to score a pill.

Around 10.30, my hotel porter appeared with another Thai

guy. The porter had changed out of his crisply ironed hotel uniform, and they both wore jeans and T-shirts.

'You come with us. We go to house.'

Neither bothered ordering a drink. I left my half-full bottle of Thai beer and followed.

'Are we getting a tuk tuk?' I said.

'No. Too dangerous. We walk. You come with us.'

We tramped in silence off the main road and into a maze of alleys that backed onto it.

A short distance from the roadway, the foodstalls and counterfeit watch vendors' stands petered out and we strolled through the dark narrow passages which gave way to small dwellings on either side.

The smell of cooking still filled the air, as local yokels prepared their evening meals.

Within minutes I had lost all sense of direction and was completely in the duo's hands. I had put my trust in these two guys and was beginning to adge up as we ventured deeper into the ever-narrowing labyrinth.

We must have been walking for half an hour before we stopped in front of a single-storey concrete house on our left. My porter pulled out a key on a chain from his jeans' pocket and opened the door.

'You come. Quickly.'

I followed them inside and found myself in a small, white-walled room with a TV set in the corner blinking out Thai programmes. A sofa stretched out in front of it. An elderly woman reposed there, in thrall to the screen. She didn't even look up as we cut through the room and entered the back of the house.

This was the kitchen. An assortment of woks and pans hung from the ceiling, and there was a small gas-fired stove alongside the far wall.

'You have money? Ten thousand Baht?'

Ten thousand was a lot of wedge. I had heard smack was dirt cheap. How much gear would I be getting for my money?

'You have the drugs? You can show me?'

The porter stayed with me, while his brother walked out through the back door into a small yard, just discernable through the tiny window above the cooker. He was back in seconds, carrying a wrap of white paper. He unfolded it very carefully in the dim light from the naked light bulb, twisting on its flex from the ceiling.

Once unwrapped, I could see the spread of white powder. Its consistency was irregular: a few solid lumps hadn't been crushed. This must have come off a compacted brick of heroin transported pretty recently down to Bangkok from the poppy fields of the Golden Triangle.

'Can I taste it?'

I didn't wait for an answer, and licked my index finger before dipping it into the powder. It was heroin all right. The slightly unpleasant, bitter taste was unmistakable.

It didn't look like I was getting a good deal here. The wrap appeared to contain 4g maximum, and 10,000 Baht was a lot to pay. It was about half what I would have paid for the same quantity of seriously cut gear in London, but I knew I was being squeezed here. I was a tourist in this situation and these two chancers were maximising their profit margin. I thought of trying to haggle. But I was well off the beaten track here, and, to be fair, they had come through with the goods. The small paper parcel was careful wrapped closed again and I handed over the money.

'You go now.'

They hustled me into the front room and out through the front door before I could even say thank you.

Now I was in trouble.

Darkness had fallen. I was in an alleyway somewhere in beautiful downtown Bangkok, about 4g of grade A scag in my pocket and without the first idea how to get back to my hotel. What could possibly go wrong here?

I started walking, and probably spent the next 15 minutes wandering in circles, before the path broadened out a bit. I wanted to find a shop that was open: I needed to buy a roll of aluminium foil to get a hit from the smack.

Finally, I chanced into a small square that hosted a couple of foodstalls catering to the locals. Fresh squid and octopus hung from hooks on their fronts and something sizzled in a hot wok beneath white writing on a red sign. There was a small grocery store on one side of the square. But it didn't seem to stock foil.

I had a 100-watt bayonet bulb moment, and bought a couple of chocolate bars, wrapped in a paper sleeve with a layer of thin metal foil underneath. That would do until I could visit another shop tomorrow.

A tuk tuk was parked by one of the stalls, its driver finishing his meal. I couldn't see the sense in walking round with my high-risk cargo – I might as well have shaved my hair and painted a luminous X on top of my noggin.

Back at the hotel, I closed the door to my room and breathed a deep sigh of relief.

Mission accomplished.

I wasted no time in unwrapping one of the chocolate bars, straightening out the creases in the foil until it lay flat in my hand. Tearing off a square from the leftover paper sleeve, I fashioned it into a hollow tube about four inches in length.

It was time to chase the dragon.

I have always had an aversion to needles: the risk of HIV and Hep. B aside, the thought of plunging a spike into my veins turns me on like necking a cup of cold sick.

The rush, when you take smack intravenously, is supposed to be equivalent to being hit with a sledgehammer. But Junkytown wasn't on my itinerary. All I craved was a little taste of something naughty, a dalliance with something nice.

I unwrapped the gear from its paper envelope, took one of the small lumps of coagulated white powder delicately between my thumb and forefinger and placed it in the centre of the foil. Now the tricky bit.

Heroin has a fairly low melting point before it turns from powder into liquid. Over-cook it, and it burns to a blackened crisp within seconds. Carefully, I held my cigarette lighter a couple of inches from the underside of the foil and flicked it on, wafting its flame

MR NASTY

under the area where the heroin lay. In my mouth I held the rolled up piece of paper to suck up the fumes that would rise as the heat from the lighter hit the gear. Slowly, it began to melt and I tilted the foil slightly so that the blob of molten heroin ran down its surface. I sucked up the trail of smoke that followed it, flicked off the lighter and held the smoke deep in my lungs for several seconds.

The hit took a few moments, but then I felt warmth spread through my body. As the scag kicked in, I felt a pleasing energy rush. I smoked for a few minutes, the white powder turning to light brown as it melted, emitting its pungent aroma.

Pretty soon I was completely stoned. I flopped back on the bed and instantly the bile rose in my throat. I rushed to the bathroom and just made it to the porcelain in time. Nausea and vomiting are routine side effects of smack. It goes with the territory, especially when you are a part-time user and your body hasn't built any tolerance for the drug. Being sick wasn't an unpleasant experience: it was mildly irritating, but the heroin dulled all sensation.

I sat on the edge of the bath and lit a cigarette. It tasted like the best I had ever smoked. My head began to nod. I suddenly felt very tired, and staggered back to the bed as the narcotic wrapped me inside its comforting embrace.

I lay there for a couple of hours enjoying the warm, cosseted feelings that heroin grants its devotees. As I drifted off to sleep at around midnight, I didn't have a care in the world.

The knocking on the door was insistent.

Finally, the loud banging forced me from my pit.

Even though half asleep, I groggily surmised that I was still wearing yesterday's clothes. I must have nodded off once too often and drifted into a deep sleep.

I slithered off the bed and stumbled over to open up, quite irritated at the hotel staff for disturbing my blissful slumber.

There were two of them.

Both uniformed Thai policemen.

It hit me like a face full of bleach: the smack was still on the table from the night before, the burnt foil right beside it.

'We wish to look in your room, sir,' the shorter of the two said in clipped but perfect English. 'We have reason to believe that you have drugs here.'

They brushed past me.

Panic rose in my throat as the bile had done hours before. I closed the door and followed the cops to the coffee table in the centre of the room. One of them had already bent down to examine the small square of aluminium foil, the telltale smear of burnt heroin all too clear on its surface.

They had me bang to rights.

The other cop had now picked up the small paper wrap and was unfolding it to reveal its contents.

'This is yours?'

I said nothing.

I had nothing to say.

I had been caught in the act. Bangkok Hilton, one way.

'It's heroin,' Shorty said to his colleague.

'Lie down on the bed. Put your arms behind your back,' the other cop ordered.

I thought about making a run for it, but noticed they both packed holstered pistols.

Anyway, where would I run to? My passport and plane ticket were in my bag in the wardrobe.

My guts churned. I did as I was told. The handcuffs clicked cold on my wrists.

This was the real deal.

They left me there, lying face down on the bed. I turned my head to one side as they continued to search my room. Shorty still held the wrap of drugs and foil in one hand.

'Where did you get this?'

Again, I said nothing. I just stared at them, the fear rising in me, catching in my throat, my heart beating nine and a dozen.

'OK, stand up. You are coming with us.'

I managed to nudge myself to the end of the bed and stood up shakily.

'Things look very bad for you my friend, very bad indeed.'

I swallowed hard and stared into Shorty's eyes. He was giving nothing away. He just stood there with a thin smile playing across his lips.

'You are going to jail for a long time. Prison will not be good for you.'

And then I saw it: a faint glimmer of hope. He was offering me a way out of this. Realisation dawned quickly. How had they known where I was? And that I would have the gear in my room?

Only one person knew where I was staying and where I had scored. My friendly hotel porter.

This was a shakedown.

I cursed my own stupidity. Of course, it happened all the time. Dealers would rat out their clients to the cops who would give them a kickback and then steam in for a bust. But why pay off a dealer if you weren't going to make something out of it yourselves?

I had some fast talking to do.

'Maybe we can work something out, guys,' I said, trying to put some conviction into my voice.

'What do you mean?'

'Well, what would it take to make this problem go away?'

The cops looked at each other.

Finally, the taller one spoke.

'Twenty thousand Baht and this problem will go away.'

'The money is in my wallet in my back pocket. Take the cuffs off. I'll show you.'

Shorty moved around behind me and uncuffed me. I pulled out my wallet and counted out what remained of my money. There was just over 20,000 Baht, plus some travellers' cheques that I had brought with me in case of an emergency. Well, this was a freakin' emergency all right.

I handed over the cash: Shorty flicked through it, making sure that all of it was there.

'If we see you out on the street, we will arrest you.'

They both turned to go. Shorty still had the drugs in his hand and it didn't look like he was minded to return them. I didn't care.

'Thank you. Thank you, thank you,' I bleated pathetically.

They opened the door and left. I sat on the end of the bed breathing hard. My first reaction was pure relief. My second was to find that porter and kick the living shit out of him.

Wiser counsels prevailed: thinking things through, the police were perfectly capable of coming back and squeezing me for another shedload of cash. Maybe some of their buddies would be dropping by to arrest me properly. Having Bangkok's finest visit my room unannounced would certainly have alerted hotel staff that the guest in room 102 was an undesirable element.

Time to switch. I packed my bag and made my way down to reception. If they were surprised to see me after the police raid, they didn't show it.

I checked out, wondering how many other guests at the hotel had been stung the same way.

The remaining three days of my trip were spent in the serene security of the Sheraton Hotel. I didn't venture out into town much, wanting to keep as much distance as possible between my warm body and Shorty's cold bracelets.

So I sucked liquor in the hotel bar until it was time for wheels up back to London.

My chemical vacation had been terminated with extreme funk. But at least I still had my liberty.

That one evening of chasing a molten blob of smack around a piece of foil was the start of something. Something that made getting busted in Bangkok seem like just another haircut for Samson.

Gather round, narco-kids, look, listen and learn: be careful of what you wish for.

It may come true.

BERLIN

STATION TO STATION

I took the steps up out of the underground at a leisurely pace, mulling over the task ahead of me. Like a mole blinking in daylight, I emerged at street level: the danger zone. I was here, in Berlin, in mission mode.

The first thing rail travellers into Berlin see is Bahnhof Zoo. Juggernaut locomotives drag in from all over Europe, ejecting their cargoes of tourists, office workers and kids looking for bright lights. It's the gateway to Berlin's hip 'n' trendy downtown, bordering the Kurfurstendamm (or the Ku'Damm as it is known locally), a tourist trap, and the city's main shopping district. More glitz than Ritz.

But Bahnhof Zoo has a darker side. A claim to fame similar to many big-city rail hubs. Its environs house riff-raff: prostitutes of all sexual persuasions and hustlers of many stripes. They all stick to the terminus's Teutonic bulk like Adam cleaving to his lost rib.

Berlin was the smack capital of Western Europe in the '80s and '90s, and Bahnhof Zoo has a thriving street trade in heroin. So, it was the first place I visited when I hit the city. I knew nobody in town. I was going into this completely cold.

A quick scan of the low-lifes loitering outside the front of the main station didn't give me much confidence. There were plenty of casualties hugging the gutter, but their internal emollient of choice appeared to be alcohol: they staggered, they swayed, they sat on the concrete in varying degrees of stupefaction.

I headed down on the left alongside the heavy traffic. Plenty of witnesses on wheels. Better to conduct this initial sortie in daylight, I reckoned, before braving the war zone of Berlin's nightworld.

I waited around for about ten minutes before selecting a target for my initial approach.

She was walking alongside the traffic which was bustling its way towards the Ku'Damm, hoping to entice some stressed businessman into a little, hem hem, executive relief.

She was tall, shading 6ft. Perhaps she was a transvestite. It didn't matter: he, she or it was neither here nor there. I gave the figure one final hard look to ensure I wasn't making an error. There was no doubt, she was wearing the hooker's uniform: micro-sized PVC miniskirt, patent leather heels and a cropped fake-fur jacket, its collar drawn up around her neck to fend off the early evening chill. I made my move, sauntering over to where she stood, surveying the passing cars.

Business appeared to be terrible.

Perfect.

'Hi. Do you speak English?'

'Ja. A little. You are maybe looking for a girl?'

She quickly snapped out of frowning at the uninterested traffic, and turned on a gleaming smile. She looked ageless, could have been anywhere between 25 and 40. Her face was hollow-cheeked. The bright-red rouge of her lips only emphasised her skin's death's-head pallor.

I could visualise the tracks and needle scars marking her forearms, concealed beneath her jacket. Her eyelids drooped slightly, quasi-comatose: a heavy heroin user.

I played to her need for cash.

'I need to score, can you help me?'

'Score, score what? A goal? You are maybe a football player?'

She laughed at her own joke.

It was prudent to humour her.

'No, I'm looking for smack, heroin?'

'To me you are not looking like you want drugs.'

True. Overindulgence in London on lager and kebabs meant I had piled on the pounds: I didn't look like a scag hound.

'I'll pay you if you help me. I have money.'

She looked at the homeward-bound punters passing her by, ignoring her and perhaps, as I'd suspected, it helped her make up her mind.

'I get you drugs, you pay me 30 Marks, ja?'

'OK, 30 Marks, no problem.'

'Good. We walk. Come with me, we go to see the man. You give me the 30 Marks now.'

'I'll give you the money when we score.'

'You don't have trust in me?'

'I've only just met you. I get the smack, you get the money. Agreed?'

'Ja. OK.'

We walked back to the front of the main station, a stroll through human debris blotting it all out with another slug from a bottle, a can, whatever.

We crossed the road running parallel to the right-hand side of the station and passed more street girls and hollow-eyed ghosts. We came to a junction. She seemed to be looking for someone, craning her thin, swan-like neck to look down a side street.

She spotted her mark and beckoned me to follow her to a weatherbeaten BMW parked kerbside.

She knocked on its window. It slid down with an electronic whirr. My hooker friend probed the driver in rapid Deutsch. Then she stood up straight and turned to me.

'How much do you want?'

'How much for a gram?'

'There is no gram, only quarters.'

'How much for four quarters?'

Too late, I recognised that excitement had overwhelmed me.

The smart thing would have been to score one quarter and check out the gear before committing to a larger order.

The girl bent down to the open window and spoke to the driver once more. He nodded and turned to look at me.

'English?'

I nodded.

'Ja, I am thinking you are English. Two hundred Marks for the four quarters.'

I flashed the cash, and reaching into his mouth, the driver removed the drugs. Dealers and users invariably carry drugs in their mouths when they are operating at street level. The merchandise is wrapped in foil and then sealed in a small rubber or polythene balloon to make it watertight. If you get into a situation with the cops then the drugs can simply be swallowed. In theory, the gear should pass through your digestive system in its sealed packaging. In practice, swallowing several balloons of heroin can lead to an overdose if the rubber seal leaks.

The street dealer extended his hand. There were five tiny watertight balloons, tightly tied off at one end, packaged about the size of half a cigarette's filter tip.

'You take four. You choose,' he said, as he reached out with his free hand and plucked the two notes from my fingers.

Transaction over, the window slid up and we returned to the Zoo.

I handed the hooker 30 DM.

'I am Chrissi.'

'Mo,' I said, once again adopting my street name as I shook her hand.

'Are you always here at the station?'

'Ja, I am here most days. I help you to get drugs, you pay me 30 Marks?'

'Yeah, sure.'

This was only a short-term commitment until I could make a proper arrangement with a connection, preferably off-street.

'Auf Wiedersehen, pet.'

It was two miles to my hotel, at the opposite end of the

shopping district from Bahnhof Zoo. I walked along the Ku'Damm.

As soon as the door closed behind my fourth-floor room, I carefully bit through the tied end of one of the balloons and unwrapped the small foil parcel from its rubber packaging. Delicately, I unfolded the foil to reveal its contents. It looked light for a quarter gram, but you rarely make full weight on a street deal. The brown powder lay in the centre of the foil. Brown meant that it was probably Afghani or Pakistani smack, but the colour looked suspicious. Instead of the verdant brown hue, characteristic of 'ghani or 'stani smack, this scag was slightly lighter. A dab of my index finger confirmed that the shit had been stepped on. I could still taste the unmistakable bitterness of the heroin, but it was intermingled with a sugary-sweet cut.

Street drugs are invariably cut to the point of being nearly useless for a hardened addict. I was just into light recreational use, but I would have preferred something purer. Needs must . . .

I moved over to the bed and grabbed a roll of aluminium foil from my bag. I tore off a section about four inches square and tapped the powder onto the centre of the foil.

The next ten minutes were spent chasing the whole quarter gram.

There was a definite buzz from the smack radiating through my body, but it was shocking gear. As the heroin melted, it charred and crisped around the edges, a sure sign that it had been repeatedly stepped on during its trip from the poppy fields of Afghanistan down to die Strasse.

I emptied a second quarter onto a new piece of foil and repeated the ritual. When the molten scag had burned to its charred conclusion I felt my head start to nod.

Welcome to Smack Heaven. Population: me.

But it was expensive. This had cost me 100 DM. I'd need an economic miracle to make many more deals like this through Chrissi. But what did it matter? I was only going to be a part-time user. Three days on, four days off to clear my system and avoid a habit. After all, I wasn't some kind of junky, I was in control of the drugs. Class A narcotics are dangerous.

You must keep control.

I lay back on the bed wondering how I'd washed up in an overpriced hotel in the Ku'Damm with half a gram of diluted smack racing through my bloodstream.

Bangkok had set me on this course. It had been a year since I had flown back to the UK, but the taste of the smack smoked in that Patpong hotel room had lingered in my memory like a melody that lingers long after the song's been sung.

I had returned to my mind-numbing office job in London and had almost immediately subconsciously begun to plan my next chemical holiday.

I wanted to explore more thoroughly the boundaries to which heroin pushed the user, but I didn't want to end up as another victim of Harry the Horse. So I had set myself some ground rules: no continuous use, no injecting and no chasing the dragon back in London. I had used a bit of heroin during my clubbing days in the UK, as an easy comedown from the pills, but my smack consumption had been limited to rare occasions, as getting a habit had not been on my agenda.

Smack has a stigma like no other drug. Word quickly spreads that there is a new scaggie on the block and, although I was determined to be a casual user, I didn't want to acquire the reputation of a junk fiend on my home turf. There was no way I wanted to wake up with a monkey on my back. I was convinced that I could control my use of the drug.

So I chose Berlin.

The city was Funkytown; its streets deluged with smack. I had cashed in my savings and had nearly 30,000 DM to fund my adventure. This was November 1997 and I had spent the past four years since leaving LA in a succession of lucrative if dull office jobs. I had religiously put all of my spare cash into a savings account each month in preparation for my next adventure. Thailand had been a mere excursion along the way and I had been building up to this for some time: what I was about to do was totally premeditated and carefully thought through, or so I figured.

Berlin is a major importer of marijuana from the Netherlands and Spain. German authorities tolerate small amounts for personal use. Most amphetamines enter the city from large production labs in Poland. Ecstasy pours in from all points east and west.

Cocaine is available in Berlin, but it's piss-poor: most of the coke-oriented business in Germany takes the form of the supply of precursor chemicals for the processing labs in South America.

The city's geographical location – the proverbial gateway between Eastern and Western Europe – makes it a pivotal trafficking point for heroin. Smack can travel from the Golden Triangle in Asia, from Pakistan, or from several former Soviet states which have rapidly ramped up production since the collapse of Communism. Organised crime gangs in the Balkans run large shipments of pills, speed and coke from Poland and Russia through Berlin. They use this narco-revenue to tool up their cabals within their own largely lawless homelands.

So, Berlin was the perfect place for my narcotic holiday. I had fundage for months; I wouldn't need to get a job. I planned to stay no longer than six months and here I was anonymous, especially to the police. I'd told my family that I was going to spend the time travelling and they seemed content that I was broadening my horizons. Little did they know that the only culture I was intending to experience was of the junk variety.

Basically, I couldn't play it straight for any considerable length of time – I lived and breathed drugs. If I wasn't taking drugs, then I was thinking about taking them. My consumption had been moderate over the past few years with the odd pill or line, but I had reached the point when getting temporarily wasted was very appealing. My motivation was quite simply that I liked drugs, especially smack and the thrill of tasting forbidden fruit.

Getting busted was always a risk. But I sussed that if things went tits up, I could always flee back to the UK. I needed to get out of this hotel though. At 180 DM a night it was too expensive.

Furthermore, I reckoned, I should be closer to where the dealers were in order to put my face around a bit. As I started to nod my way towards a deep, heroin-induced slumber, I made my plans for the next day. Find a new place to stay. And find Chrissi.

Next morning, Chrissi was job one. Depending on where I could establish a connection, I could then sort out someplace suitable to stay.

I arrived at the Zoo at midday and spent an hour walking through the lost souls cluttering the pavements around the station. A couple of hustlers sidled up and talked at me in German. Were they offering horizontal jogging, gear or what? I ignored them. I had scored off Chrissi before and she was on the level.

Just after one o'clock, I spotted her coming out of the main entrance dressed in last night's outfit.

She saw me and waved, approaching immediately.

'The deal was good, ja?'

'It was OK, the gear was cut though.'

'It is a good deal for Bahnhof Zoo. Most of the stuff here is shit.'

'That's what I want to talk to you about. Can we get a coffee somewhere?'

Chrissi tilted her head to one side and looked at me, a glint in her eye.

'We can get a room if you like.'

'No, it's OK. I just want a coffee and a chat.'

She looked disappointed, but took her rejection with a stoicism born of trudging mean streets.

We walked back inside the station and took a couple of seats at a small snack bar. Once we were settled with a couple of espressos I launched into my spiel. 'I want to score some more smack, but I'm looking for better quality.'

'Quality is not good around here. Sometimes it takes me two or three quarters just to get straight in the morning.'

So, she was a user.

'Where do you usually get your gear from?'

'I have a guy in Kreuzberg, where I live. It is over on the eastern side.' Berliners still divide the city into east and west, despite the fall of the Berlin wall and reunification. This confirmed my instinct that Chrissi wouldn't bother with the street dealers around the station unless she was desperate for a quick fix.

She looked like she was in need of a lunchtime shot. Her hand shook as she sipped the hot coffee; she had the hungry eyes of an addict needing to score, and score fast.

'I'll pay you good money if you introduce me to your dealer.'

'I don't know. He doesn't trust people he doesn't know.'

'That's why I need you to introduce me.'

She paused for a few seconds.

'I'll introduce you and you buy me two quarters.'

That was going to cost me 100 DM. Pricey, but I would get better gear and save cash long term. I nodded my agreement.

'OK. We get taxi. C'mon.'

For many Berliners, the district of Kreuzberg is also, unofficially, divided into east and west. The eastern half houses anarchic squats where May Day riots are common. Its western counterpart, by contrast, is a neighbourhood that aspires to Poshopolis.

In the very north of Kreuzberg is Checkpoint Charlie, the notorious cold war crossing point between Communist East and Free West Berlin. Now the wall has come down, Kreuzberg is home to 200,000 Turkish immigrants. The community adds a cosmopolitan flavour, but is also a conduit for the heroin that the Afghani and Pakistani cartels pump into Berlin through Turkey. Most of the action in the district takes place in the streets around Viktoria Park, a long-time haunt for pot dealers.

We cruised down Yorkstrasse, Kreuzberg's main drag, dotted with cafés and nosheries busy with the lunchtime crowd. Almost imperceptibly, the snack bars became less trendy and the buildings more dilapidated as we drove east onto Bergmannstrasse with its second-hand clothes shops.

We stopped at Chamissoplatz, a beautifully intact district, remarkably untouched by Allied bombing during the Second

World War. I paid the driver and joined Chrissi in front of a large, ornate building, festooned with Gothic motifs.

A row of buzzers to one side of the door suggested it had been converted into flats. The property looked slightly run-down, but it was certainly a step up from some of the squats we had passed en route.

Chrissi spoke into the intercom and we were buzzed in.

'The elevator is broken,' she said as we moved through the foyer. 'It never works. We walk.'

On the third floor, Chrissi knocked on a sturdy black door. A good sign. Dealers like to put as big a barrier as possible between themselves and the law, who could bust their way into the premises any time.

'I have brought someone with me. It's OK, I know him.'

She was speaking English for my benefit. The door opened and a pair of beady eyes scrutinised me. They were set in a hawk-like face, its olive complexion radiating a healthy aura absent from the skeletally thin frame stood in the doorway.

'Come in,' he said.

We followed our host through into the lounge. Chrissi gave me a hard look, letting me know that she would be doing the talking. My potential connection sat by a small wooden dining table on one side of the room. Chrissi and I took our places on a battered sofa facing him.

'Bill, this is Mo, a friend of mine. Mo this is Wilhelm, but most people just call him Bill, Kaiser Bill.'

She laughed at the last part, but Bill was frowning.

Perhaps better not to join in.

'I've told you that I don't want you bringing your friends to me. I don't know this guy,' Bill said. 'He could be anybody. How long have you known him?'

'A few months,' she said. She lied convincingly. The lure of some free smack honed her thespian skills.

'Sure, sure,' Bill told her, 'but this is the last time.'

He extended a bone-thin arm, and I leant forward to shake hands.

'OK, I tell you the rules,' Bill said. 'It's 50 Marks a quarter,

MR NASTY

don't come here with 49 and expect to get anything. You don't ask to shoot up here as there are no needles allowed in my flat. And I stop dealing at midnight so don't be ringing my bell all night like a junky. I will be asleep.'

'I understand.'

'Good,' said Kaiser Bill, and opened a small wooden box on the table in front of him.

'Do you want one each?'

'No I'll take six. Four for me and two for Chrissi.'

Bill's eyes widened.

Six was obviously more than a routine order from his clientele, who probably spent their days prostituting themselves, or stealing from others to scrape together the Deutsche Marks for their next shot.

He withdrew half a dozen small foil wraps and spread them on top of the table. I counted the 300 DM and handed the banknotes to him. Chrissi pocketed her two wraps.

'OK, just remember the rules, otherwise find yourself another dealer.'

'I'll see you again tomorrow, Bill,' I said, to cement the relationship.

'Ja, ja. Whatever.'

Outside on the pavement I bade Chrissi auf Wiedersehen with a 20 DM note for her cab fare back to the station.

I suspected that she was heading straight home for a fix, but never mind, she'd earned it.

I walked back towards the centre of Kreuzberg and prowled the streets around Viktoria Park. I found what I was looking for on Gneisenaustrasse. It was an unremarkable estate agency. My stilted German was not up to negotiating a lease on a flat, but luckily the girl behind the desk spoke fluent English.

One listing caught my eye. It was for a six-month lease on a small flat above a café in Riehmers Hofgarten, quite near the park. We drove over, and I signed on the spot. Three hundred Marks a week was more than I wanted to pay, but the fully furnished apartment was in a quiet street.

MR NASTY

That afternoon, I moved my stuff from the Swissotel in the Ku'Damm to my latest home, and then settled down in my new surroundings to have a smoke.

The gear was good, much better than the rubbish I had scored at the Zoo. I flicked on the TV. Before long, the goggle box was combining with the smack and my brain was mush. German television mixed tacky game shows with zealous news reportage delivered with the light touch of a Panzer division.

I grew bored, switched off and nestled down along the length of my new sofa. The smack enveloped me and I set up another piece of foil.

I wanted to get totally twisted.

All thoughts of food were absent. Heroin kills appetite: culinary, sexual, everything.

I was happy to lie there, letting the afternoon drift by in a downy cloud.

One more day on the gear, I decided, then I'd take a break for a while. Heroin takes 72 hours to completely clear your system despite the fact that the actual high only lasts six to eight hours. I'd let the shit pass through my bloodstream so I'd be clean again.

Taking heroin is like sliding into a hot bath, then being dried by an angel who wraps you in a euphoric embrace. All your cares and worries evaporate into a background void, leaving you to live forever in a cotton-wool world . . . until you wake up one day feeling the force of your habit driving you to get things together for your next smoke. Addiction is a vicious price to pay for the narcotic pleasure the temptress supplies. It is slow to take hold when you are snorting or smoking, but rapid if you are injecting the drug.

Smack – you've gotta have it.

I felt safe chasing the dragon. But I was already burning my way through half a gram of gear a day. Smack's bitch grip clamped itself around my psyche: I had talked myself out of taking a three-day break and reduced it to 24 hours off the horse.

I knew that I was already running the risk of short-term

dependency. And yet, I easily convinced myself that it would take several weeks before I was hooked. Plenty of time.

Narco-time.

During the next couple of weeks I fell into an easy routine of scoring from Kaiser Bill every couple of days. My usual order was a gram but, by the second week, my tolerance was building, so I now needed three quarters a day to reach nirvana.

Since that first tense encounter, Bill proved reasonably friendly. I was scoring in quantity, and he quickly adopted me as a preferred customer.

After four or five weeks I was still comfortable with the fact that I wasn't hung up on the gear. Heroin does that to you. The smack lulls you into a false sense of security and you start to inhabit a place where the hours and days pass by in soft focus. Your stoned existence becomes normality to such an extent that when you eventually crash and burn in the ferocity of dependency and withdrawal, you aren't just trying to claw your way back to the reality of being clean. You have to pass through that stage and travel further on to regain the existence of living high on the horse. It's a long, long way to fall from that high to the living hell of being strung out. It's almost impossible to imagine the world of fear and desperation that comes with paying the price for continual smack use. The inevitable fact is that eventually the drug will turn on you and sink its teeth into your jugular, bleeding all of the desire, joy and hope out of your life and shackling you to the only thing that is now of any importance to you: your next fix. It overrides everything else and consumes you completely. But that was only for junkies. I was cool. I had the situation locked down. I wasn't going to let the smack take me over. Score and smoke, score and smoke, score and smoke. Day after day, week after week. Goodbye to all the boredom, the fear, the pain of everyday existence. Hello to heroin's loving arms, wrapped around me, protecting me, taking me higher and higher to that special place where I was insulated from the outside world. Just one more day. Just one more hit. Just one more step towards disaster.

I was walking down Yorkstrasse one lunchtime on my way to pick up the medicine when I heard my alternate identity being hailed.

'Mo. Hey, Mo. Over here.'

I turned to see Kaiser Bill sitting in a compact black Opel hatchback on the other side of the street. He looked smug.

'This your car?' I asked him through the open driver-side window.

'Yeah, sure, I've just bought it. Get in. We can go for a drive.'

I climbed in.

The ride was a couple of years old. It did cross my mind to wonder how a junky could afford a new set of wheels, but I had enjoyed my now customary morning smoke, and suspicion quickly evaporated.

'I've got four quarters on me which you can have,' said Bill, ever the businessman.

'I'll wait until we get back to the flat.'

'No problem, I just want to get some dope first,' he said.

We drove through the streets until we hit Viktoria Park. A 60-metre-high monument topped the hill that towered over lawns there: young families and children rubbed shoulders with small-time pot-peddlers who skittered furtively from deal to deal.

Bill got out and headed towards the monument, a neo-Gothic cross affording fantastic views of north Berlin.

He disappeared.

Five minutes later he re-materialised by the car. He got in and fired up the engine.

'Do you want to come back for a puff?'

Before I could reply, a black, leather-clad arm had shot through the open driver-side window and locked around Bill's neck.

Shit, it was a cop.

He was shouting in German while trying to grab for the keys with his free hand.

Bill was having none of it and flicked the car into first gear.

We were moving forward now, accelerating. Bill's head was bent towards the window, still trapped in the police officer's tight embrace.

The cop wasn't going to let go. He was screaming at Bill to stop the car.

We rolled down a gentle hill. Bill managed to push the stick into second gear, but he couldn't steer properly with the weight of the cop around his neck. We must have been dragging him along the ground by now, but he still clung on like a barnacle.

Fifty metres before we hit it, I saw the wall.

Events seemed to unfold in slow motion as the bricks loomed.

The cop pulled down hard on Bill's neck. Then he saw the oncoming obstacle.

He let go.

His body hit the tarmac with a slapping sound.

Then we hit concrete.

The car ploughed straight through it, bricks and dirt crashing through the windscreen, shattering it on impact.

We stopped dead.

Both of us sat there in stunned silence, surveying the wreckage around us. The car was a write-off, its front crushed. My passenger door had buckled and was hanging from one hinge.

At least we weren't hurt.

Suddenly the driver's door was yanked open and Bill was hauled out.

A cop wagon pulled up alongside. Flight was pointless.

I kicked open the Opel's mangled door. Immediately a policeman flipped me around so that I was facing the car again. He was speaking in rapid-fire German that I couldn't understand. On the other side of the car, Bill faced me, deadpan. He put his hands on the roof. I did likewise.

The cop rifled my pockets and patted his way down and around my body, checking for weapons I didn't have.

Herr Law flipped me back round to face him.

Bill's cop had found a small bag of pot.

Now we were both handcuffed and hustled into the back of the wagon, where we sat on wooden benches opposite one another. Bill looked solemn as another cop joined us to ride shotgun.

This was catastrophic.

Anything I said could incriminate me further, so I zipped it. For ten minutes the talking stopped. As calmly as I could, I speculated on my fate and what charges I might have to answer. I wasn't holding any drugs on my person. Whereas Bill, I suspected, still had the smack on him somewhere.

The van's doors opened and the cops manhandled us both out into the daylight, through a pair of swing doors into the booking-in area of the cop shop.

The sergeant sitting behind his desk stared impassively.

'I am English. I don't speak German,' I said.

I sounded calmer than I felt.

'So, you are English and you expect us all to speak English too,' the desk sergeant said. 'I think that it is not so good an attitude after you have taken one of my officers for a drive through the park. Empty your pockets on the desk.'

I did so. They fingerprinted me and snapped my mug shot. They re-cuffed me and dumped me on a bench. Two plain-clothes officers took Bill down a corridor. They could be beating him with rubber truncheons for all I knew. I was definitely in schtuck.

I didn't know Bill well enough to judge whether he would take me down with him.

The next hour crawled like a funeral march. Eventually a female officer uncuffed me.

She led me through a door to one side of the custody suite, and I found myself in a passage lined with small offices, some with their doors open, others closed. I was led into one on the right and sat down in front of a small wooden table.

Opposite sat the desk sergeant who had booked me in, and one of the plain-clothes detectives.

'So, Mo, if that is your real name . . .'

It was more luck than smarts that I hadn't been carrying any ID.

'. . . I am Detective Kellerman and this is Sergeant Weisz. We would like to ask you a few questions about this afternoon if we may?'

His English was as faultlessly formal as his sharp grey suit.

His extreme courtesy flicked a warning light on my interior dashboard.

'Shouldn't I have a lawyer?' I asked.

'Please, there is no need for such formalities at this stage,' Kellerman insisted. 'We just want to have a chat. Your friend has been most cooperative with us and we just want to confirm some details. Did you know that the vehicle was stolen?'

Bill had nicked the car? This just got better and better.

'No, I assumed that it was his car,' I said.

'I see.'

'He told me he'd just bought it.'

The two cops exchanged glances and then Kellerman continued.

'Your friend was observed buying illegal drugs in Viktoria Park – drugs which were subsequently recovered from his person – together with a quantity of powder which we believe to be heroin.'

He was talking in that weird cop language which seems to be universal in all police stations. The sky is never azure, but always medium blue in colour.

'We would like to ask you if you are carrying any drugs on your person which you would perhaps like to tell us about?'

'I'm clean. I don't do drugs. Your officers have already searched me. I don't have anything to hide.'

'But that's exactly the point,' Kellerman said. 'Perhaps you do have something to hide and have already hidden it. We would like to conduct a more thorough search just to make sure that what you say is true.'

Things that make you go ooooooh.

I was led out of the office and down to the end of the hallway to another room. It was empty – except for an unremarkable chair.

'Please remove your clothing and place it on the chair,' Kellerman said.

Another cop had joined him and his silent sidekick. I clocked the newcomer's hands: they wore thin, putty-coloured latex gloves.

Lovely. This was going to be a full cavity search.

Seething, I reluctantly stripped, folding my clothes slowly and carefully over the chair.

The silent sidekick started going through my jeans' pockets. He was methodical and meticulous.

'Put your arms out straight in front of you.'

Gloveman was checking for needle marks. He looked closely at my forearms, before examining in between my fingers and then moving down to my feet. Users frequently inject themselves in places less obvious than their arms. Some slide the needle underneath their fingernails to avoid telltale tracks.

'Turn around,' Kellerman said.

'Now bend down and put your hands on your knees.'

I did as I was told and inhaled sharply as the cop's cold finger probed where the sun don't shine.

Being strip-searched evokes a combination of humiliation and anger in an individual, particularly if they have nothing incriminating on them. I was seething. I had been stopped on numerous occasions in the past and had my pockets rifled, but this was my first full body search.

'Please stand up and put your clothes back on.'

The three of them stood and watched as I dressed.

They led me back to the interrogation room.

'How do you know Bill?'

'How does anybody know anybody?' I said. 'He's just a guy who's around.'

'What were you doing in a stolen car?'

'I've already told you. I didn't know the car was stolen.'

'What do you know about the drugs?'

'Nothing,' I said, 'until you told me just now.'

They liked Bill for this, so we spent 45 minutes at the cat–mouse interface. The dynamic duo suspected I must be guilty of something. But I wasn't about to help them prove it. I hadn't been driving, and I didn't have any gear in my possession.

They were detaining Kaiser Bill for now. Kellerman was talking up a charge of attempted murder, but I doubted if they could make it stick. Bill would take the rap for driving the Opel without consent and possession of the drugs.

He would get bail, but not today.

Eventually Kellerman seemed to tire of my vague evasions. He leaned back from the table.

'Supposing we let you walk out of here. What are you going to do?'

'Go straight home and stay out of trouble,' I said.

I hoped I sounded earnest enough. I tried to look cowed and apologetic.

'I think you will be straight out on the street again looking for drugs. However, we have nothing to hold you on so you are free to go. If we see you again though, you won't be getting off this lightly.'

I walked through the swing doors of the pigpen to freedom.

I hadn't succeeded in scoring but told myself I could do with a break from the Chinese rocks, and returned to my apartment without taking any detours. That was enough excitement for one day.

I woke at 2 a.m.

Something was wrong.

Cramps were shooting up my legs from my toes to my groin. I was bathed in sweat but shivering with the cold. I shrugged off the duvet and staggered through to the bathroom.

I checked the mirror.

The sweat was dripping off the end of my nose, dark circles surrounded my eyes. I retched and sank to my knees beside the white porcelain toilet.

This couldn't be going down. I had only been using for a few weeks.

But it definitely was happening. Smack . . . bang. An icy fear spread through my polluted veins. Regret and self-recrimination overwhelmed me in an instant. Just how fucking stupid was I to have landed myself in the nightmare of dependency?

I had broken all of Mr Nasty's rules: I had used continuously, steadily upping my intake until my body was habituated to smoking nearly a gram of gear a day. Like I said, it's a long, long way to fall when you crash and burn. The physical pain was tearing my body apart but it was the total headfuck that was worse: the realisation that I was now enslaved to the gear. Some say that heroin withdrawal is all in the head. If you are mentally strong, then you can just tough it out, just like having a bad dose of the flu. Whoever says that hasn't had their psyche instantly dismantled and re-assembled in such a way that all your nightmares are there to stay, permanently. Cameron White had been obliterated by the nuclear blast of addiction and in his place was a clutching, retching, soulless smack monster.

Cramps lanced through my arms and legs once more, buckling my knees and reducing me to a shivering, crawling mess. This was a whole new world of hurt. Every nerve ending in my body, which for so long had been deadened by the smack, was now alive with pain. There was a blast furnace of agony where my skin touched my clothes as my desensitised body suddenly awoke from its slumber and kicked my teeth out. And I knew that this was just the beginning.

Shit, I had to score to stop the pain and stave off the withdrawal symptoms now wracking my mind and body.

I stood up and moved back into the bedroom, collapsing on the bed as a wave of nausea hit me.

I counted back in time.

It had been 15 hours since my last hit. Time enough for the horrors to set in. I had to get busy before the Jones kicked in with a vengeance – by then, I would be fit for nothing. I estimated that, at most, I had a couple of hours.

I dragged myself into my clothes, slipping on an extra jumper to fend off the chill running through my veins. One thing drove me on through the pain: the need for the one thing that would make me well again. Out on the street there was a tense five-minute wait before I hailed a cab.

'Bahnhof Zoo, bitte.'

I collapsed back into the seat. I had no choice but to score at the Zoo. Kaiser Bill was probably still in a cell downtown. Even if he'd got loose, it was well past his midnight curfew and, after the day's events, I couldn't see him answering his bell.

I focused on trying to impose my will over the violent tremors arching though my aching limbs.

This was payback for sleeping the daydream of heroin narcosis.

The traffic was light but I was running in the narco-time zone: it seemed like forever until we stopped at the front of the station. I clambered and stumbled out. The driver must have thought I was just another junky.

He was right.

I straightened up and paid him. Aimlessly, I began looking at the faces of the dispossessed and the damned, searching for Chrissi. She wasn't around.

Maybe she had gone home early, maybe this was her night off. She could have been with a client, or perhaps she was lying dead in a toilet somewhere, a spike in her cold arm.

I was starting to panic.

I leaned against a railing.

There was a girl walking the street in front of me. For a moment I thought it was Chrissi, but then I saw the bump in her belly. Sweet Jesus, she must have been six months pregnant.

I weaved towards her.

'You speak English?'

'Nein.'

'Please.'

'I speak a little. Not so very good.'

'Can you help me? I need to fix. Heroin. Please.'

She stood there watching me shivering and shaking.

'You are sick?'

'Yes, I am very sick. Please help me.'

I was on the verge of sobbing as another spasm shot up my spine.

'Give me money, 100 Marks. I go for you. Wait here.'

I was too sick to play by the rules that dictate you never part with your dough until you have the drugs. I handed over the hundred; she lumbered off around the side of the station. I sat against the front wall of the Zoo with the rest of the scummy ratbags, trying to stop my legs from shaking uncontrollably.

It crossed my mind that the pregnant hooker hadn't asked for any money for herself.

Probably wouldn't be seeing her again . . . I scanned the other faces for another likely mark.

But then she returned, kneeling in front of me with her hand out. I took the two small foil wraps and she helped me to my feet.

'You go now. I get you what you want.'

'Thank you. Thank you. You've saved my life.'

'Ja, ja. You go home now. Get off the street.'

She was turning away from me as she spoke, obviously over her good Samaritan phase.

I hailed a cab and headed back to Viktoria Park and home. My hand was shaking so badly I could hardly get the money out of my pocket to pay the driver.

I ran up the stairs to my flat and immediately started tearing the place apart looking for the foil. I just couldn't calm down. Every nerve ending in my body felt like raw meat on a skewer.

Eventually, among the debris, I found some foil pushed down beside the cushion of the sofa.

With trembling hands, I unwrapped the gear.

There was no brown powder.

Just cigarette ash.

Shit.

I opened the other wrap: same story.

The bitch.

No wonder she hadn't asked for a tip. She had ripped me off. She could see that I was sick, but had turned me over. Götterdämmerung!

What now? I didn't feel up to going back to the Zoo again after dark. And, by morning, I would be too sick to pick up.

I had to act now.

I slowly made my way down the stairs, every step jolting pain through my legs.

I had done some exploring of Berlin during the previous few weeks and had sussed that there was one other place where I had the chance of scoring cold.

It was nearly 3 a.m. and most cabs were off the clock, so I walked for about half an hour, my arms wrapped around me, my teeth chattering. Finally a cab pulled in and I climbed inside.

'Mitte, bitte.'

Mitte is the happening new city centre on the east side of town. Oranienburgerstrasse was the main drag, lined with restaurants, bars and clubs. It also had a small, but busy, tarts' strip.

It wasn't far. I had already walked most of the way. The taxi coughed me out on the main street. I walked down it, my eyes darting left and right into dark doorways searching for a friendly face.

There was a girl up ahead on the corner of a street junction. She saw me approach and put an unlit cigarette to her lips. I can only presume that she asked me for a light in German.

I shook my head. I couldn't speak.

She took a closer look at me and then walked away.

'Junky,' she muttered under her breath.

I pushed on, desperate.

The absence of traffic meant that there wasn't much trade: most of the girls had gone home.

Another shadow crossed my path.

She looked to be about 19 or 20, her bleached hair showing dark black roots and her heavily made-up face giving her a hard edge.

'P-please, can you help me? I need to find some heroin.'

'Heroin? There are no dealers here. Go to Bahnhof Zoo.'

'Please, don't turn away. Come back.'

I was jogging to catch up with her as she walked away.

'Please can you help me?'

I was nearly crying now from the effort of simply standing up. I doubled over as my stomach cramped, tightening into a small, knotted ball.

'I have some, but you pay me.'

She had stopped walking and I straightened up.

'Sure, how much?'

'One hundred.'

She reached into her jacket pocket and took out a small balloon of gear.

It was only a quarter. A hundred Marks for a lousy quarter. She could see that I was sick, desperate, and she was sticking it to me.

I had no choice.

But a quarter wouldn't be enough.

I needed to smoke at least double that to strike the balance between my body and the drug once more.

This was hopeless.

'I have a spare works for you.'

'Works?'

'Ja, a needle. It's clean. See.'

She held up the syringe still in its sterilised plastic wrapper. Maybe there was a way out of this nightmare. If I shot the dope into my body, its effect would be exponentially more powerful than if I smoked it. It could carry me through until morning. Then I could get over to Bill's – the cops would probably have sprung him and I would be able to score.

I fumbled for the money, dropping coins all over the pavement. She handed me the wrap and the needle, and took the cash.

There were more taxis now, picking up the clubbers spilling out onto the street.

I hailed one and headed home.

It really takes something to plunge a metal spike into your body even if it is a 0.5mm insulin-injection syringe. As I sat there on the toilet, the works in my hand, I wasn't sure I could go through with it.

I had started cooking up as soon as I had got home. I had seen it done many times before – several of my school friends had descended into the bottomless pit of addiction during my now dim and distant days of growing up in east London, so I knew exactly what to do. I took a metal dessertspoon from the kitchen drawer and as carefully as possible emptied out the wrap into its

MR NASTY

218

centre. I had unwrapped the syringe and sucked it full of water from a glass I had poured. I then squirted the water over the gear. It had been cut with so many impurities that it wouldn't dissolve.

I held my lighter under the spoon, and slowly heated it until it began to boil gently, so the liquid became a transparent, golden brown. Ripping the end off a cigarette filter, I placed it in the centre of the small brown pool, and touched the tip of the needle on the sodden foam mass. Very carefully, I drew the liquid up into the pump of the syringe, the cotton of the cigarette tip an impromptu filter to drain any nasty toxins lurking in the street smack.

So I sat there, my upper arm tied off with my belt and my veins throbbing in the crook of my elbow.

I could do this.

Just one shot and I would be feeling better.

I dug the needle under my skin at an angle. Shit, I missed the vein. I withdrew it and tried again. The wafer-thin metal sliced into the blue line running from my elbow down to my hand. It didn't hurt.

I pushed down the plunger slowly, all the way, until blood spurted back up the needle from its pressurised confinement in my vein and dripped into the pump.

I loosened the belt and then it hit me.

Like a sledgehammer.

My pain instantly dissipated. This was the most intense high I had ever experienced.

I went to stand, but slipped back, cracking my head against the toilet cistern. But I felt nothing. The drug enveloped me. My arms and legs were floating as I lay on the bathroom floor.

I don't know how long I stayed there. Maybe a couple of hours. It was only when I finally crawled into my front room that I realised that the needle was still in my arm.

I plucked it from my flesh and carried on crawling to the bedroom. As I lay back, the possibilities flooded my mind.

If shooting a quarter could give me a high like this, then I wouldn't need to be smoking my way through a gram a day. After all, if I only used sterile needles, where was the danger? It was just a pinprick.

I had just given myself my wings, and I was as incorruptible as the professionally embalmed.

Yeah, I was hooked on the shit. I needed to max out my money: injection was an economy manoeuvre, it made sense. Didn't it? It's absolutely incredible how getting that fix just washed away the preceding hours of pain and desperation. Heroin is a vicious mistress. She will trick you, hurt you and ultimately kill you.

The next day dawned: pouring rain.

It matched my mood: I was physically dependent on smack, a junky – the lowest of the low. Amateur psychology aside, I now needed to arrange my days around the need to score enough gear to keep me straight. I waited until ten and then wandered over to Kaiser Bill's. Thinking about my future was like looking down the wrong end of a telescope. The practicalities of my dilemma were all that concerned me now.

He let me in on my second ring and I made my way upstairs. 'Scheisse,' he said, 'you look like crap.'

'That's no way to treat your best customer, Bill. Anyway you don't look so great yourself.'

'That's because I spent the night at the police station. They bailed me at eight o'clock this morning.'

'What's the damage?'

'Taking a motor vehicle without consent, and possession.'

'What about intent to supply?'

'Nah. They're letting the pot ride and treating the horse as being for my own personal use. Anyway, what can I do for you? I need to get some sleep.'

'Just four quarters.'

He pulled his small wooden box from a sideboard next to the dining table and counted out four wraps.

'I don't suppose you know where I could get a few sets of works?'

If Bill was surprised, he masked it.

'I never keep spare needles in the flat. I know a chick who gets her works from the needle exchange in Friedrichschain. She's due in this morning to pick up. I'll ask her if she's got any spare. If not, I'm sure she can get hold of a few extra.'

'Cheers, Bill.'

I needed a supply of sterile syringes if I was to turn the small apartment into my own personal shooting gallery.

HIV and AIDS are rife among the drug community: I wasn't keen to die at the end of a dirty needle.

Oh no, not me: I was adopting a much faster form of suicide. After my initial panic over my addiction I became more accepting of it. I had fucked up and become hooked, but life went on. The heroin-induced haze in which I conducted that life went some way to cushioning the impact of my progression to becoming a full-time junky. A habit tends to focus your mind on only what is important to you as an individual: your next fix. Nothing else matters and self-analysis of your situation becomes secondary. OK, in an ideal world I wouldn't have chosen to be shooting up on scag, but I had dealt myself this hand and I would just have to play it.

The days rolled into weeks and I soon established a routine. I would have my wake-up fix as soon as I got up, usually a full quarter. At around two o'clock I'd shoot about a third of a gram with another third at about nine in the evening. Soon I was doing nearly a gram a day. So much for saving money.

Bill came through with a dozen spikes and told me he could get me more at short notice. The syringes were supposed to be disposable and thrown away after being used once. But they were slow to blunt, and I could use the same spike half a dozen times. The weight fell off me and, within four weeks of my first shot, I had lost 20kg. I was skin and bone.

I stopped while shaving one morning (this happened about once a week by this stage) and stared at my reflection in the mirror. My face was pale and gaunt, but it was my eyes that shocked me. They stared back at me blankly, except for some near-imperceptible thing, a subtle glint, a subliminal hunger, a craving for smack.

MR NASTY

How far would I go?

I had already stretched the envelope of addiction. Just how far down the razor's edge was I prepared to slide? Every day, I woke up with a monkey on my back, my hands shaking as I prepared the first scag of the day: I ensured that I always had enough in reserve for my morning fix.

Bill was open for business seven days a week. I always knew that I could cop. As long as I had the money.

One Sunday, when I had finished self-administering my opiate breakfast, I realised that I had screwed up. I pulled my money belt from under my bed. Inside was my last 5,000 DM traveller's cheque. But no cash.

Fuck-o-rama, I could have sworn that I had a couple of hundred in there. I must have been burning through my wedge faster than I thought.

No problem, go to the bank with my passport and cash the cheque. But that wasn't on; it was Sunday. Unlike London or New York, Berlin wasn't a 24/7 society.

All right then, I'd just have to find a bureau de change which was open and cash the traveller's cheque there. But that wasn't on either.

I tramped all the way up to the Ku'Damm where I was likely to strike lucky amongst the tourist crowd. I hit on every bureau de change open, but none of them would cash a cheque that size.

'You need to take it to a bank on Monday,' came back the inevitable answer.

But Monday was too fucking late as far as I was concerned. It was pouring with rain and I was now an hour overdue for my two o'clock shot. I had 40 DM in my pocket.

I walked back down to Bahnhof Zoo. Maybe I could find someone to split a quarter with me if I anted-up my 40 Marks. But the station was nearly deserted.

It was Sunday afternoon and the weather had turned. The working girls had seen it for the washout that it was and stayed home. The alkies were still there braving the downpour, but I couldn't get a sniff of any junk.

The Jones was starting to hit me as I cabbed over to Oranienburgerstrasse in Mitte. The ride chewed up 10 DM of my money, but I was shy of the 50 DM I needed for a quarter anyway.

Mitte was as barren as the Zoo had been.

I felt like everyone was doing this to me on purpose. Maybe all the dope monsters were hiding around the next corner ready to surprise me with a gram of Afghani brown.

I was losing it, big time.

I couldn't go to Bill's. He never gave credit under any circumstances and would cut off your supply if there was even a hint of hassle. I sat down on my haunches in front of a café and stared glumly at the pedestrians who passed me by. To them I was just another loser, a no mark, human rubbish.

I thought about begging and tentatively put my hand out. I was ignored for five minutes and packed it in.

There had to be some way to get some scratch together.

A young couple passed me by. I had seen them before somewhere. Now, where was it?

At the Zoo, I had seen them outside the front of the station. What were they doing here?

I watched them walk to the far end of the strip, and then return towards me. By the way the boy's head moved from one side of the street to the other, I sussed he was looking for something. If they had been at the Zoo and were now trying here, then they were looking to score. I stood up and started to follow them.

The rain dripped from my lank hair, and I must have looked half dead; withdrawal was fraying my edges like old, worn carpet.

'You need some help?'

I was behind them when I spoke and they turned to face me. They seemed young, about 18, dressed in the clubber's daytime attire of baggy cargo pants, trainers and trendy sweat tops. They were as bedraggled as I was. And surely on the hunt for something they shouldn't be.

'You speak English?'

'I am English.'

They looked at each other and then the girl spoke to her partner.

'Go on, Neil, ask him, I'm freezing my tits off here.'

'What are you looking for?' I asked, taking control of the situation.

'We're looking for some pills. We're here for the weekend and were up for going out tonight. A mate told us that we could score around the station, but that was a blow out. Someone there suggested we try here.'

They looked disconsolate. Poor dears.

'I can score for you, but it'll cost you 20 Marks for me to do it.'

Their faces visibly brightened.

'Yeah, but the pills are 50 Marks each. I know the guy in the sex shop over there. He deals them under the counter. How many do you want?'

'Fifty? That's a bit steep. How many d'you reckon, Maggie?'

'Just get two then.'

'OK, give me the 100 Marks for the pills and the 20 for me.'

I was already leading the way over to the gaudy shop across the road with enticingly advertised 'Kino booths, 5 DM.' We stopped outside and Neil handed over the money.

'You go in with him, Neil.'

He made as if to follow me up the steps into the shop.

'No, you stay here,' I said. 'My mate gets a bit twitchy if he's dealing to someone he doesn't know. You can stand by the door, I'm not going anywhere. I have to come out this way.' But I didn't have to come out that way at all.

Most sex shops have two entrances, one at the front and one at the rear to accommodate the shyer punter who may not want the world and his wife sharing his discreet porno moments.

I walked up the stairs and ducked through the shabby bead curtain.

I toyed with the idea of going back to them and saying I couldn't score but would keep the 20 Marks for my trouble – with the 30 Marks in my pocket, that would have given me enough for one of Bill's quarters.

But then I thought: fuck 'em.

I would keep the lot and get myself three quarters. Maybe it would teach them a lesson. Didn't they know that drugs were bad for them?

I legged it through the back door.

I could picture them standing in the rain, waiting for about 20 minutes before Neil plucked up the courage to enter the sex shop, only to be met with the blank-eyed stare of the assistant. And no sign of me.

I kept running all the way to Kaiser Bill's.

I was laughing at first, but then it gradually sank in. What was I doing? Was my need for the gear that bad? I had ripped off a couple of kids to feed my craving.

The rain pelted down as I returned from Bill's. I just had enough to get me through the rest of the day and for my morning fix.

I sat in my flat cooking up with trembling hands. It was now five o'clock and this shot was well overdue.

Shit, the smack had me locked down.

My every waking moment revolved around getting it together to score, then trailing back to my bolthole and cooking up my next hit.

My elation at getting the money together to feed my habit evaporated. Even the smack was no longer lightening my mood with its euphoria. The amount that I was shooting now was just enough to keep me straight. I was a full-blown addict, helplessly dependent on the needles full of scag I spiked into my arm. I had always viewed smackheads with the utmost contempt, yet here I was hustling with the street freaks for my next shot of Harry Horse.

I had sunk to the rock bottom of the barrel. I started to weep. It was uncontrollable, the sobs heaving my shoulders in a dance of despair. My great experiment, my grand plan, had gone spectacularly wrong.

I had to get myself clean.

Starting tomorrow I would start reducing the dose of heroin and wean myself off it.

Tomorrow.

But tomorrow was another country, the land of the future; and it always will be.

You'll be astounded to learn that I didn't stop the next day, or the day after that. I returned to Kaiser Bill's every day to collect my four quarters.

With rent to pay and my daily expenditure on gear, within three weeks I was down to my last 300 DM. I still had my return air ticket to London, so getting home wasn't a problem. But I had to get clean before I could go back. I was a junky on holiday, but I sure as hell wasn't going back to the UK as an addict.

It was a Monday morning when I woke up on my first day clean. It was March 1998, and I had been in Berlin for about four months: plenty of time for me to have developed a monster habit.

There was still the small problem of withdrawal to go through, but that could be dealt with. After all, it was just like a bad dose of the flu, nothing more. The smack had once again worked its evil magic on me and made me forget the pain of my first time in withdrawal.

The first 12 hours were not too bad. I was twitching uncontrollably, my arms and legs jitterbugging spasmodically to a rhythm in my brain that I couldn't switch off. A bottle of vodka helped dull the pain. Then it came on like a shit storm.

Lightning bolts of electricity shot through my arms and legs. My stomach was a tight knot of pain. I lay on my bed, my legs scissor-kicking, my body refusing to keep still for a second. My bowels, which had been constipated, packed stip-solid for weeks, decided that it was time to open the floodgates: I found myself glued to the toilet, shivering.

I wasn't going to make it.

It would be another 72 hours of this torture until the gear was out of my system. Every nerve ending in my body seemed to amplify any external reaction. They stabbed knives into my feet when I walked and eviscerated my back when I lay down.

I couldn't take it.

I don't remember leaving the flat, but I was at Bill's place leaning on the buzzer. I still had an hour to go before midnight, and prayed that he hadn't decided to turn in early.

He was in. Thank God. He buzzed me upstairs.

'Jesus, Mo. What's happening?'

'Tryin' to clean up. Can't hack it. Need to score,' I blurted out as I sat hunched on his sofa, the perspiration rolling off me as I shook to my core.

I still had the 300 DM and could afford four quarters. Anything, just to stop the pain.

'You've got to stick with it, Mo, if you want to get clean. How long have you been off?'

'A day.'

'Oh Jesus. Look, I've got something that will help you if you want to get through this.'

'What? Give it to me.'

'I don't give anything away. Do you know how many people turn up here as sick as you, begging for me to stand them a shot?'

He went to the sideboard and pulled out a small green plastic bottle of pills. 'Temazepam, 25 of them. They'll help you sleep through the worst of it. Take three of them now, and then three more every time you wake up. They'll put you out for a few hours at a time and get you through the next two days.'

Temazepam, commonly known as poor man's heroin. Inside the green bottle were high-strength tranquillisers which, when taken in quantity, mirrored some of the effects of smack. The favoured method of absorption, in Glaswegian housing estates, was to stick a needle through the outer gel capsule into the liquid centre, suck up the fluid and then shoot it straight up.

The side effects could be horrendous, ranging from blood clots to gangrene. But I was prepared to take anything I could lay my hands on and paid Bill the 100 DM he asked for.

I cabbed home and collapsed on the bed after downing a tumbler full of vodka to hasten the effect of the pills and stop the fucking pain.

I don't remember the tablets kicking in, but I went out like I had been hit by a train.

MR NASTY

The tazzies kept me under for about five hours. I woke and immediately washed down three more with vodka.

During the next day and a half I completely lost track of time. Every time I woke, I just took three more pills and, within 30 minutes, I was asleep.

I must have slept through the worst of the withdrawal, but when the tranquillisers ran out it was hideous. My body alternated between red-hot sweats and a frosty chill which iced my bones like shards of glass.

After the pills were finished, sleep was impossible. Hour after hour, I lay awake, occasionally praying for death.

I had been a big swinging dick in London, New York and LA. Now I was reduced to sweating this poison out of my system in a grotty flat a thousand miles from home.

I cursed my mental frailty for letting things get this far. I hated myself for my weakness. My weakness for the drug which had finally overpowered me. I was nothing. Less than zero. Another junky lying in his own filth with a face full of pain.

Even rock bottom has a bargain basement. And when you've scraped the bottom of the barrel, you can pick it up and see what's crawling around beneath.

I lay there for another two days before the pain started to clear. I was still very weak and shook with every faltering step I made. Another sensation was taking over though. Hunger. Not for smack but for food. My appetite had been suppressed for months and now it was in overdrive. All I could find was a box of cornflakes. I ate them without milk, cramming them into my mouth by the handful, gorging on them – anything to get some energy into my emaciated body.

I must have lost about 30kg and my skin hung on my skeleton like a dusty rag.

By the fifth day I was back on my feet again and made a tentative visit to the local supermarket to stock up. The sunlight pierced my eyes as if I had fixed razor blades to my retinas. I bought some bread, butter, corned beef and some ice cream. It was all I could keep down.

MR NASTY

After a week off the scag, I was beginning to return to normal. Sleep still eluded me: I stumbled around my flat like a zombie all day and lay awake all night feeling sorry for myself. I couldn't stay here any more. Tomorrow would bring a knock on the door as the rent was due.

I was still a bit shaky as I packed my bags, but I was beginning to feel like a human being again. I was emerging from the twilight half-death that the heroin deity gives its disciples, in return for their unswerving loyalty.

I made my way by taxi to the British Airways office in the centre of town and got myself on the seven o'clock flight to London that evening. Another chemical holiday, another bitter lesson learned.

If you decide that smack is your drug of choice, be prepared to pay the piper. There are people who have maintained a scag habit for decades. They are the lucky ones.

Allegedly. The others end up being scraped off some skanky toilet floor after a hot shot of cut gear or horse too pure for their depleted systems to handle. Few emerge unscathed. I was no different. I was mentally and emotionally devastated.

It took me nearly a year to get back on my feet. A year of endless therapy sessions, of waking up screaming in the middle of the night thinking that I could still feel the pain of going cold turkey crumbling my bones and crushing my spirit. I suffered alone. I told neither friends nor family of what I had been through. I was actually ashamed of myself. I had always tried to control any given situation and manipulate its outcome. Drugs had taken control of me and my weakness had been exposed. I conducted a cosmetic exercise of patching up my smashed ego, but couldn't quite make it to a full recovery. I capitulated to the fact drugs weren't finished with me just yet. There's no such thing as a cured addict. All addicts who manage to get themselves clean are in a constant state of recovery. Lapses are more common than continued abstinence and temptation lurks amongst the shadows. I had been to hell and back, but I still wasn't done. I often wondered what the fuck was wrong with me that I couldn't just walk away from the whole crap-shoot and, more importantly, stay away. Drugs had punched so many holes in my mental defences that my psyche leaked away its willpower like a cranial colander.

My physical recovery was essential and I joined a gym and got back in shape. You've just got to suck it up and take the pain.

The mental side of things was a lot more complex. Over the years, my personality had warped and twisted to such an extent that I quite simply couldn't function within the constraints of normality. I felt that living in the narco-world gave me life while the nine-to-five slowly killed me. I felt I wouldn't ever be able to guarantee that when the opportunity of my next score knocked, I wouldn't grab it with both hands. Subconsciously at first, and then with more conviction, I began to accept that this would be how my life would unfold: a cycle of addiction and normality, addiction and normality.

Sometimes you can push too hard and too far.

So far that you go over the edge, never to climb back again. Was that how it would end for me?

SYDNEY

MR NASTY?

After Berlin, it took time to rebuild my shattered perspective on life. Back in London, my internal stylecops initially vetoed any involvement with anyone connected at any level in the drugs scene – but how long would that last?

A few quiet pints and a game of darts down at the local pub was as good as it got, and I hated it. Pulling myself out of my malaise was a slow and painful process. I held down a series of menial jobs, drifting on subsistence wages, as I struggled through the spring and summer of 1998. I had fallen a long way. Where once I had skyrocketed from one hot-shot position to another, I now found myself cleaning floors and flipping burgers. To be honest I wasn't really up to much else.

My drug-fuck was total: crushing depression weighed me down like an anvil. But I stayed clean for six months.

People around me noticed the change, and their kind words urged me on to better things. Therapists encouraged me to explore the inner child within my psyche; addiction counsellors prodded me towards thinking that I was a decent member of society. The great and the good poked around the inner workings of my mind in a vain attempt to crack the code and understand why I did the things I did. Why my index finger permanently hovered above the self-destruct button. They didn't get very far. My recovery was largely due to the inherent survival instinct that had carried me this far and which would fool me into thinking that the concept of mortality simply didn't apply in my case.

Slowly I began to rise from the dark, entombing hole into which I'd dug myself.

After getting through this initial crapped-out phase of wallowing in self pity, I found myself a reasonable job as an information technology consultant with a pioneering international new-media firm. But as my prospects improved, I found myself growing restless. I was tired of the UK. My outlook was jaded under its perpetual steel-grey skies. I was over London. Maybe this was what prompted my continual wanderlust, the need to seek thrills in situations where the ice is thin and danger always wears a new mask. Perhaps I needed to make a break for it and find my own feet once more. This was my disease: my perception that I was somehow unique, somehow superior to the office drones that surrounded me and filled me with contempt. Oh no, I wasn't like them with their mortgages and marriages sustained by familiarity and fear. This wasn't how my life was meant to be. It was driving me fucking insane. I was Cameron White, Mr Nasty. I'd had it all, lost it all and now I wanted it back. I just needed one more chance. My last chance.

Ploughing through another draggy afternoon at work, an ad in one of the office trade mags caught my attention: 'IT Recruitment Consultants Wanted: Sydney, Australia.'

Why not? The company would sort out a long-stay business visa for the successful candidate. The climate was fabulous. Maybe I could learn to surf. I looked up the website and fired off a résumé. Then it was back to work. I was Joe Citizen, on the square and good as gold.

Three weeks later Sydney called. The consultancy's managing director would be in London next week, was I available for interview? Too bloody right, mate. It really was that easy. I like to think that I've made my own luck, but if the truth be told, chance has always favoured me: my toast has usually landed butter-side

MR NASTY

up. The next Monday we were face to face. Cards on table: I had zero experience of the recruitment business. 'No bloody worries, mate, you'll be apples. It's 99 per cent down to attitude, right?' That I had in spades.

They would train me and hold my hand for the first couple of months while I found my feet Down Under. Even the basic salary would provide a good standard of living.

The company flew me out to Australia for two weeks to see if I liked it. What was not to like? Quickly I set about tidying up loose ends, and prepared for a voyage of discovery where the water runs down the plughole the other way.

My life had been devoid of drugs for six months after returning from Berlin, while I was recovering from heroin addiction. By now, however, the devil was dancing on my shoulder, invoking my dark side. I found myself starting to indulge once again.

I stayed away from smack – the memory of lying in agony in that Berlin flat still provoked residual retching – but psychologically I was edging back into narco-mania. The odd speed dab here, a few cheeky lines of coke there.

Chang was still my drug of choice, but I was determined to keep any all-night, every-night insanity firmly in the rear-view mirror – my heroin addiction was a past indiscretion that I would never repeat. I was a classic case though: countless addicts replace addiction to one drug by getting hooked on another. I actually fooled myself into thinking that doing coke was OK, as it was safer than smack and I could control my usage. I had as much chance of controlling the weather.

I seriously thought I had grown up. In fact it was the actual drug experience that was changing for me. The highs weren't quite so high and the lows less capable of overwhelming me. But there was something missing, something not quite right. I hadn't felt the adrenalin rush from being in the wrong place at the wrong time for so long that I'd almost forgotten how it tasted when that enervating mix of fear and excitement pounds through your system and takes you full tilt on some madcap, twisted ride.

My intentions for my new life on the other side of the world were honourable and true. But my heart beat faster every time I fantasised about stepping across the velvet rope that separated mere existence from truly living. I was addicted, not to drugs per se, but to the adrenalin of the drugs world. However, I was changing. It was subtle at first, but then I started to look around me for the first time. I started to view this new opportunity in Australia as a genuine chance to break free: but drugs hadn't finished with me just yet. During my dealing days in London, my motivation had been simple: the thrill of the deal, the money I earned and my expenditure of that money on what I wanted – drugs for my own consumption. However, the balance between the factors which drove me on through the drug world had altered and the equilibrium had shifted. My need to consume drugs, my addiction to the narcotics themselves, now far outweighed the deal itself or the money on offer. It sounds bizarre, but I was actually lessening my desire to experience that surge of adrenalin that I thought separated me from mere mortals and was replacing it in my hierarchy of needs with a basic, animalistic dependency on drugs. Maybe, just maybe, this change would offer me an escape route.

It was early 1999: the cabin crew sprayed everyone with disinfectant before we disembarked at Sydney International Airport.

'How do you know the poms have landed?' the okker next to me asked.

'Dunno,' I shrugged, reaching into the overhead locker.

'The 747 turns its engines off, but the whining goes on.'

Let's get the niceties out of the way.

From Bronte Beach to the showy affluence of Double Bay, from the quiet rustle of old money on the Lower North Shore to the screaming gay scene of Oxford Street, Sydney's vibrant beauty makes it a city for the young and young at heart. If you want to score in Sydney there are two drug districts. To the west of Sydney's urban sprawl, the heroin-ridden Western Suburbs, 'The

Westies,' in local argot, where Cabramatta is 'Smack Central'. To the east, the more tourist-friendly freak show that is Kings Cross. There are around 30km between Cabramatta and the Cross but their destinies are inextricably linked and increasingly preordained.

There are other locales, Redfern for instance, which host thriving narco-minimarts. But don't go there. The inherent ultra-violence can take you off the street. Permanently.

The rewards of scoring in Cabra? Cheap, high-grade high-purity heroin. And it's as easy to cop as getting the wrong numbers in the lottery. Dealers and runners descend on the local station every time a train pulls in. It's a feeding frenzy and highly unlikely that you will actually need to ask anybody for your drug of choice 'cos it comes to you, Blue.

If you choose the Western Suburbs as your playground, you'll probably be buying from a teenage foot soldier working for one of the Triad-related gangs who dominate Sydney's heroin trade. Distinctive tattoos on the hands and face are an instant tell.

You are unlikely to get ripped off in the epicentre of the city's scag trade, but you may find that you are one of the few Western faces cruising Cabra's streets. So be prepared to stand out from the crowd. Which leads to the downside of scoring in Cabra: police CCTV. Cameras are omnipresent in the borough as the predominantly Asian population seeks to regain its identity and reclaim the streets.

Cabra cops have a policy of targeting buyers rather than dealers. Street-level runners are blatant about their business but also ultra street-savvy. Smack here, as elsewhere, is sold in balloons carried in the runner's mouth so they can be swallowed quicksticks.

Very few cops here, or any place else, are going to hang around for three days monitoring a street dealer's turds on the off chance of fishing out a baby bust. And Cabra dealers are tough to catch: most can swallow their stash in a flash. Therefore the chances of arrest for the inexperienced buyer are quite high, particularly as the New South Wales Police Force is usually on some crusade to sweep the streets clean.

The amounts you'll be offered vary from a cap (roughly one tenth of a gram) for 30 of your Australian dollars; a quarter gram (perhaps the best deal for most users) at about A$70; through to a whole gram for about 250 Aussie buckeroos. To score whole weights (grams) you will need a good connection. But if you were serious about that, you'd know it already, wouldn't you?

I like to think I'm pretty street-smart, so Cabramatta held no fear for me. From April 1999, I was scoring hash tar there regularly. I had only been in Australia for three months and was already amping up my narco-activity, but it was really addiction that drove me now. Increasingly, I was able to keep off-street and conduct business by mobile phone. We'd only meet to pick up outside of Cabramatta.

I was booted and suited most of the time, holding down my lucrative head-hunting job, plundering IT companies in the Central Business District (CBD) and north Sydney of their senior staff. More often than not, my personal deals would be conducted in districts close to Cabra, such as Fairfield and Canley Vale, congruent stations on The Westies' smack train. Back in those mad millennial dotcom days, Charlie didn't visit Cabramatta. My drug of choice however remained cocaine.

Cocaine was available, via some fairly sketchy connections in the CBD, at A$200 a gram. But to describe the quality as appalling would be like saying the Pacific was damp. Sometimes describing the merch as 'cocaine' meant that the powdery substance on offer may once have sat in a room near some real cocaine for a few minutes.

Even moderately pure coke was all but impossible to get hold of in Sydney at the end of the 1990s. Ecstasy, 'eckies' if you're talking Australian, and speed were pretty easy scores, but there, too, quality was sub-standard. E was mainly shipped in from Europe; speed distribution controlled by Hell's Angels and other biker gangs.

Amphetamines in God's Own Bloody Country are largely produced by the distillation of cold and flu remedies: so not only is Australian speed about four times the price of its Euroland counterpart – at street level, expect to pay around A$100 a gram – but consumers are basically buying concentrated ephedrine. Oh yeah, the buzz is there, but the comedown is hideous.

To all intents and purposes, I'd decided to stop bothering with Australian coke as a regular purchase. It was, to use the rhyming slang the locals love, 'pony', as in pony and trap. Occasionally, I would come across some decent gear and would stock up, but for six months or so I kept my head down and grafted hard while partying on the weekends at some of Sydney's excellent clubs. Things were changing, however, and it became apparent, to me at least, that there was a massive shift in the focus of the major Australian gangs. Smack was on its way out and cocaine was set to replace it.

With the Asian gangs retaining a stranglehold on the heroin market, they could apply the laws of supply and demand. As we passed into the new millennium, smack droughts were becoming increasingly regular as the gangs stockpiled supplies to keep the streets dry. The authorities and press saw these droughts as attempts to drive the price of the gear up and, around New Year 2000, a gram of decent horse hit the A$600 mark in Melbourne. But this was just a side effect of the cartels' real motives. They were sitting on huge amounts of heroin for different economic reasons. Cocaine was coming, fast.

I was first offered coke by one of my Cabra connections early that year. With my predilection for gak, I naturally made a buy and found the quality surprisingly superior to the rubbish people had offered me in the CBD. This chang was about 50 per cent pure. Not great, but good enough for me to rapidly develop an increasingly rapacious habit. Not cheap at A$300 a gram either, but since I was pulling in about A$250,000 a year, my bank balance could stand it.

I was something of a novelty in the Western Suburbs: a mad pom in a suit scoring in an area where you learned to swim in hot water. I was also – unknown to me at the time – a guinea pig. As the jazz salts became purer and more available in Cabra, I quickly became a preferred customer.

My first exposure to the new powers in Australian drug distribution came as Sydney was looking forward to its Olympic bonanza: the economy was climbing like a cable car, the future looked bright and the coke was starting to flow. I was meeting a connection in Canley Vale in The Westies on an almost daily basis to pick up a couple of grams of medium-grade toot. But the word had gone out, and I was attracting discreet attention from certain parties in the distribution chain. In my Alexander McQueen suit and Armani shades, I looked like legitimacy incarnate. However, I was ignoring one of Mr Nasty's basic rules and sticking out like a sore thumb. Certain people wanted to see exactly who I was, because I represented the epitome of their new target market. Call it market research.

I had phoned ahead to my contact, a Vietnamese kid called Kiet. I first hooked up with him on the streets of Cabramatta during some of my early drug excursions to the Western Suburbs. Kiet must have been about 18: a smack addict, thin and eager to foster a dealing relationship with a prize catch like me: a cashed-up city boy willing to risk a ride on the smack train to The Westies to pick up his gear. We had quickly established a routine whereby we would meet away from the war zone of Cabra, where my presence would merit unwanted curiosity from the cops and low lifes, who would see me as a prime target for a rip-off. I had made Kiet as a foot soldier for one of the Triad gangs controlling the heroin trade at street level in the area, and wasn't to know that he'd been mentioning me in dispatches to his lords and masters.

Kiet was waiting for me at Canley Vale station. He was not alone. There was another Asian guy in the passenger seat of Kiet's four-wheel drive. He was introduced to me as Xian, but I could call him Jim. I came to know him as 'Asian Jim'.

'Let's go for a drive.'

I felt like I was wearing a silk shirt in a cold wind. Jim was pure gang member. He had the required tattoos on his hands and neck and was giving off the obligatory 'don't fuck with me' vibe. But I had to front this out – go with the flow to get my blow. We drove through suburbia for about 20 minutes before stopping outside a palatial home in a tree-lined Poshopolis suburban road. We parked up and Jim turned to me in the back seat.

'There's someone who would like to meet you.'

It was more a statement than an invitation. I was out on a limb. How could I refuse? John Cale's 'Sane fear is a man's best friend' flipped onto my internal jukebox as I dumbly nodded my acquiescence. Jim and I got out of the Landcruiser and headed into the house. Kiet stayed put, leaving me in uncharted territory with a stranger. This was breaking so many rules about scoring that I couldn't keep count. Jim rang the bell and spoke Chinese into the intercom beside the main entrance.

The foyer, and indeed the whole of the house as far as I could make out, was decorated and furnished in an oriental style. Japanese artworks hung on the walls alongside antique Chinese chairs and screens, and low coffee tables.

There was a reception committee in the foyer.

'I presume you are Mo?' said the urbanely dressed Caucasian as he tagged me with my adopted street name.

It reminded me of a stupid joke:

> Why do Australians go up at the end of their sentences?
> Because so many of their ancestors went down at the beginning of theirs.

I shook the man's perfectly manicured hand. His grip was bone-crushing. This individual was utterly self-confident. He was a player. His clothes suggested a premier-tier distributor: expensive, but not flamboyant. He was casually kitted out in a dark-blue linen suit, grey silk shirt, no tie and no socks, expensive sandals.

I wasn't smirking now.

He beckoned me into a lavish sitting room that opened out onto a good-sized pool, and indicated an exquisitely ornate, cushioned chair.

'I'm Steve.'

'Hi.'

'You don't fit the bill as one of our usual customers, Mo.'

He awaited my response.

'Really?'

There are seven different ways to say that word in English. Each means something different.

'You are buying quite a bit of coke from my runners.' He emphasised that they were his runners to put me in my place, show me who had the juice here. I knew the score and nodded concurrence.

'OK, Mo, here's the situation.'

Steve spoke pianissimo. I had to crane my neck towards him to hear what he was saying. This was someone who was used to being listened to.

'Is all of this gear for you, or are you supplying other people?'

The reality of the situation hit home. I wasn't here for my novelty value. I wasn't here because I was a regular customer. I was here to be evaluated as a potential recruit for Steve's distribution channel. More likely, on behalf of whoever was pulling Stevie's strings.

I suspected that my host was hot-to-trot but mid-level in whichever organisation owned his ass. This wasn't his house either, I surmised, but doubted that its real owner would be making an appearance. I did, however, have the uncomfortable sensation that I was being observed by others, unseen, somewhere within this palace of iniquity.

'Personal use, Steve. It's all strictly for personal use.'

'You like to party?'

'Work hard, play hard, fuck hard,' I laughed. 'That's my motto.'

Jim had taken a seat in the corner, and an Asian flunkey entered the room with a porcelain pot that he placed on the glass-topped table between us. There were gang tattoos on the tea boy's hands. In fact, they were identical to the tattoos on the hands of both Jim and Kiet.

'Tea, mate?'

Steve was going to be mummy.

I flashed back to Camden, trying to chill out Murph on the

brick-phone while the Widow McQuigley rolled around beneath her kitchen table. I remembered the tea on her table and had a Munch Screamy moment but canned it. I didn't have to drink the tea anymore. I didn't have to put myself in situations where I was playing patsy for the mob. My take on the whole situation was starting to change.

Whoever 'Steve' was, it was evident that he was in bed with some serious individuals.

He dismissed the servant with a quick flurry of an Asian dialect. It sounded Vietnamese to me, but I couldn't be sure.

My personal fear factor rose up another notch. I was already amped-up, out of my depth, operating away from the neutrality of a street deal, and I could feel the steady pull of Steve's tractor beam dragging me into a situation where my control of events would be limited, to say the least.

Apparently I had passed some sort of test because Steve now leaned forward and produced a snap-lock bag containing half an ounce of rock cocaine.

Most of the coke purchased at street level is a bastardised version of rock. For shipment in its pure form, coke is usually compacted into solid kilo bricks.

If you get hold of it like that it means that you're probably handling cocaine in its purest incarnation: 90 per cent plus. Straight off the boat.

Steve poured a lump onto the glass table. It looked like a couple of grams. He produced a cut-throat razor, the sort favoured by old-time barber shops, or Glaswegian psychopaths who want to give someone a facial chibbing.

For five minutes there was silence, apart from the clicking of metal on glass.

Once Steve had finished using the blade to reduce the rock to talcum powder, he cut two lines. They were huge, about a quarter of a gram each.

He reached into his jacket pocket and produced a snorting tube and handed it to me. I leant forward and hoovered a line up each nostril. It took about ten seconds for the coke to enter my bloodstream and explode in my brain with synapse-searing intensity.

This was grade A kit.

'Enjoying yourself, mate?'

Steve was grinning. He must have been in his 40s. His hair had silver streaks and he was well tanned. Every move reflected the poise of an individual who's used to having the upper hand. A nod and a sniff was all I could muster by way of reply. I must have been under the ether. Perhaps I was still naively hoping that Steve wasn't going to make a move on me. Just keep your mouth shut and it'll be OK? Fat chance.

'Mo,' Steverino said, 'I am more than happy for our arrangement to continue on its current basis, but from the look of you I figure you must be working within a corporate environment. Perhaps you know some like-minded individuals, people like you who may want a taste of this as well.'

He cast his eyes downward towards the miniature mountain of white powder on the table between us. When his gaze returned to mine, any pretence of friendship had caught the first bus out of town.

'Think about it, Mo. I can sell you an ounce at this quality for four grand. Even if you step on it, you can make a tidy profit and have your own fun as well.'

Again, more fact than offer.

'My guess is that four grand wouldn't be too difficult to get hold of for someone like you, and an ounce shouldn't be too difficult to move on a regular basis. You would be sitting on top of the pile if you persuaded more like-minded individuals to join your enterprise. Then we could start talking about kilos.'

It wasn't just the chang jangling my nerves now. I recognised the pattern here. You buy coke. You deal with it. One day your dealer gives you up to their connection: 'Someone wants to meet you.' You take a ride. Your new best friend offers you hospitality in the form of mind-warpingly good Avianca. They suggest that you could move some product. You'll be dealing volume, so you get more gear, better and cheaper. But you have to deliver the market and the cash. Regularly. My interior warning lights lit up like a Christmas tree. Bells rang, klaxons sounded and the price of parachutes skyrocketed.

Time to be canny, careful and wise. Steverino may well have had the capacity to use that razor for more than just racking out a few lines. He had an outward appearance and demeanour that could make him pass for a perfectly reasonable kind of guy, but he was giving off the subliminal aura of a plenty-scary individual. You catch it for a fraction of a second, a glimmer in the eyes, a hand gesture made with intent. This guy would slash and burn without hesitation if he felt his authority wasn't being respected. A straight refusal was definitely not going to be a shrewd move on my part.

'I don't know,' I said. 'I would have to ask around a few people, see if they were interested.' It didn't sound like a convincing response to me, but he seemed to accept it at face value.

'No problem. Take your time. Xian will make sure you get back to the Vale.'

The meeting was over. We stood, shook hands and I was driven back to the station in a state of semi-terror and coke-induced psychosis by Kiet, who had waited in the car outside.

'Shit, shit, shit on a shitty stick,' I muttered to myself during the train journey back to the CBD.

It was mid-afternoon and my job as a head-hunter meant that I was expected to be out and about schmoozing IT clients for much of the working week. Not socialising with Asian Jim and his homeboys.

To say I had misgivings about accepting Steve's proposal would be like describing the universe as largish. I had more chance of winning the Melbourne Cup, without a bloody jockey on my back, than moving the amounts he was talking about. This wasn't like New York and Los Mescaleros. I had no built-in customer base in my workplace. Most of my colleagues led lives of unbelievable virtue. My coke usage was mainly a solo operation. But I knew that he was assuming I would accept. In fact, I figured that I had no choice in the matter. The lure of virtually pure rock was tempting, but I didn't want to get involved with these larrikins.

MR NASTY

Steve had shown his hand as a distributor for one of the gangs. He certainly wasn't the top man, yet he still scared the living shit out of me. I could only guess at how frightening a proposition his paymasters were. Steve was just a front, an acceptable, legitimate face. They basically wanted to use me as another route into the CBD.

I had no choice than to sever my links with Kiet as my coke connection. I just wouldn't call him again. I would have to get my supply from another source. Only it wasn't quite that simple.

My meeting with Steve took place on a Friday afternoon, and I had scored a gram off Kiet for the evening's entertainment. Saturday morning dawned and I was faced with the problem of establishing a new connection.

There was a guy called Bugsy. I had scored some dope from him a few times before, and he had mentioned that he had some coke connections. He was a bit of a wildcard. Bugsy must have been about 50: tall, lean and mean. He always wore a black shirt and suit, his dealer garb topped with a long leather trench coat.

I had heard stories about him extracting payment from delinquent customers with an aluminium baseball bat. But he had always played fair dinkum with me. I punched up his number.

Bugsy's stomping ground was to the west of Kings Cross, so we arranged to meet in the city, a quick trip up Oxford Street.

'I'll sort you out with some sonic snuff, ya bastard. No worries,' he snarled, and we arranged to hook up outside the block of units where he lived later that day.

'We gotta travel, mate,' Bugsy said. 'I gotta pick up some flight bags. My ute's in the shop, so grab a cab, OK?'

My nerves resumed yesterday's twitching and shifting when Bugsy told the driver our destination.

'Canley Vale station, mate.'

Cut my legs off and call me Shorty: I had only phoned this psycho because I wanted to avoid The Westies at all costs. Now here I was riding straight back into bandit country.

Bugsy yabbered on his mobile, arranging to pick up. I should have been listening, but I was re-running yesterday over and over again like a movie behind my eyes.

Thirty minutes later, we arrived at Canley Vale station. And guess who was waiting in the Landcruiser?

Kiet.

In fact, I'd hit the daily double: Asian Jim was riding shotgun. You didn't need to be psychic to feel my vibes redline. Sure enough, Bugsy sensed my tension.

'Don't worry, Mo, these guys will drive us to the gear. It's cool.'

For every narcopolis, there's a gangland.

If the guys in the Toyota were surprised to see me with Bugsy, they were cool enough not to show it when we climbed in. There was no conversation during the journey. I offered many silent prayers to a multitude of gods that we weren't going back to see Steve in the house of horrors. After about ten minutes we stopped outside an apparently innocuous block of flats. Thank God, Buddha and all the little fishes my fears proved unfounded.

'Let's roll.'

Bugsy led the way as we clambered out of the car. Our destination was on the top floor. A solid steel door barred our way. Asian Jim buzzed the intercom and yammered Vietnamese into the speaker. We waited about ten seconds then the door clicked and we were buzzed in.

The first thing I noticed, and it wasn't easy to miss, was the high-calibre machine gun on the tripod in the foyer. The barrel was pointing straight at us. Bugsy read my vibes: I was cranked up tighter than the high e in a soprano's anxiety.

'Take a chill pill, Mo,' he said. 'I'll get sorted and you can get yours on the way back into town. Just let me pick up, yeah, mate?'

I wasn't going to argue.

Kiet had gone back to the car and Asian Jim led us around the gun and into a room off the hallway. There were two guys sitting on a sofa bed in a sparsely furnished lounge. Both Oriental. Both sporting gang tattoos on their hands.

Bugsy produced a wedge of cash. It looked like a couple of

grand. One of the dealers left the room and we stood in absolute silence for a couple of minutes. The man returned with a snap-lock plastic bag containing what seemed to be half an ounce of blow. But it wasn't powder. This was rock.

Bugsy beamed at me as he pocketed the bag.

'You are gonna thank me for this, mate. This gear will take the top of your bloody head off.'

Asian Jim remained silent throughout the exchange. Even as Bugsy and I left, he zipped his lip – but he gave me a knowing look as we circumnavigated the hallway artillery and exited the building.

Asian Jim stayed behind, so it was just Bugsy and I who got into the back of the car with Kiet in the driver's seat. We sped off back towards the station.

'Crazy fucking gun, eh?'

Bugsy had his psycho grin on again.

'If any fucker tries to get through the steel door with some thermal bloody lance, they'll get blown to fucking bits by that motherfucker. Nobody takes their gear over.'

There must have been a substantial amount of gak in the flat and I nodded, wondering whose gear he was actually referring to.

Unwittingly, I had been led straight back into the lion's den. Skip the starter, go straight to the main course: Cameron White on a platter of mixed veg.

Bugsy got the Charlie out of his pocket. Yep, it was rock all right and it looked pure, with a slightly sallow tinge that indicated that it was probably straight out of Bogotá.

'Have you got a blade on you, mate? I'll cut you off a slice, or do you want a taste first?'

The grin had disappeared from Bugsy's face now, and the inside of the car was suddenly crackling with tension. Jesus Christ. Now what? Everything had been going OK. Not perfect, but OK. Now Bugsy had picked this moment to go all moody on me. Something was up.

That's the trouble with doing business with someone who is quite clearly psychotic. They shift up through the gears until they are running in insanity overdrive. It happens at the drop of a hat and without reason: Bugsy had just crossed the line into demonic dealer mode.

Kiet was watching me in the rear view mirror.

This was a test. Bugsy had chosen this moment to see if I was the real deal. If I was just another punter mooching for a one-off score, or worthy enough to be on his preferred client list? All dealers need the reassurance that their customers can take the heat if the nightmare scenario goes down and they're busted. I had learned from my dealing days in London that a little intimidation can go a long way to inspiring the required level of dealer–customer loyalty. If I asked for a taste it would prove how big my balls were, but it could also trigger Bugsy's unpleasantness.

A split second, then I was compelled to call.

'No worries, Bugsy, just cut me off a weight.'

Now, I did carry a blade. Well, actually it was a Swiss Army penknife that my employer used to dole out as a promotional gift for clients. It wasn't a weapon to be used in anger. I used it to chop out lines. Bugsy stared wide-eyed for a second or two at the penknife.

'For fuck's sake, Kiet. Look out, we've got public enemy number one with us. That's not a bloody blade, mate. Now this . . . [Bugsy reached into his leather trench coat and pulled out a gleaming machete] . . . is a bloody blade.'

It was more than 18 inches long. This wasn't Bugsy's tool for chopping out lines; this was the passport to an impromptu amputation for anyone who fucked with him.

Kiet was still watching in the rear view and there was a second of real stress (me) before an explosion of laughter (them).

Bugsy surfed the mirthquake as he cut me off a lump of coke, and he was still chuckling when Kiet dropped us at the station so we could cab our way back into town. I laughed along with Bugsy, but couldn't help wondering if he would have shredded me had I questioned his integrity by asking for a taste. The penknife had defused the situation. Being the butt of a gag, I reckoned, beat ending up as diced meat.

Another deal done, but I wasn't going to continue business with this lunatic anymore.

Bugsy was clearly unstable. And he was in bed with the people I wanted to avoid at all costs. I would have to make another new connection. I only had one route open to me now: time for a coke hunt in the Cross. I had scored weed there before from the dipshit dope dealers, but hadn't carried out a mission where cocaine was on my menu. This had every chance of turning into a black-bag operation. The initial subconscious changes that had started ocurring within me were now amping up their voltage, replacing the adrenalin fix of dark deals and quick scores. Satisfying my narco-impulse was turning into hard work.

Kings Cross is a stone's throw from the CBD, but couldn't be more different if it was twice as odd. The Cross's main drag stretches north from William Street, and runs down to the massive Bourbon and Beefsteak Hotel on the corner of Darlinghurst Road and Macleay Street.

Sydney's sleaze district first attracted the wrong crowd during the early 1970s when US servicemen from Vietnam would dock at the nearby naval port for some rambunctious R&R.

The Cross still houses legal brothels, porn shops and strip joints. After darkness falls, it kicks off its heels and comes to life. Human flotsam and jetsam drift out to play amid the strip's gaudy neon. This is a freak show where the drug food-chain's bottom-feeders shift in the shadows. It caters for all tastes, but act like a drug tourist and you will get ripped off. All the dealers on the street are merely runners for their distributor. If you seem green, they'll take your money and scram. So, don't buy off the street. If in doubt, ask a hooker: there's no shortage.

It is worth A$100 to get a working girl to introduce you to her connection as, like elsewhere on this narco-planet, street prostitution and drug dealers are tighter than a photo finish. Get a connection and, more often than not, they will deliver what you require at a predetermined point away from the mainstream action. Discreet. Safe. Nice.

There used to be a thriving marijuana dealing business on Roselyn Street, which bisects the main drag. The now notorious bars where weed was openly sold, like Café Amsterdam, were closed by tabloid pressure in the run up to the 2000 Olympics. There are still weed dealers in the area, though, and occasionally you'll hear someone mutter, 'Smoko, mate?'

Dope deals are usually pretty straightforward, and it is unlikely that you won't actually get what you want, but A$20 only buys a tiny satchel of stuff. Anybody who offers you heroin or cocaine here should be studiously ignored. They're clowns. Buy from them and you are too.

The Cross has two sides to its strip, geographically reflecting who controls each. Two individuals have had the juice of late. Let's call the player on the eastern side of Darlinghurst Road Smithy, and his west-side counterpart Jonesy. The shifting fortunes of both identities are a key indicator of the shift in emphasis within Sydney's drug culture. Both appeared untouchable as they battled for supremacy. Now, the power behind their thrones has come to light.

Jonesy dealt exclusively in smack, while Smithy seems to have embraced cocaine and, last time I looked, operated with apparent impunity from local law enforcement personnel. The Cross has always been the epicentre for police corruption in New South Wales. Rumours abound of massive pay-offs to the boys in shiny buttons. It was explained to me like this:

> Look, mate, when a new politician comes in and takes over in New South Wales, they've won on a ticket of cleaning up the corruption and vice, OK? Well, at a certain point during their administration's honeymoon, a box is delivered, and someone suggests they should take a bloody long look. Inside the box are prints of cabinet members, friends and associates doing things they certainly shouldn't be. At the bottom of the pile of pictures is a sheet of paper. It's a few suggestions from the people who own the negatives.

Hard evidence is curiously scarce, but given many true blue Aussies' pride in their convict heritage, rumours that the constabulary may be bent aren't exactly astounding. Call it vibes, call it karma, but the drug subculture lures its own.

It didn't seem convenient, in the sense of keeping my head firmly attached to my neck, to keep scoring in Cabra. So I made some useful connections in the Cross.

From the get-go, I perceived the smack trader's fortune waning as a massive influx of severely cut cocaine hit street level. The droughts imposed by the Asian gangs severely ate into Jonesy's smack business.

Both players had substantial assets along the strip: massage parlours, brothels and girlie bars where the sex and drug trades operated like conjoined twins. The past few years have seen a mass liquidation of real estate assets by both operators in a bid to gain control of the jewel of the Cross: the sprawling Bourbon and Beefsteak, a labyrinth of restaurants, gaming rooms and bars which would be the ideal springboard into legitimacy for either player and, more importantly, a perfect staging post for an all-out narcotic assault on the CBD and pastures further afield.

Events beyond his control took Jonesy out of the game and into prison. His lords and masters, the Asian gangs supplying his smack, were less than pleased at his attempt to legitimise his business interests and move away from the new cocaine market they were then developing. A clear indictor that smack was now yesterday's product.

The word was that Jonesy went down for the murder of a low-level rival rather than narco-related charges. Any way you look at it, he is gone and Smithy rules the roost in Cocaine Central: my rare encounters with Smithy have led me to believe that the Asian gangs are now expanding their influence in the heart of the city, as planned.

The inhabitants of the Cross make the boys and girls in Cabramatta look like stock brokers. If I had stood out in Cabra, then in the Cross I might as well have had a neon arrow pointing down at my head. I was scoring every day, as street deals invariably didn't operate on a volume basis. It wasn't long before all the coke dealers along the strip knew who I was and what I was there for. The jungle drums went into overdrive as the coke-head pom in the suit started making waves. I was attracting attention again and being monitored by the forces of darkness.

This was December 2000, and it was then evident that Charlie was in charge of the distribution channel in the Cross. The street was flooded with runners selling A$60 caps of cha-cha-chang to the world and his wife. Jonesy's demise meant it was nearly impossible to score heroin on the street here anymore.

I was summoned to the court of the now dominant Smithy for the same reasons that I had been hauled to an audience with Steve out in The Westies: I was working in the CBD, so provided a potential distribution channel amongst the suits.

The two meetings I had with Smithy took place in his office above one of the girlie bars on the west side of the strip, which he now controlled almost in its entirety.

I first met him when a runner collared me one evening as I was making my post-work pick-up run in the Cross. Once again it was the usual request: 'There's someone who would quite like to meet you.' Who was I to refuse?

The adrenalin was already starting to pump through my veins, but where once I would have savoured the thrill, I now felt only fear.

I followed the runner down Darlinghurst Road and up some dimly lit steps. We must have climbed about four levels before I was eventually led out into an office area.

Smithy sat behind a desk that looked like it had been lifted from a Victorian accountant's office.

Feather-quill pens? Check.

Ink wells? Check.

Mid-level street distributor plus Samoan giant who looked like a couple of small cars welded together and then supercharged with steroids? Double check.

Everyone clear on their job? Oh yeah. Let's go.

'Take a seat, Mo.'

The conversation was polite but to the point. Cue the offer of pure rock cocaine. Cue sample. Four grand an ounce – too similar to be coincidence?

At the time, I didn't make the connection. I just wanted to get the hell out of there. Once again, I had been propositioned to move high-grade bugle within the CBD. Once again I declined the offer. I may have been a user, but my journey through Planet-narco had finally convinced me, for all my past braggadocio, that I was not cut out to be a dealer at any level any more. The rush was gone. Mr Nasty was shedding his skin.

Permanence and narco-commerce are oxymoronic. It was dawning on me that my sell-by date was looming. Fast.

The thought hit me then that this guy was a little too close to the action to be the player he was supposed to be. Anybody within 50 metres of the drugs on the street was nothing more than a distributor.

But Smithy drove a Bentley and a Jaguar XK8, so he must have had some juice backing him up. He was being squeezed by the Asian drug-gang suppliers to get more product to market and, in turn, he was squeezing me to further his ambitions. I recognised it as the threat it was and not the opportunity he presented it as. Burrell had done the same thing to me in New York and back then I had played the game to see where it took me. But now, I wasn't playing by Mr Nasty's rulebook: in fact, I had torn it up. I knew that if I stayed in the drugs world then my luck would eventually run out and I would be banged up or blown away like the human debris I had by then become. I could almost hear the clock ticking. The tantalising walk along fear's tightrope was replaced by anger and feelings of depression that it had come to this. Who the fuck was this guy to put the hard word on me and how stupid was I to have landed myself in this situation again? I was tired of it all.

There were other factors to consider.

Not only was my dependency on the thrill of the deal waning, but despite my best attempts to prolong my bachelorhood, I had fallen in love.

It had started as an office affair, the kind that spring up all the time and usually wither and die once the throes of unkindled passion fade to black. This was different.

I had found a wonderful woman who enjoyed the party lifestyle as much as I did, but managed to fuel her enjoyment of clubs and music without relying on artificial stimulants. She knew about my drug use and accepted that it came with the package, but I knew that if we were to have a long-term future I would have to clean up my act.

As the relationship blossomed, I noticed that I wasn't scoring as regularly anymore. My appetite for drugs, once such a dominant force in my life, was dissipating with my new mood of optimism. I realised that I wanted respite from my headcharge along the knife-edge of living close to the danger zone. My craving for adrenalin was replaced by the curious desire to see how my life might have been if I hadn't sold that first pill in a London club. What was going on? Had I just lost my bottle? Had the drugs finally burned away too many brain cells? No. I was simply facing up to the real world for the first time in over a decade. You know what I mean. It's the world that you live in. It's the world of a fair day's pay for a fair day's work. The world of having a sensible car and a small runabout for the wife. The world of two weeks' holiday a year with the kids and time off for Christmas. It's that world. Sure, I knew that I wasn't going to become a homemaker, complete with a pipe, slippers and a cocker spaniel called Toby. My old tendencies would sometimes seethe under the surface of my desired sense of karmic harmony. I had to accept it, deal with it, to move on and start my life for real.

I began to look ahead, away from the shallow delusions of a short-term future, which were all that my chemical romance with Charlie Chang offered.

Sydney was a paradise. Why the fuck was I wasting a golden opportunity, again? How many more chances like this would I get? Perhaps this was my last chance to live a life not perpetually thrown into a narcotic-fuelled turmoil.

I found myself mentally reprising and regretting my drug

induced journey round the globe: London; Amsterdam; New York; Los Angeles; Bangkok; Berlin; Sydney. Places I had visited all too briefly before hustling myself onto the next voyage down a sewer in a glass-bottomed boat.

The impetus within me was to make one final run for it. Not on another drug excursion, but towards a better life away from the endless power-slide towards self-denial and, ultimately, self-destruction.

When you get involved in drugs you are entering a downward spiral. It's a steep descent and you quickly gather momentum as you move from dealer to user to abuser to addict. At the lowest point of the spiral you drop off into freefall. Once you enter this stage there is only incarceration or death to look forward to, but while you are still descending the spiral, even if you are just clinging onto its bottom tip, there is the faintest opportunity to start the slow climb upwards.

My own mortality was catching up with me. Along with the sense that I could make a go of it as a normal member of the legitimate world. I still managed to clutch onto some semblances of a normal existence. I could still start to climb back up the spiral.

Work was OK: I was good at what I did for a living. I was well paid and could afford life's little luxuries. Which shouldn't solely consist of cramming as much brain-numbing powder up your schnoz as possible.

Berlin still weighed heavily on my mind. It would be all too easy to stretch the elastic band of destiny to breaking point. I had been right out to the edge of junk culture and had found that it wasn't worth visiting again. But it would have probably been all too easy to book a return ticket if I didn't get myself together and fly straight, sooner rather than later.

Every journey has an end. It was Christmas when I dealt my final hand in the drugs business. At a trendy apartment off Oxford Street, an easy walk from the Cross, the party people were all revved up and ready to go-go; but drawing blanks contacting their coke connections on their mobiles.

'Hey, Cameron, you're the bloody Martini man: you can score anytime, anyplace, anywhere, right, mate?'

Take a wild guess as to who trudged up to the Cross in the pouring rain to score for everybody that stormy night?

They wanted distributor-level coke, not street caps of crushed caffeine pills. So I was back in Smithy's office, but this time of my own volition. Once again, I found myself facing the same proposition. Nothing new there – except a greater level of urgency from Smithy. He craved outlets for his merchandise in the CBD, he needed them. Had to have them.

At Smithy's right shoulder, staring me right in the eyes was a familiar figure, Asian Jim. Reflected back at me in his eyes was the person I had turned into over the years: cold, reptilian, inhuman, Mr Nasty. I made my personal choice that night when I looked into Asian Jim's eyes: I was looking at my own mirror image. Maybe I had been that person once: the hustler, the player, the dealer. I couldn't be that person any more though.

Asian Jim stood before me. I noticed that his forearms were criss-crossed with deep wounds: fresh slashes a few inches across, made by something razor-sharp and wielded with extreme malice. His eyes followed my gaze to his mutilated arms. 'Don't worry about it. I stepped out of line.' Jim had been carved open like a leg of lamb by the people he worked for, the same people who now wanted me to work for them.

I was looking at someone, something, that I could be and would be if I didn't turn myself around: a victim.

He would carry those scars with him forever. But what about the scars that I carried? They weren't physical in their manifestation, but they cut deep nonetheless. I needed to start healing them before my personal fragmentation dragged me under one last time.

How long would it be before the cops scraped me off the floor of some scuzzy public toilet, a dollar bill up my nose or a syringe spiked into a vein? How long would it be before I was discovered lying in the filth and rubbish of some back alley with my head caved in and my body sliced to ribbons? In reality, it was only a heartbeat away. The possibilities of my own fatality were about to become a reality. My time in the narco-world was up and I knew it.

After a decade in the dead zone it wasn't an OD or a beating that gave me my epiphany. It was quite simply the acceptance of who I had been, who I was now and where I was ultimately heading – none of which looked to me like the kind of person I had envisaged myself being or becoming when I was seven years old and the tallyman came to call.

I had travelled from the Ecstasy-buzzed streets of London, where I'd first carved out my niche in drug land, to the imminent cocaine-driven warfare of Sydney.

I wanted no part of it anymore. I wanted to be away from the streets, the hookers, the runners; the men who treated making a profit as the main benefit of taking a life.

I had run so fast for so long that the tank was now empty. If I was to refuel, it had to be on my own terms, not at the whim of dealers who sought to make me a part of their crazed master plan to take over the world by drug domination.

I had so nearly had the life force squeezed out of me on so many occasions that I had learned to treasure it. Perhaps even to nurture it for better things in the future.

'You want this gear to go?' Smithy asked.

He had a quarter ounce of rock cocaine laid out on the desk in front of him. I could almost feel it calling to me, feel its mind-sizzling intensity as I snorted it, line after line. Asian Jim was giving me his laser-beam stare. I don't know where it came from, but at that moment a faint recollection dredged itself up from the recesses of my psyche and lodged itself at the front of my mind. I recalled an interview I had read with the Formula One racing driver James Hunt. He had been asked why he had retired from racing at the height of his powers. Hunt had replied that every driver reaches a pivotal moment where the realisation dawns on him that he is putting his neck, his very life, on the line each time he steps into the car on race day. Once that simple fact becomes part of a driver's mind-set he has lost that indefinable 'edge' that makes him not just a competitor but a winner. He may decide to continue racing, but he is no longer willing to take that additional, split-second gamble; that calculated moment of recklessness that can make the difference between being in pole position and just another runner in the pack.

I was experiencing the same illuminating, shocking self-perception in that moment.

I had lost that intangible quality that had spurred and protected me during my time in the drug world. Call it a survival instinct, street-savvy, pure luck. I had lost the mojo that had always made me ready to roll on race day.

'I'll have to get some more cash together for the quarter.'

'Sure thing, Mo, but don't keep us hanging. We need to start thinking about moving some serious weight from now on. Understand?'

'Yeah, I understand.' In that moment I understood everything. Completely. The simplicity of the choice before me was suddenly very clear to me. Life or death? Make your mind up, Cameron.

'I'll catch you later.'

'Be seein' you soon, Mo.'

But they would never see me again. I hadn't scored the gear. I hadn't made the choice to continue a life that would inexorably lead to my self-destruction. Fuck the people at the party. Fuck 'em all.

I walked out of the office and down the stairs leaving Mr Nasty behind. He's still there, somewhere: in my nightmares, hiding behind the sometimes fragile veneer of my existence, lurking just out of sight as the shadows draw in. Maybe he'll come out to play someday. I pray that day never comes.

What were you expecting? A happy ending? An instant turn around from my life as a drug monster? After I had walked down the stairs and out of Smithy's clip joint that night, my life didn't just fall into place. I wasn't rewarded for my decision to leave my drug years behind with an instant invitation to join the world of simple pleasures that go hand in hand with leading a normal life. I am burdened with the legacy that a life cutting a swathe through the drug world has left with me. Not a day goes by when I don't reflect on the destructive forces with which I have been involved.

But, I'm working damned hard to try and get there. If I'd picked up the coke for the party people on that December night in the Cross, I would have just dropped off the bottom of the spiral, into freefall and oblivion. I know how close I came in that moment and made the decision to start clawing my way back to the surface. I am not going to leave you feeling warm and fuzzy with a saccharine-coated view of how my life is now picture perfect after walking away from drugs. The truth is that it isn't. The three years that I have been away from the business have involved a continuous struggle to climb my way back up through the madness of my own destructive compulsions. I'm getting there, day by day, inch by inch.

Life's not easy, but I have discovered the factor that was absent from my personal philosophy, the missing link that I strove to find for all those wasted years.

Hope.

I hope to get through each day drug-free and savour the sense of achievement that it gives me. I hope to be a better person to the people I love and who love me in return. I hope that one day my dreams won't be clogged with the phantoms of my previous existence. I hope that I continue living my life, not merely existing within the framework that fate provides for me. I hope that each day clean I become a better person for it.

I live in hope.

POSTSCRIPT

THE POLITICS OF JUNK CULTURE

It's not easy living clean. But that's just the way it is for me now.

Drugs are everywhere. They surround me. Would I find it easy to live in a world where drugs were legalised and available to the masses? It's hard enough to get by without the pull of the drug world, illegal as it is now, sucking me back into its embrace.

I smoke cigarettes and drink alcohol, destructive legal drugs in their own right, without enough care for my long-term survival. If someone cracked open a fresh wrap of Charlie bought at the local licensed drug boutique, would I just get up and walk away? It's easy to say, what's the difference? A shot of vodka and a puff on a ciggie will end up shortening your life expectancy just as surely as banging a line of toot will. There is no solution to the drug problem where everybody wins. In my opinion, a progressive approach to legalisation will result in less crime, fewer deaths and a better society; but it doesn't mean that drugs are a good thing. Humanity in its wisdom will always devise ways of screwing itself, one way or another. Now is the time to face up to a problem of our own making and try to limit the damage somehow.

When all is said and done it's got to come down to the choices

MR NASTY

259

we make as individuals. The difference with me is that I have to make that choice every morning when I wake up, not just on a Friday night when the boys and girls are up for a party. If you choose to take drugs then that's your lookout and you should be free to make that decision for yourself. I am not about to preach abstinence. I can only speak from my own personal experiences, which have made me come to terms with the frailty of my own weakness.

I'm no different from any of you. You could have lived my life if you had succumbed and taken a wrong turn here or there. I'm not denying it was a ride while it lasted, it's just time to step off the ghost train.

Much of the drugs business is a front: its back end, violence and madness.

As both a narco-merchant and a user I have learned to live with moral ambiguity and residual guilt. Of course I realised that what I was doing would affect the lives of my buyers. But I found it too easy to blur the lines between right and wrong with serious money on the table and my drug of choice at my fingertips.

The ethics of my trade are deeply dodgy. Looking back, it seems that I was wrapped up in a solipsistic world of profit making and increasingly self-destructive extravagance as I made the transition from dealer to user. The pull of untold riches drew me in like a love-starved cobra. Like any narco-businessman, I rationalised that if I wasn't supplying the gear, somebody else would.

After the business in London nosedived and the cash from my early days of dealing dried up, I can't say that I didn't scrutinise my ethics more closely. My problem was that I chose to ignore the irrefutable outcomes of my self-analysis.

All drugs are destructive. Living is destructive, yet does that make us wish for death? After I left Smithy's table without my party bag, I wondered about the lives I'd taken down to my level. Were they my victims or my co-conspirators? Is humanity the problem or the solution? I don't pretend to have all the answers, only observations from my experiences of how the drug problem has played out in the past and how I see it developing in the future.

In my opinion, all drugs should be decriminalised so their supply can be carefully controlled. As it becomes clearer and clearer that the current approach to narco-commerce won't win the drugs war, I believe de facto legislation becomes increasingly inevitable. Decriminalisation would liberate the significant police and medical resources which are employed in dealing with the effects of drug abuse, and simultaneously reduce crime and make room in hospitals for the ageing population.

It's paradoxical, but to implement a successful international political solution to policing the narcotics industry, politicians need to de-politicise the problem and recognise that it's primarily a medical issue born of social and cultural catalysts.

Yes, monitoring and maintaining a state-run recreational-chemical network is a massive cultural challenge. But I believe it is one we must grasp with both hands. Or prepare for the whirlwind.

Let's examine the Petri dish of Sydney's narco-zone so we can see, in microcosm, how continued drug prohibition is empowering the suppliers while devastating the user population.

As Asian migration into Australia has increased to harmonise the nation's geo-political position, so, inevitably, has the prevalence of gang activity. New Asian crime cartels like Sing Wa run drug-trafficking, prostitution and migrant-smuggling operations, and have taken over the former predominance of traditional Hong Kong-based Triad organisations like the notorious 14K syndicate. The power that drives these organisations originates thousands of miles away in Asia, but the destruction within communities in Australia is not lessened by the geographical distance separating them – it's no different from the Colombian cocaine cartels' far-reaching influence on the drug markets of the US and Europe.

The Triads, Sing Wa and the powerful Singaporean-led Ah Kong syndicate don't have a total monopoly on Australia's narco-market – the Japanese Yakuza are gradually building a presence too. Even here we're just scratching at the surface of Sydney's free-market narco-world, where these established illegal corporations face constant competition from hungry and innovative rival up-and-comers: last time I looked, some less formally organised criminal outfits which have built a presence within the migrant Vietnamese community in the Western Suburbs of Sydney.

New groups are constantly emerging and evolving in Australia, based on the Triad and Yakuza concepts, or at least using their name to exploit the growing Asian population.

One of the biggest challenges for police intelligence is keeping track of the gang members as they cross borders. Australian Customs officials have, more than once, picked up known Yakuza members entering the country with around A$1m in cash. In 1994, the number of recognised Yakuza entering Australia amounted to 40. These 40 were only noticed because they were well known, so one might wonder how many unknown Yakuza associates come and go unnoticed by the authorities.

Europe faces a parallel problem: as the volume of immigrants from Second World nations shaking off the shackles of Communism rises, so it becomes exponentially more difficult to reliably vet immigrants for prior criminal histories or gang memberships. And this concealment of unscrupulous individuals' criminal pasts makes their reality more deadly.

Many Australian cops and politicians dismiss or underplay the influence of the Triads, and other Asian-based crime syndicates, operating within their national borders. However, throughout the world the narcotics enforcement industry hypes the monetary value of the contraband it seizes, and bigs up the significance of any narco-traders its police operations place in custody. It's in their interests to do so – politicians and career civil servants need to play to the media gallery. Like any other branch of government, the bigger the problem, the greater the perceived need for resources to solve it: there are careers and livelihoods on the line here, team-building issues of status and turf, powerful individuals' concerns about their reputation and legacy.

There is a vast, taxpayer-funded, economically inefficient industry devoted to tracing the origin of narco-transactions. Take, for example, Operation Dogshark, which in 2001 aimed to smash the Sing Wa combination's people-trafficking and drug-dealing operations. Through Operation Dogshark, Sydney police evaluated Sing Wa's assets at A$40m. The reality is, according to more accurate information within the public domain, that figure should be multiplied, conservatively, tenfold to reflect the cartel's power. Sing Wa is an economy within an economy, a society within a society: as long as drug prohibition continues, the violent crime and huge illegal cash flow it perpetrates will continue to pollute Australia unchecked.

Yakuza narco-money has been used to buy up and develop real estate, particularly on Australia's tourism-fuelled eastern seaboard. So much legitimate Asian money pours into developing resorts, like Surfer's Paradise in Queensland, that it's difficult to track laundered criminal cash.

Casinos remain illegal in several Asian countries, including Japan. Australia, with its thriving gaming industry, looks a good punt as a dirty money laundry. The drug world and the world you think you live in are in actual fact one entity.

Once drug prohibition ends, as I believe it will, resources will be available to clamp down more successfully on other criminal and terrorist money-laundering operations that pose a more pressing threat to the general population's safety.

One obstacle to developing and enforcing a coherent plan to deal with gang activity springs from difficulties, well-documented elsewhere, of obtaining evidence against the Triads and their competitors. The absurdity and futility of drug prohibition remain inherent as long as disparities in national laws vitiate the cross-continental narcotic enforcement programmes vital to any successful resolution of illicit cartel trafficking. For instance, Japanese privacy laws limit its police force's ability to provide information on citizens to foreign law enforcement agencies.

You'll be astounded to hear that, twice, Japanese Yakuza members have successfully sued their own government for releasing information on their financial status to authorities in foreign jurisdictions.

The threat is very real as the gangs target their own populations within Australia as a core customer base and decimate them by instigating high levels of drug addiction within these communities, along with the concomitant violence and crime that are addiction's tagalong by-products.

Life is cheap in Cabramatta.

People, not usually Italian-Americans, joke that the Mafia has become disorganised crime. But in the twenty-first century, the Triads and their rivals boast tight infrastructures. We underestimate them at our peril. By continuing drug prohibition we empower them. And simultaneously economically handicap the police and medical services we rely on to clean up the carnage these organisations spread.

It is estimated that Asian crime organisations, even though they may not be entirely located within Australian shores, are in control of 90 per cent of Australia's heroin trade. According to the CIA World Fact Book, 80 per cent of heroin seized within Australian jurisdiction can be traced directly to the Golden Triangle.

Instead of dancing to the tune of tabloid-generated hysteria every time some hapless suburban teen overdoses on a dodgy disco biscuit (less likely to happen in a properly regulated environment), the Sydney authorities need to shift their attention to understanding how crime syndicates connected to Asia work.

As in the US and the UK, many Asian gangs in Australia began life as defensive groups. The young males protected vulnerable members of their own minority ethnic community from physical attack, intimidation and harassment. The perpetrators? Ignorant and frightened bigots within the majority population. We all have a stake in the blame-game.

Yet as recently as 1994, Australian police had no Vietnamese officers serving in the field. A majority white cop force confronted not just language and cultural barriers but, more importantly, the mistrust of a people who could not relate to the troops deputised to protect them on the ground. It's not that the Vietnamese can't relate to white Australians, it's more to do with the fact that the tool of Australian domestic authority, the police, has failed to cater for the socio-cultural needs of Asian cultures when it polices large, predominantly Asian areas, like Cabramatta.

Asian individuals are not alone in their reluctance to report cartel-related crime to the authorities – they have well-grounded fear for their personal safety. In the past, many have had bad experiences with authority figures, either within their own homelands or in Australia. Their experience reflects the lack of clear thinking at the highest levels about the role drugs play, while they remain prohibited, in funding and empowering the gangs. The perpetration of a 'them and us' demarcation between Asian communities like Cabramatta and the Australian authorities only strengthens the gangs who can actively recruit from and secretively operate within communities which close ranks against external agencies like the police. Drugs are fuelling the gangs financially and also providing them with additional control over an addict population which provides the core, base layer of their hierarchy.

If governments were to decriminalise drugs and take control of their distribution, the decision about their availability would become one made to benefit society rather than engorge the bottom line of a warlord supporting a vicious, and usually totalitarian, regime many miles away. Which is how it is now.

Sydney's police force has reeled in the past from allegations of corruption. Cabramatta has become a focus for the police. There they have set out to clean the streets of that suburb and, in turn, burnish their own public image.

The move from heroin to cocaine in Sydney is more than a clampdown on smack, as part of a political public relations exercise by the Australian authorities. Smack is a pain in the butt to deal. It is still relatively cheap to buy at street level, so profit margins are low. Additional heat from the authorities has not helped, but the increasing scarcity of high-grade heroin in Australia has more to do with, inevitably temporary, DEA and Interpol lock-downs on the Golden Triangle.

Economic sanctions against supplier nations may work for a while, but they are always doomed in the long term. Remove one seller and another will take its place. But remove the buyer and the market collapses.

Tragically, for the puritan tendency, the genie is not only out of the pharmacological bottle but also dancing in the streets. Governments need to decide who is actually playing the tune: the authorities or the cartels?

While governments fretfully procrastinate, the South American drug bosses have a problem in their numero uno North American market: despite increases in DEA seizures, the market is saturated.

The Caribbean and Mexico are no longer the safe staging posts in the distribution chain they once were. Euroland is tough to reach by sea or air, and the South American cartels prefer to move product in bulk using transoceanic shipping.

The combination of established gang-led internal drug distribution networks in Australia and the Latino cocaine kingpins' desire for new outlets has led to the formation of a truly unholy alliance.

Maximum purity cocaine is shipped from South America eastwards around our narco-planet. Australia is a destination, a market, another stop on the route.

By selling to Oz direct, the South American cartels bypass existing distribution networks in Asia. This removes interference from the DEA and other international agencies. A more direct distribution channel creates fewer opportunities for the cocaine to be cut or stepped on by profiteers within Australia's traditional distribution chain. This equates to a burgeoning and relatively easy-to-access market for the manufacturers – and much greater profit margins for the Asian gangs as bulk distributors.

Smaller distributors will be 'removed' as the Asian gangs drop their façade and bring death and destruction to this laid-back playground on the far tip of the world.

I've seen the future and it hurts.

Unless action is taken right now, we're condemning our children to a harsh realm.

We can take control. We can establish a system coordinating police, doctors, pharmacists and social workers so that users can beat their addictions.

And don't think that Australia's problems aren't yours, wherever you may live. There's always going to be someone who wants to float your boat for a price: the Russian crime syndicates, the Italian Mafia, Afghani drug warlords, South American cocaine cartels. The list goes on and on and their market spans the globe: the guy who sits next to you in the office; your next-door neighbour; the people you pass in the street; and you.

But what the hell is he talking about? How can you advocate the legalisation of highly addictive drugs like crack cocaine and heroin? Surely this is the end of civilisation as we know it? Not necessarily. It's not going to be a case of simply walking down to your local minimart and picking up a few rocks and a gram of smack to go.

I really believe it's a case of drawing a line in the sand. Heroin substitutes, in fact heroin itself, are already widely available on a prescribed basis in many parts of the world. I've already stated that the drug problem should be treated as a medical issue, prioritising the issue from the end user's perspective and cutting demand.

The fundamental principles of supply and demand will reduce the function of criminals in the drug chain with state-sponsored provision and pricing negating the high profit margins currently enjoyed by narcotics traffickers and dealers. If legal supply undercuts the criminals then they will automatically look for other avenues of operation. It's not the ideal scenario, I know, but with the drugs business representing such a large proportion of current criminal activity it is the only way to go if the problem is to be dealt with on any level.

The key to future drug policy is in control and reduction. The problem of drugs will only start to be manageable once control mechanisms, in the form of legalised provision, have been introduced. The criminality of the drugs industry snuffs out just as many lives as the drugs themselves. Users will do anything within their power to get their gear and dealers will do likewise to give it to them. Legalisation would kill both birds with one stone and nullify the dual motivations for criminal activity. The street corner dealer will no longer be required if users are guaranteed a controlled supply of their pertinent narcotics and the addicts themselves will no longer be forced to embark on mini-crime waves to feed their habits. Most addicts find themselves surviving within the welfare system and should therefore be provided with free prescriptions, while the pricing level for the legal supply of controlled narcotics should be set at a level which is affordable for users who do have jobs. The fact is that, currently, the manufacture of illegal drugs is fairly inexpensive. It is the illegality of trafficking the drugs and the high risks involved as they move down the supply chain which causes them to be so expensive to the end user. For example, 1kg of near-pure cocaine will cost approximately US$2,000 if purchased in Colombia. By the time it has been trafficked to the US, cut several times en route, and packaged in small quantities for sale on the street, that kilo could realise as much as US$250,000. Drug crime is so rife because the amount of money that the drug-using population needs to raise to feed its collective habit is vast. Controlled pricing in relation to the socio-economic demographics of drug users will make legalised distribution an affordable proposition from the addicts' perspective and negate the need for criminal activity on their part.

As far as I can see it is only within this framework of legalised control of supply that a reduction of the drug problem can commence. If the demise of the illegal channels of distribution can be brought into effect then users will only have the option of state-regulated access to their daily fix. It would then be practical to turn the screw. It sounds cruel, but I have been an addict, I know the mind-set, I know the way it works. If continual supply to a given addict were to carry on indefinitely then there would be little incentive to stop using. If an environment for controlled withdrawal is created then there is a much greater chance of success. This would be enhanced by the fact that users would not be able to supplement their addiction with illegally procured drugs. One source, one mechanism for control. Society has already faced up to the issue of dependency on prescribed drugs such as Valium with the solution of medically supervised, controlled withdrawal, so it is not such a quantum leap to introduce the same protocols for illicit drugs. It would be too simplistic to think that all addicts could stop using by controlled withdrawal alone. Many people use drugs to escape the reality that the drudgery of their everyday lives gives them. Withdrawal programmes need to address a wider set of sociocultural issues. People need help putting their lives back together after addiction. Controlled distribution needs to go hand in hand with a change in our attitude towards addicts. If you don't examine the causal problems that lead to dependency, apart from merely the proliferation of illegal supply, then it just isn't going to work for some users. If we go down this route we have to make ourselves accountable for the drug problem and therefore the solution. The process of rehabilitation has to include the provision of greater opportunities for this underclass of addicts to gain a foothold in society. This will require investment in redeveloping the potential of a whole section of the community. I think that it is this investment of money and resources more than any other that causes governments to stutter when it comes to considering legalisation, as it means redefining society itself. We're never going to live in a utopia, but we need to address this issue if we are going to move forward with regards to the broader implications of the drug problem.

Sure, you say, but methadone reduction techniques only work in a small percentage of cases. That's true, but the failure of methadone treatment is within our current framework, where addicts are able to choose their levels of continued usage via the illegal marketplace. Dealers won't trade for peanuts and risk a prison sentence for 'unregistered supply' if their customers are getting catered to for free or even for a nominal charge from registered sources. Limit supply within a medically controlled environment and treat the disease of addiction. And I firmly believe that addiction is a disease. Ask almost any addict if they would trade the misery of the daily grind of substance abuse for a life clean of drugs and they would say yes. What the addict always lacks is motivation and it's a fact that they would need to be forced to confront their problem. Coming off drugs isn't a cakewalk by any stretch of the imagination. Most addicts want to stop using but can't face actually going through with it. Unfortunately, that's not going to reduce addiction levels. This goes beyond the practice of tough love. Isn't it preferable to induce a little 'enforced motivation' to quit in users rather than let them slide over the edge of addiction?

Add to this the fact that the creation of nationalised drug production entities would ensure the safety of drug use by manufacturing pharmaceutically untainted products. We would then not be looking at the high level of hot shots and overdoses currently experienced amongst users. Once society can begin to define users as patients rather than addicts, then dependency rates will start to fall.

Rather than throwing money at trying to stem the flow of drugs into society, funds could be better spent at treating and reducing the number of addicts. This methodology comes at a price. There are already millions of registered addicts around the globe. The additional numbers who would flood the system if supply was regulated would signal overload for the medical authorities. Who's going to pay for the infrastructure which would need to be created to cater to the huge numbers of legally recognised addicts? Think about it. Not only will the policing bill be dramatically reduced as drug crime falls, but there are far more lucrative options available for governmental revenue generation within state-controlled narcotics provision, not least taxation of drugs made available.

Class B drugs, such as marijuana, need not fall under the medically controlled criteria ascribed to highly addictive drugs.

MR NASTY

Dope is easy and cheap to produce, as much so as cigarettes and probably equally harmful to the user. Yet society already allows cigarettes to be freely available in our shops and supermarkets and levies considerable revenue via extreme levels of taxation. The same is true of alcohol. If cigarettes and booze were banned there would be uproar, so, conversely, would it really be so perverse for us to legalise the sale of a spliff through licensed means? Heroin and cocaine could be made under strictly regulated licences by the likes of Glaxo Wellcome et al. They would surely jump at the chance to broaden their product range in return for paying a fee to the powers that be. The tax dollars generated through these new revenue streams could be directly allocated to managing the addict population.

Some of this may seem extreme, but pause for a moment. We already live in a global society where drugs, be they prescribed in many shapes and forms or readily available to all comers in a bottle or a stick of tobacco, are legally within reach of customers. The pharmaceutical conglomerates make billions with a 'pill for every ill', yet millions of people are dependent on tranquillisers. We are already dealing with the trials and tribulations of a marketplace where many drugs are legal. I am merely advocating an extension of policy to include substances that are far more detrimental to our health and dangerous to our society.

We need to accept the fact we have lost the war on drugs. The problem is so endemic in society that it is now impossible to halt the supply and demand of narcotics within the current framework of counter-criminal policy. I am not naive enough to think that the drug problem will ever go away completely, but we can start thinking about controlling it. It is only through regulated control of the problem that we can then establish mechanisms to reduce it. As our inherent frailty and weakness as human beings manifests itself in ever increasing rates of drug addiction, we have to accept that this is a problem of our own creation and now is the time for progressive thinking and radical action to provide a solution.